Bring Back the Birds
What You Can Do to Save Threatened Species

Russell Greenberg and Jamie Reaser

D0973213

STACKPOLE
BOOKS

Published by
STACKPOLE BOOKS
5067 Ritter Road
Mechanicsburg, PA 17055

Printed in the United States of America

Chapter One is based on *Birds over Troubled Forests,* by R. Greenberg and S. Lumpkin, Smithsonian Migratory Bird Center, 1991.

Cover and interior art by Julie Zickefoose
Cover design by Tracy Patterson

First Edition

10 9 8 7 6 5 4 3 2 1

To Judy Gradwohl for sharing the adventure and Gene Morton for helping to dream up the Smithsonian Migratory Bird Center over beers at the Zebra Room.—R. G.

To my mentors for their inspiration, encouragement, and unyielding patience: Leonard J. Soucy, Jr., Edward E. Clark, Jr., Mitchell A. Byrd, and Paul R. Ehrlich and to my mother, Wilhelmina "Billie" Reaser, the bravest person I know.—J. K. R.

Library of Congress Cataloging-in-Publication Data

Greenberg, Russell.
     Bring back the birds : what you can do to save threatened species / Russell Greenberg and Jamie Reaser. — 1st ed.
          p.   cm.
     Includes bibliographical references (p. 296) and index.
     ISBN 0-8117-2519-7
     1. Birds, Protection of. I. Reaser, Jamie. II. Title.
QL67605.G66   1995
333.95'816—dc20

94-43772
CIP

Contents

Neotropical migrants like the Prothonotary Warbler depend on national laws and international treaties to protect ever-shrinking habitat throughout their range.

Foreword

They're beautiful; they're fascinating; they represent a couple of hundred million years of a stately evolutionary history. That's reason enough for me and, I suspect, for most readers of this book. But it is unlikely to be enough to convince a politician, or hard-nosed businessman, or *Wall Street Journal* editorial page writer. Many products of the deteriorating North American educational system have not been introduced to the diversity of life in any detail and have little understanding of how humans depend on biological resources. They see no reason to be alarmed by the news that an extinction episode is beginning that may rival the biological holocaust that exterminated the dinosaurs 65 million years ago. That's where you come in—you can help explain to other people why the wide variety of plants, animals, and microorganisms on Earth ("biodiversity") should be protected, and why birds not only deserve protection but can help confer it on other organisms.

There are four general reasons for preserving biodiversity. The first is ethical. Many people believe that, as the dominant species on the planet, *Homo sapiens* has a moral responsibility not to casually exterminate other populations and species. There is no scientific justification for this view; it is quasireligious: you either believe it or you don't.

The second reason is aesthetic. Most people find beauty in other organisms, in blooming dogwood bushes or singing thrushes. This appreciation creates substantial economic activity. The production and distribution of bird seed, garden tools, binoculars, cameras, nature films, and natural history books, as well as ecotourism, all create flows of wealth.

The third reason is that humans derive direct economic benefits from biodiversity. All crops and domestic animals have been withdrawn from nature's vast "genetic library." Roughly a third of all medicines come from that library or are modeled after chemical compounds that plants evolved to fend off their enemies. And many industrial products, from woods and fuels to various oils come from the same library. Above all, that library contains a vast potential for yielding still more valuable products. Sadly, we humans are burning it down.

The fourth reason is the most important from an anthropocentric viewpoint. Other organisms are working parts of the ecological systems that supply us with an array of free services without which civilization cannot persist. Those services include controlling the gaseous quality of the atmosphere so that the climate does not change too rapidly, running the hydrologic cycle that brings us dependable flows of fresh water, generating and maintaining the soils that are absolutely essential to agriculture and forestry, recycling the nutrients that are required to keep us fed, controlling the vast majority of pests that could attack crops or transmit diseases to people, pollinating many crops, and maintaining the genetic library. When we wipe out other populations and species, we are threatening these critical ecosystem functions. In many areas their delivery has already been impaired.

How do migratory birds fit into all of this? Their existence and aesthetic value are clear enough, as is their economic contribution to the natural history industry. Birds, of course, make a great contribution to the control of pests—the eastern United States would become a much more unpleasant place to live without the controls that migratory birds exert on populations of forest insects.

If migratory birds were exterminated, populations of other predators *might* eventually increase to the point that they would take over many of the pest-control functions exercised by the birds. That is, however, a gamble few biologists would be willing to take, and even if the role of migratory birds in maintaining ecosystem functions could be replaced, some fail-safe redundancy in the system would be removed.

Above all, however, migratory birds serve to monitor the health of ecological systems. Just as canaries once warned miners of potentially lethal accumulations of methane, declining populations of migratory birds may signal the potentially lethal faltering of human life-support systems. Popular interest in such birds makes them ideal miners' canaries in that respect, and that interest can help ensure that political action is taken to halt their decline and thus preserve functioning ecosystems. All of us must work hard to see that the politicians do the right thing: we owe it to ourselves, our children, and our grandchildren.

—*Paul R. Ehrlich*

Acknowledgments

This book would not have been written were it not for the guidance and encouragement of Rick Bonney. Mary Deinlein and John Sterling created the maps and developed the text for the bird biographies. Sue Ruff and Mary Deinlein reviewed and provided helpful comments on various chapters. Mandy Marvin assisted with editing. Shirley Briggs, former President Jimmy Carter, Edward Clark, Emile DeVito, Sam Droege, Peter English, Bill Hilton, Robert Horwich, Eugene Morton, Stanley Senner, and Kim Sturla took time from their busy schedules to prepare original essays. Mark Oberle assisted in communications with Mr. Carter's office. Ian Warkentin reviewed several chapters and provided constant support.

Amateur ornithologists count Broad-winged Hawks and other raptors at key sites along their migration routes.

1

Migratory Birds

Whenever a man hears it he is young, and Nature is in her spring; wherever he hears it, it is a new world and a free country, and the gates of heaven are not shut against him.

Thoreau wrote those words of a Wood Thrush, a familiar summer bird in eastern North America. They capture the feeling of many of us for whom spring is heralded by the sudden sighting of a Black-and-white Warbler following a chickadee flock, and for whom the ethereal songs of Veerys, the plaintive whistle of a circling Broad-winged Hawk, or the flashing black, yellow, and red feathers of Western Tanagers among the green foliage are the essence of a summer's walk in the woods.

These are among the more than one hundred fifty species of New World tropical (Neotropical) migrants: birds that breed in North America and winter in Latin America or the Caribbean. They are part of our internationally shared heritage. Throughout the course of a year, many of these birds experience an astonishing array of habitats, from boreal coniferous forest and Arctic tundra to desert, ocean, or tropical rain forest. As they migrate great distances, they confront amazing challenges to their survival—bad weather, scarce food, and lurking predators and parasites.

Today, however, the threats to Neotropical migrants from human-caused changes to the landscape dwarf these natural dangers. Indeed, as natural habitats are rapidly eliminated in Mexico and increasingly fragmented in North America, Thoreau's own Wood Thrush is declining precipitously. This book describes what bird enthusiasts—amateur and professional alike—know about Neotropical migrants and what must be done to save them.

For millions of years, birds have migrated across the Americas, breeding in the North, wintering in the South, and spending spring and fall traveling between. Shorebirds swoop and hover over the grasslands and marshes during the summer and congregate on mudflats and shorelines in the winter. Songbirds bring summer vibrancy to the northern forests and winter diversity to the southern. Everywhere, these beautiful birds and their still-mysterious voyaging inspire human admiration, sometimes poetry. But it all seems to be falling apart.

A few types face imminent extinction or are already extinct, including Bachman's, Kirtland's, and Golden-cheeked warblers, the Least Bell's and Black-capped vireos, and the Eskimo Curlew. The curlew was largely hunted to its near-extirpated status. The other species are in trouble because they are losing their homes. These birds spend both winter and summer in small, geographically restricted areas. Luckily, these critical cases are exceptional—most Neotropical migrant species still number in the millions. But just as today's small, managed herds of bison are barely a shadow of the enormous migratory herds that once crisscrossed the Great Plains, so, too, are migrating populations of birds declining. Longtime birders attest to that decline over the last decade, and the data for forest-dwelling migrants bear them out.

Item: The U.S. Fish and Wildlife Service's Breeding Bird Survey, conducted by volunteers who cover eighty thousand kilometers (fifty thousand miles) of road each year, shows that the number of Neotropical forest migrants in eastern North America declined at a rate of 1 to 3 percent a year between 1978 and 1987. Similar declines have begun to show up in numbers of Neotropical migrants captured at banding stations during migration. Although the annual rate seems small, if the trend continues, millions of birds could vanish within our lifetimes.

Item: Rock Creek Park, in the center of Washington, D.C., is one of the largest natural urban parks in the world and boasts vast stands of mature deciduous forest. Rock Creek's breeding birds have been counted for more than forty years, and a recent analysis of the records revealed some shocking facts. Of fifteen Neotropical migrant species present in the 1940s, more than one third have disappeared from the park. Numbers of other migrants have dropped by 80 to 90 percent and breeding densities have fallen by half. Once 60 to 80 percent of Rock Creek Park's breeding birds were migrants; now fewer than 40 percent are. In contrast, resident and short-distance migrants still breed in numbers similar to those of forty years ago, and none have become extinct. Similar patterns have been found in several other long-term urban study areas.

Item: The vulnerability of certain migratory bird populations was revealed when the *Exxon Valdez* spill occurred seventy kilometers (forty-six miles) away from where a majority of the world's Western Sandpipers flock to the Copper River Delta.

Item: Throughout the eastern United States, remnant patches of forest no longer support viable populations of such migrant species as Cerulean and

Worm-eating warblers. Although some remote sites, such as the Great Smoky Mountains, have supported stable populations of forest migrants, others, such as the Sequoia groves in the southern Sierra Nevada, have experienced severe declines or local extinctions.

Item: The number of migratory bird flights over the Gulf of Mexico detected by radar during three years in the 1980s was about half that of three years in the 1960s.

Past Comebacks for Migratory Birds

Although there is cause for concern, migratory birds have come to the brink before and, responding to concerted conservation action, have largely recovered. Shorebirds—easy targets heavily concentrated in a few estuaries along predictable migration paths—were favored game birds for the first three centuries of European settlement of the New World. The fate of a few species was sealed because they were large and relatively tame, and night hunting with lights allowed harvesting in large numbers for the stew pot. The long-distance migrants—the ones that stop only rarely on the way to southern South America, put on a tasty layer of fat for the trip. The Eskimo Curlew, or "doughbird," made a particularly easy target and a nice handful for commercial meat markets. Other long-distance champion migrants, such as the Hudsonian Godwit, Upland Sandpiper, yellow-legs, and Golden Plover, were also favored targets and declined dramatically at the turn of the century. The Migratory Bird Act of 1918 protected most shorebirds, but many have recovered only to face increasing threats to their habitat.

Duck, geese, and swan populations also crashed to near extirpation. Not only were populations heavily harvested, but critical wetlands where millions of waterfowl held their noisy winter conventions were lost. Even after hunting was regulated by international treaty in 1918, waterfowl populations kept declining because of the continued draining of wetlands. Although the first government-run duck sanctuary was founded in Lake Merritt in Oakland, California, in 1870, it wasn't until the first decades of this century that national wildlife refuges were established. Drought and waterfowl declines spurred the purchase of wetlands in the 1930s and again in the late 1950s and early 1960s. Although the drastic declines of a hundred years ago have been arrested, wetlands are increasingly contaminated with chemicals from agricultural runoff or are disappearing altogether.

A number of raptor species experienced well-documented declines and reproductive failure from 1946 through 1972, a period that corresponded with the introduction and use of chlorinated hydrocarbons (particularly DDT) as insecticides. When these compounds were largely banned in the United States, populations of Bald Eagles, Peregrine Falcons, and Ospreys, as well as Sharp-

Hudsonian Godwits fly from Canada to South America, stopping only a few times along the way.

shinned and Cooper's hawks, began to slowly increase. Yet raptors continue to receive concentrated doses of a growing number of other agricultural chemicals that damage or destroy their reproductive functions, and even DDT and its metabolites are showing up again in North American birds.

THE NEW WORLD MIGRATION SYSTEM

Most birds that migrate between wintering grounds in the tropics and breeding grounds in North America are insect-eating landbirds. Swallows, swifts, Nighthawks, Whip-poor-wills, and flycatchers feed in the air on flying insects; vireos, orioles, and warblers glean insects from leaves. Various species of raptors, thrushes, and hummingbirds are also Neotropical migrants. The wood warblers, some fifty species in all, are perhaps the most exciting group of migrants. Names like "Cerulean," "Bay-breasted," "Golden-cheeked," and "Painted" reflect the warblers' striking nuptial plumages.

Large numbers of shorebirds migrate, too. Each fall sandpipers, plovers, godwits, and curlews leave the mudflats and beaches of North America for the rich tropical bays and estuaries—the Bay of Panama and the mouth of the Orinoco River—and the grasslands and marshes of southern South America. A few ducks make their way to tropical wetlands. Meanwhile, the hardy mariners—phalaropes, jaegers, and Black Terns—leave land behind and head out to tropical seas for the winter months.

Various species of raptors are also Neotropical migrants. Although most raptors brave the northern winters feeding on mammals and birds that remain active throughout the winter, many species that feed on more seasonally available prey, such as insects or reptiles and amphibians, head south. Some hawks, such as accipiters and falcons, prey on the smaller migrants. Millions of Broad-winged and Swainson's hawks, Mississippi and Swallow-tailed kites, and Turkey Vultures funnel through the Central American isthmus, creating migratory displays that dwarf the more famous hawk-watching sites of North America.

Why Birds Migrate

Migration allows birds to take advantage of the abundant food of the temperate-zone summer and to avoid the lean fare of winter. Avoiding cold temperatures is a less important reason for wintering in the tropics (many small birds survive even the boreal winter) than the scarcity of prey and limited foraging time of short winter days. Snow cover makes the food supply of many birds unavailable. But during the summer, immense numbers of insects and spiders flourish in the forests and fields of North America. Rich in protein, these arthropods provide the nutrients many birds need to produce and rear young. Neotropical migrants in particular feed on bountiful summer hatches of flying and crawling insects that thrive on succulent new leaves. The long days of summer give birds plenty of time to search for food and may enable them to raise more young.

The Origins of Migration

The Neotropical migration system probably began with a general cooling of the earth ten million to thirty million years ago, when a largely subtropical climate in North America was gradually replaced by a cooler but distinctly seasonal one. Many of the Neotropical migrants, such as pewees, *Empidonax* flycatchers, tanagers, grosbeaks, wood warblers, and vireos, are closely related to species living in Central and South American mountains. These same migrants may be relics of a very diverse tropical bird fauna that populated the large expanses of subtropical savannas and forests that covered North America. But the cooling trend may have caused wide-scale extinction or forced adaptation to exploit the new seasonal environment. Migration is one such adaptation. The ebb and flow of the glaciers fragmented and isolated the forests of North America, allowing new species to form and thus contributing to the high diversity of migratory birds.

Shorebirds also flourished and diversified in the expanding and contracting tundra ecosystems during the Pleistocene. Unlike most landbird populations, which breed and winter in forests, the tundra-breeding shorebirds search out wetlands, shorelines, or warm grasslands to winter. The staggering numbers of shorebirds that feed on crane flies and midges in the Arctic summer find relatively local and restricted habitats in the winter compared with landbirds. Their solution has been to migrate farther, and many species winter primarily in the wetlands of South America, where they achieve remarkable densities. They arrive in the southern, or austral, summer to find grasslands and wetlands largely

Although the temperate-tropical migration system is old, some Neotropical migrations may be quite recent. Lincoln's Sparrow probably started migration to the highlands of Mexico and Central America during the late Pleistocene.

unoccupied by locally breeding shorebirds. The few breeding species tend to be specialists—dissimilar in their habits from the waves of incoming northerners.

Ever-Changing Migrations

Although the migratory systems are probably ancient, species can shift specific migration patterns rapidly. For example, Song Sparrows are fairly sedentary; some individuals and populations remain resident on North American breeding sites. However, their more shy and less well known relatives, Swamp Sparrows and Lincoln's Sparrows, travel widely. The marsh-dwelling Swamp Sparrows pile up along the Gulf Coast, while the bog-loving Lincoln's Sparrows fly as far as the mountains of Central America. These are impressive differences among species that probably descended from a common ancestor since recent ice ages.

Consider also that during the ice ages, many common migrants of the eastern deciduous forests were probably restricted to small pockets in the Deep South as coniferous forest spread over most of the East.

Once a species undertakes migration, range changes can occur swiftly. Even the most impressive long-distance flights, such as Blackpoll Warblers' migration from Alaska to the Amazon Basin or the Pectoral Sandpipers' journey from Siberia to Argentina, likely evolved from short-distance movements. Each generation of birds traveled farther and farther, perhaps to avoid competition from related species.

Birds do occasionally lose their way. Many are blown off course, and some inherit a poor sense of direction. Scientists suspect that these vagrants may act

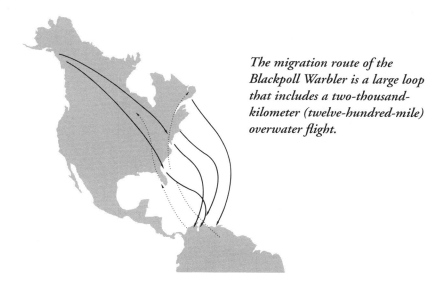

The migration route of the Blackpoll Warbler is a large loop that includes a two-thousand-kilometer (twelve-hundred-mile) overwater flight.

as prospectors, in the evolutionary sense, for new breeding and wintering sites. Migrants from the East are frequently sighted along the coast and in desert oases in the West. Populations of several eastern migrants now breed in small pockets west of their recent historic range. Every year small numbers of Siberian shorebirds, such as Curlew Sandpiper and Rufous-necked Stint, show up along the coast of Alaska; occasionally they breed. A similar exchange occurs between North America and Asia. As a result, we have Dunlins that breed in Alaska and winter in Asia and Pectoral Sandpipers breeding across Siberia and wintering in South America.

The Diversity of Migratory Behavior
Motion characterizes the lives of North American birds. Most species breed and winter in different sites, sometimes moving only a few miles up and down the slopes of a single mountain range. Some species, like the Yellow-rumped Warbler, move only as necessary to avoid harsh weather.

Whether the movement brings birds to unfamiliar habitats varies considerably by region and species. For landbird migrants from western North America, no sharp distinction can be drawn between tropical- and temperate-zone migration. Habitats in western Mexico and the Central American highlands are very similar to their breeding habitats in the western United States and Canada. As they move south, only gradually do winters become more moderate. Eastern North American species, on the other hand, tend to jump into the tropics more abruptly. Most species fly across the Caribbean or the Gulf of Mexico to winter in Caribbean lowlands or South and Central American highlands, which have very different plant and animal species from the conifers that account for more than 70 percent of North American forests.

Some species leave their breeding habitat soon after eggs are laid. In June the arctic grasslands are teeming with life, while the nearby shorelines are birdless. By mid-July hundreds of gulls, sandpipers, and phalaropes are twirling and probing along the gravelly arctic shores. They will move on—most teeming along shorelines or wintering in wetlands, but a few hardy species, such as the phalaropes, will head out to sea.

Unlike restless temperate-zone birds, many tropical birds are generally sedentary. Some birds of tropical forest understories, such as antbirds, spend their entire lives within 200 meters (660 feet) of where they hatched. But even in the more climatically stable tropics, birds that depend on seasonal foods must migrate to survive. Most, like Resplendent Quetzals and Bare-necked Umbrella Birds, move up and down the mountain slopes following the fruiting season of their favorite trees. A few species, such as the Yellow-green Vireo (close kin to the familiar Red-eyed Vireo), migrate long distances between tropical areas in Mexico and the Amazon Basin.

MIGRATORY BIRDS IN THE TEMPERATE ZONE

All aspects of migratory bird biology, from behavior to physiology and ecology, are tied to an annual calendar of events—migrating, breeding, and molting. Each activity occurs in its own season. The waxing and waning of hormonal levels run the annual clock. The onset and duration of each phase of the annual cycle are fine-tuned by such environmental factors as weather, changing day length, and social behavior, which in turn influence the ebb and flow of hormones.

Harbingers of Spring

Migration begins in North America as a trickle in late February, with the flood of returning birds cresting in late April and early May. When you see trees full of brightly colored migrants on a crisp spring morning, you are experiencing but a tiny portion of a massive migratory wave. Radar tracking has shown that some eighty thousand birds per mile of migration front arrive on the Louisiana coast each day during peak migration. The migrants filter slowly northward, traveling an average of only thirty miles a day and taking as long as six weeks to reach their breeding grounds. In large flocks, these birds track the insect larvae hatching on newly leafing trees as spring rolls northward. In the East, migration paths

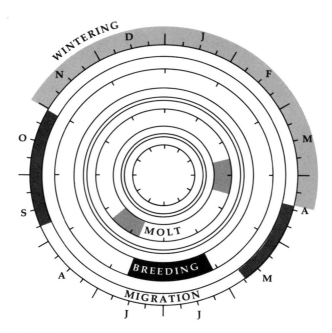

The annual calendar for a typical Neotropical migrant: Each season features energy-demanding activities requiring high-quality habitat.

tend to move slowly up the slopes of the Appalachians. By early June migration is virtually complete.

Shorebirds tend to feed at fewer, larger stopover sites during migration. Sites that have remarkable concentrations of shorebird food support millions of birds during a short period. The coming together of birds and invertebrates creates spectacular natural events, perhaps the most famous of which occurs on the shores of the Delaware Bay. Here hundreds of thousands of Red Knots and other sandpipers come to feed on the eggs of the spawning horseshoe crabs in mid- to late May.

Raptors rarely concentrate at feeding sites during migration, but large numbers often funnel along narrow flight corridors. These hawk highways are defined by prominent topographic features, such as north-south ridges. At strategic spots along these routes, such as Hawk Mountain in Pennsylvania, Cape May in New Jersey, the canal area of Panama, and the mountains of Veracruz, Mexico, raptor enthusiasts can watch large numbers of birds, primarily in the autumn.

Most of the Red Knots that migrate along eastern North America stop to refuel at Delaware Bay. This great concentration makes the population vulnerable to a chemical or oil spill.

Species that migrate the shortest distances generally arrive first on their breeding grounds. Within species, breeding residents usually arrive before the migrants passing farther north. And among breeding residents, males usually arrive earlier than females, and older birds before younger ones. The earlier migration begins, the greater the risks the migrants face, such as a late snowfall or several days of cold rain that may temporarily reduce or eliminate prey. Males, particularly older males, risk the harsh demands of early arrival to win the intense competition for a good territory. Usually slightly larger than females, males may be better able to withstand a surprise spring storm. But massive die-offs of migrants faced with unseasonal weather are not infrequent, and breeding populations can be reduced for several years after.

Where Migrants Breed
During the breeding season, Neotropical migrants spread unevenly across North America. The grasslands and desert scrub that dominate most of the West are populated by only a few Neotropical migrants, such as the Lesser Nighthawk, Scissor-tailed Flycatcher, and Western Kingbird. The chaparral and oak wood-lands of the Pacific Coast, with their mild, rainy winters and hot, dry summers, also support relatively few migrants. Riparian woodlands and montane forests attract more migratory species, including Western Wood-Pewees, Swainson's Thrush, and a few species of wood warblers and vireos. But the vast majority of Neotropical migrants breed in the great eastern deciduous forests that stretch from the Gulf Coast to southern Canada, and from the Atlantic Coast to the Great Plains, and in the boreal forests that extend across Canada to central Alaska. Without these summer visitors, our forests would be virtually silent. In northern coniferous forests, for instance, Magnolia, Blackburnian, and other warblers constitute nearly three quarters of breeding birds.

Most shorebirds that winter in the tropics or the south temperate zone over-shoot the forests and grasslands of temperate North America and fan across the vast expanse of arctic grassland and marsh commonly referred to as tundra. The melting of snow in late May and June exposes a muddy brown carpet of apparently dead grass and shrubs. Within a few weeks, however, the intense arctic spring is in full swing and birds used to probing muddy estuaries are gobbling up an explosion of crane flies and midges.

Niches
For the most part, Neotropical migrants are not common backyard birds. Some striking species, such as Orchard Orioles, Indigo Buntings, and Eastern King-birds, are common in fields or woodland edges, but Neotropical migrants are primarily creatures of the forest. Within a forest, each species feeds differently, searching different layers of the forest and using unique search-and-capture tech-

niques for insect prey. In a typical northern hardwood forest, for instance, the Ovenbirds methodically patrol the leaf litter. Above them, American Redstarts dart about flushing small leafhoppers. Vireos inhabit the same branches as the redstarts and slowly peer about for larger insect prey. Nearby, rapidly hopping Black-throated Blue Warblers search the foliage in the understory, and Black-throated Greens work the canopy.

Even in seemingly simple habitats, birds carefully divide the space and prey. The great diversity of shorebird bills, for example, gives each species access to different kinds of invertebrates hiding in the mud. At one extreme is the halt-and-scan gait of a plover as it searches the surface of the mud for its prey. At the other extreme, Whimbrels and other curlews probe the burrows of ghost crabs with their long, decurved bills. Small sandpipers pick at the surface, while dowitchers probe like sewing machines, feeling for subsurface prey. Meanwhile, tiny phalaropes spin in circles offshore and peck into the vortex they create, pulling the planktonic prey into their beaks.

Controlling Insects and Other Pests

Songbirds are the unsung heroes of northern forests, protecting them from foliage-eating menaces. Adult migrants may eat a wide variety of insects and spiders, but almost all feed their young with caterpillars. Feeding voraciously on new foliage, caterpillars shunt almost all of their food energy directly into growth, using very little to build chemicals, hairs, or coloration (caterpillars are usually translucent, but their leafy stomach contents make many appear green). Without noxious defenses, caterpillars are a near-perfect food for nestling birds; their relatively large size also means fewer trips for the parents. Even so, the average pair of warbler parents must search several hundred thousand leaves in the ten days it takes to raise a nestful of babies to fledgling status. In fact, scientists have shown that birds, mostly migrants, can reduce the number of caterpillars on a tree by as much as half. In a world without migratory birds, insects would consume the forests' abundant harvest of foliage with impunity—no need to hide, sneak out at night, or employ defense colorations or chemicals.

A few species of moths periodically infest North American forests. Every twenty-five years or so, for instance, spruce budworms reach epidemic proportions and defoliate boreal forests. With superabundant food, populations of several Neotropical migrants, especially Cape May, Bay-breasted, and Tennessee warblers, breed successfully and may even produce larger clutches of eggs than usual. Although these birds were once regarded as the reason for the budworm population crash that follows each outbreak, it is more likely that the diminishing leaf and food supply, aided by a tiny wasp that lays its eggs inside budworm bodies, holds spruce budworms in check. However, the voracious birds are important in reducing budworm numbers and limiting damage to the forests.

Not surprisingly, experiments in which sections of mudflat were protected from birds have shown that high densities of voracious shorebirds control both the abundance and the composition of the animals that hide in the mud. Faced with a rather complete array of seafoods, the birds understandably favor some and ignore others.

Nesting Birds

Migrants are very particular about where they place their nests and often draw from a very specific inventory of building materials. For instance, all Worm-eating Warblers build multilayered nests in a painstaking ritual that includes selecting and beating dead leaves and scratching in the humus for a certain type of hair moss. The resulting nests are always carefully tucked under the shelves that form beneath shrubs growing on steep slopes. Nearby, in more open leaf litter, Ovenbirds sit in a small grass-and-leaf cup under an arching roof of rootlets and leaves. Overhead, pewees construct nests of lichen-covered plant fibers that resemble a small knot on a limb; Great-crested Flycatchers line old woodpecker holes with weeds, grass, plastic bags and paper, and cast-off snakeskins; and Red-eyed Vireos suspend their homes of woven bark and fiber from tree forks.

This specialization in nesting habits protects some of the eggs or young from predators, which quickly learn where to look for nests. And the more nests of the same type in the same area, the more likely the area is to attract the attention of a predator.

For most Neotropical migrants, the breeding season is short and intense, an intensity reflected in the cacophony of sound in the predawn chorus of bird songs. The following actions that punctuate the three-month breeding season of Prairie Warblers are typical for Neotropical landbird migrants:

• Establish territories. Males arrive on the breeding ground about five days before females, and within a day or two select and begin to defend territories against other males.

• Form pair bonds. Upon arrival, female Prairie Warblers move about inconspicuously, approaching singing territorial males; often they form pair bonds within a few hours. More so than males, the females tend to return to different areas than they used previously.

• Build a nest. During a few days of courtship and pair formation, females select nest sites, then divide their time for the next five to seven days between foraging and nest building. Males spend their time feeding, singing, and otherwise defending their territories and mates, who are now receptive to copulation, from other males.

• Lay and incubate three to five eggs. Soon after finishing the nest, a female lays the first of the eggs, which she produces at about twenty-four-hour intervals. Incubation begins when the next-to-last egg is laid and continues for about ten days. In Prairie Warblers only females incubate, spending up to 80 percent of the day on the nest. Females must feed incredibly fast to minimize the time eggs are exposed to temperature changes and predators. Sometimes males bring food to nest-bound females.

• Raise the young. Once eggs hatch, both parents bring food to the growing nestlings. Warblers fledge quickly, leaving the nest nine to twelve days after hatching, when they are barely able to fly. At this point, leaving the nest is probably safer than staying. At about ten days past fledging, the young warblers become hyperactive and exploratory. The parents split the brood and have little further contact with each other. The male feeds some young and the female the others until they are forty to fifty days old and foraging independently. All family ties are then severed as the adults molt and the young gather in loose foraging groups, preparing for migration.

Not all warblers and other Neotropical migrants follow the typical Prairie Warbler pattern. Female hummingbirds, for instance, visit males only briefly to mate, then go off alone to raise the two young that hatch from pea-size eggs. And members of even apparently monogamous species may have complicated sex lives. Bigamist males, dividing their attention between two families, turn up in most well-studied bird populations. More surprising is that sophisticated genetic "paternity tests" reveal that many young birds are fathered not by the pair male, but by other males who sneak onto a neighbor's territory to mate with the female. In a final twist, some female warblers are already carrying stored sperm during the spring migration.

It is among the shorebirds, particularly the sandpipers, that alternative lifestyles are thoroughly explored, and it may be migration itself that causes this diversity of breeding behavior. Different species in the genus *Calidris,* nesting side by side in the tundra, show the complete range. Dunlin, for example, are monogamous, with both males and females caring for young; Pectoral Sandpipers are polygynous, with males defending territories that have one to several females; Buff-breasted Sandpiper males display in "leks," or arenas, to attract mates. The Buff-breasted Sandpiper males retain their plain plumage and small size, and attract females by raising their wings to create a white flash that can be seen up to a mile away across the flat grassy tundra. After mating, the females tend the eggs and care for the young on their own.

The Ruff is famous for its varied and spectacular plumage and large size compared with the female, but other shorebirds exhibit the rare phenomenon of complete sex role reversal. The phalarope females are large and colorful, and the smaller, dull-colored males tend the eggs and nest and care for the young.

The diversity of mating arrangements is common in birds that have "precocial" young, such as shorebirds, whose young hatch out mobile and are generally able to feed themselves. These young look a little like Easter chicks, but the downy plumage of rich rusts, golds, and whites perfectly matches the lichens of the tundra. Their ability to feed themselves and their camouflage reduce the need for parental care and free one of the adults from duties after mating. However, in many shorebirds the pair bond is maintained for further mating attempts and protection of the young.

A second condition for the more unusual mating systems is related to how far the species migrate to winter. Departure from monogamy occurs primarily in those species that migrate long distances, such as from North to South America. After mating, individuals of one or the other sex can do better for themselves by making a safe early trip to a benign wintering ground than by staying and being of marginal assistance in family duties up north.

Threats to the Nest

Neotropical migrants are threatened by predators and parasites. The open, woven-cup nests built by many migrants are more vulnerable to egg predators like raccoons, opossums, and squirrels than the nests of many resident species, which tend to be high in trees or in trunk cavities. And unlike many larger residents, small Neotropical migrants cannot defend their nests from avian egg predators, such as Blue Jays, grackles, and crows, but depend entirely on clever nest location and stealth. Predators can take a heavy toll: the contents of some 80 percent of Prairie Warbler nests end up in the stomachs of predators. Losses hit Neotropical migrants particularly hard because their short breeding seasons rarely permit time to produce more than one brood a year.

Many nesting Neotropical migrants are also threatened by parasitic cowbirds—the Brown-headed Cowbirds living in much of North America, the Red-eyed in the southwestern United States, and a newly arrived Caribbean immigrant, the Shiny Cowbird. Cowbirds thrive by tricking the adults of other species into raising their young. Female cowbirds seek out unattended nests to lay their eggs among those of the nest's owners. Some species, such as American Robins, Gray Catbirds, and Blue Jays, recognize these alien eggs and roll them out of their nests. Yellow Warblers desert the parasitized nest or build a new nest over it. But less discriminating hosts, including many warblers, vireos, and fly-catchers—virtually all Neotropical migrants—incubate the eggs and raise the cowbird young with their own, but at great cost.

Parent birds operate on the "squeaky wheel" principle: the biggest, pushiest nestlings who beg loudest and longest get the most food. Because cowbird young hatch earlier and grow faster than host young, they usually are the squeakiest wheels in the brood, and host young are crowded out or starve. Studies of vireos and phoebes, for instance, revealed that parents rearing a cowbird fledged only half as many young as their unparasitized neighbors. Among Prairie Warblers the situation is worse. On average, parasitized nests produced less than one fledgling, compared with more than three young fledged from unparasitized nests. When cowbird parasitism is widespread, as it has increasingly become, losses of this magnitude can be devastating.

MIGRATING TO THE TROPICS

Adult birds must replace worn-out feathers once or twice a year. Most migratory birds molt completely before the autumn migration; the rare spring molts are limited to decorative body and head feathers. In some species, spring plumage changes do not actually require a molt. During winter, the bright spring plumage is covered by dull edges that gradually wear off to reveal the colors, much like a picture rubbed with a coin. This transformation can be subtle, as in the Cape May Warbler and Orchard Oriole, or staggering, as in the Bobolink, which changes from drab to brilliant.

Following the molt, the migratory bird embarks on a feeding frenzy. A small bird may double its body weight with fat that is used to power long-distance flights. At the same time, migratory birds become restless at night, showing movement in the direction in which they will soon be flying. Scientists have shown that caged migrants, deprived of signals from nature, maintain this directional restlessness for about as long as the species migrates in the wild.

Finding Their Way

One of the great mysteries of migration is how birds find their way, with amazing accuracy, over vast distances to return to the same breeding and wintering grounds, often to the same territories, year after year. The adaptiveness of this site fidelity is understandable: a good place one year is likely to be a good one the next. But how do they do it?

Young birds generally do not learn the routes and stopovers by following their parents. By the time migration begins, young warblers have left their parents and are ready to journey alone or in loose groups. Nearly a half-century's research has revealed that a warbler's tiny brain contains a multisensory atlas and is predisposed to use a number of different road signs.

Night-traveling migrants find their way primarily by the stars. Indigo Buntings, for instance, learn a sky map as they observe the rotation of the stars. To navigate, they use the axis of the rotation of constellations around the North Star. If the night sky is overcast, birds may use other methods, including orienting by the sun at dusk, tracking major topographic features such as the coastline, monitoring wind direction, and sensing the flux of magnetic fields. While general direction and duration of a migratory trip may be inherited, the precise route and endpoints are probably learned.

Neotropical migrants spend up to two months of each year migrating from wintering ground to breeding ground. Many birds, especially the smaller ones, undertake the demanding and risky migration flights at night, refueling and resting during daylight hours. Flying at night may reduce predation by raptors, to which small birds are particularly vulnerable, and may also allow the birds to avoid high-altitude winds. Unpredictable weather poses other risks. Millions of migratory birds can perish from exhaustion or starvation if a cold snap eliminates insect prey or a cold front or hurricane prolongs an over-water flight beyond the birds' reserves of stored energy.

Routes to the Tropics

Many Neotropical migrants embark on nonstop flights exceeding twenty hours over as much as six hundred miles (one thousand kilometers) of the Gulf of

Western Hemisphere

Mexico to reach the Yucatan Peninsula. Unless surprised by storms or severe cold fronts, migrants make the trip easily. Others take the more circuitous overland route around the gulf into Mexico. Although this route may be three times longer, birds can stop to rest and feed along the way.

Some particularly ambitious species fly over the Atlantic from the eastern seaboard to the Caribbean islands or South America after migrating from as far west as the Northwest Territories and Alaska. Different species leave the coast at different points, but most depart north of North Carolina on nonstop, overwater flights of eighteen hundred miles (three thousand kilometers) or more.

Although most species follow roughly the same fall and spring migration routes, some species' migrations define large loops. For example, the Connecticut Warbler flies down the Atlantic coast in the fall and up the Mississippi Valley in the spring. This is an extreme example of migrants' tendency to follow a more westerly course to their breeding grounds. Instead of taking dramatic long-distance, nonstop flights as they do in the fall, most species island-hop across the Caribbean, make short flights over the gulf, or travel the overland route through Mexico.

MIGRANTS IN THE TROPICS

The staggering numbers preclude precise counts or even very accurate estimates, but perhaps two billion to five billion birds migrate south each year. Some migrants, primarily those that breed in western North America, spend the winter in northern and western Mexico. Others winter on the islands of the Caribbean, and a few reach northern South America or even as far as the Amazon. Many shorebirds and a few landbirds winter in the temperate regions of Argentina and Chile. The winter destinations of some forest landbirds are not known. It is thought that some, such as Veerys and Connecticut Warblers, winter primarily in the forests of Matto Grosso in southern Brazil.

In forested habitats, the number of landbird migrants relative to resident bird species falls as one moves farther from North America. Migrants constitute half or more of the birds present in some parts of Mexico, the Bahamas, Cuba, and Hispaniola; 20 to 40 percent of the birds in Guatemala and Belize; 10 to 30 percent in Costa Rica and Panama; and as few as 1 percent in Trinidad, Venezuela, Ecuador, and Peru. These figures also reflect absolute number of individuals and species. In a typical lowland forest of Mexico, it is not uncommon to find ten to fifteen species of migrants, whereas a similar forest in Panama may have only two to five species at one third or one fourth the density.

Given the high risk of migration, it is not surprising that most migrants winter as close to their breeding grounds as possible. But other factors also come into play. As one moves south toward the Amazon, the diversity of resident bird species increases and migrants face more competition for food. A typical forest in the Amazon might have a hundred species of small insectivorous birds, a Mexican forest thirty species, and a Caribbean island only five.

Visiting birds may also find tropical forests as unfamiliar as we do. Deep in the tropics, migratory birds find insects well armed with a dazzling array of defenses. Unlike North America with its abundance of colorless, defenseless caterpillars, tropical forests have larvae that are usually distasteful or tightly bound in rolled-up leaves. The only other large, soft-bodied insects are large roaches and katydids with elaborate camouflage, biting mouthparts, and long spiny legs capable of delivering a severe blow to an inexperienced bird. Few migrants can cope with such fierce prey on little training and with temperate-zone-adapted beaks, and rely upon spiders and small insects in tropical forests.

Shorebirds fly south to the estuaries of large tropical rivers. By flying even farther, some species can find an array of temperate habitats, ranging from mud-flats to grasslands, where the austral summer is in full swing.

Geography dictates that an enormous number of Neotropical migrants are packed into a small area each winter. The potential breeding grounds in North

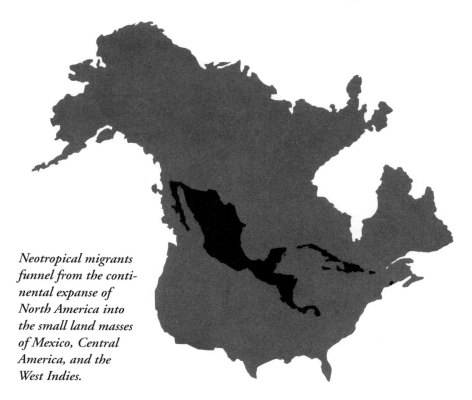

Neotropical migrants funnel from the continental expanse of North America into the small land masses of Mexico, Central America, and the West Indies.

America encompass over 40 million square kilometers (16 million square miles), but the entire land mass of Mexico, the Bahamas, Cuba, and Hispaniola is only about 6 million square kilometers (2,400,000 square miles), and more than half of all Neotropical migrants funnel into this small area.

A few species, such as Black-and-white Warblers, range over large areas in the winter. However, it is more typical for most members of a species to winter in one relatively small area, separate from closely related species to reduce competition for food and space. For example, although sixteen species of *Dendroica* warblers winter in northern Latin America and the Caribbean, it is rare to find more than two or three at one spot.

Where related species share the same region, they are usually separated by altitude or habitat. In several migrant species, notably American Redstarts, Hooded Warblers, and Black-throated Blue Warblers, males and females occupy different habitats. Males generally live in forests and woodlands, while females inhabit shrubby areas.

It was once widely believed that migrants used primarily edge and second-growth habitats on the wintering grounds; we now know that migrants inhabit virtually all Neotropical habitats. Many species (such as Wilson's Warbler and Northern Oriole) prefer second-growth and edge, a few (Common Yellowthroat and Indigo Bunting) are found primarily in farms and fields, and some (Kentucky Warbler and Acadian Flycatcher) depend on closed-canopy forest and edge.

As a rule, wintering and breeding habitats are structurally similar for many species. Kentucky Warblers hop on the forest floor, whether beneath palm trees in Panama or under oaks in the deciduous woodlands of the southeastern United States. Other species make striking habitat shifts. Least Flycatchers, summer residents of New England's forests, winter in the scrubby cattle pastures of Mexico.

Tropical Niches

The lifestyles of most breeding migrants, with their nuclear families, all-purpose territories, and hard work, seem a natural metaphor for a conservative society. But freed from the constraints of breeding and offered myriad new resources and habitats, wintering Neotropical migrants can be wild and unpredictable. The switches in feeding and social behavior displayed by some migrants during their annual tropical sojourns would surprise watchers of temperate-zone birds.

Most migrant songbirds remain insectivorous and search for arthropods in places similar to the ones they frequent on the breeding grounds. Insect-eating migrants often pass the winter on individually defended feeding territories. But a flock of hundreds of Eastern Kingbirds descending on a fruiting tree, a common sight in the tropics, is a far cry from the more familiar single kingbird looking over an open field from a treetop. Red-eyed Vireos, Swainson's Thrushes, and even, occasionally, Swallow-tailed Kites turn to fruit eating in the winter. Most of these frugivorous migrants travel in groups, searching for the mast crop of productive trees. In fact, some scientists speculate that trees time their fruiting to the passage of large numbers of migrants, which then disperse the trees' seeds.

In contrast, individual Gray and White-eyed vireos defend territories containing fruit trees (elephant tree and gumbo-limbo) and eat a few energy-packed *Bursera* fruits every day all winter long. Each vireo thus becomes a dependable seed disperser.

A pollen-stained Tennessee Warbler feeds from the shaving brush–like combretum flowers.

Migrants that feed on nectar may defend individual plants, or a wandering flock may descend upon the massive flower display of a canopy tree. A high-energy food, nectar is often readily available in the tropics, and flowers fuel the high-energy lifestyles of Cape May and Tennessee warblers, Northern and Orchard orioles, and many others. Orioles, in fact, possess specialized brushy tongues that draw nectar from flowers.

Even specialized arthropod hunters dramatically change their feeding style from season to season. Blue-winged, Golden-winged, and in particular, Worm-eating warblers specialize in searching for insects hiding in the curled, dead leaves that hang in tropical shrubbery. In a tropical forest, many large arthropods are active at night and spend the day cocooned in dead leaves. With long, strong bills, Worm-eating Warblers partially open the bundles and snap up their meaty contents.

Kentucky and Hooded warblers occasionally find food by timidly loitering on the fringes of army ant swarms that mow through the leaf litter. Specialized tropical antbirds and woodcreepers squabble for frontline perches, which offer first access to the flushed insects. Over their heads, Black-and-white Warblers follow the large mixed-species flocks that quietly patrol the mid-level and canopy.

Migratory birds were long thought to be opportunists, using a variety of unpredictable food sources and occupying marginal habitats underpopulated by tropical residents. Nothing could be further from the truth for many species. Instead of searching nomadically for new food sources, many species are site-faithful, if not territorial, throughout the winter. Nonetheless, most migrants can survive for a short time in inhospitable places. And there are a few vagabonds, like Yellow-rumped Warblers, that roam the countryside in loose groups, feeding on insects in fields, tree foliage, and even in the air. They also swoop into fruiting poison ivy or wax myrtle, as they have the rare ability to digest wax. At other times, Yellow-rumped Warblers probe for nectar in eucalyptus or elder flowers.

Closely related species wintering in the same place may also differ remarkably, with some being quite specialized and others more opportunistic. Bay-breasted and Chestnut-sided warblers winter in forests and second-growth woodlands in central Panama. As in North America, Chestnut-sided Warblers defend territories and forage for insects on the undersides of leaves. In contrast, Bay-breasted Warblers wander through the forest, often in groups, searching for insects in ever-changing ways. And when a tree produces attractive fruit, Bay-breasted Warblers congregate for a fruit-eating frenzy. Why are these species so different? One possible explanation is that breeding and feeding in coniferous forests, where trees possess needlelike foliage, render Bay-breasted Warblers less well prepared for hunting insects on broadleaved foliage than are deciduous-forest-breeding Chestnut-sided Warblers. Bay-breasteds make it through the winter as jacks-of-all-trades but masters of none.

THE CONSERVATION PROBLEM
The New World's forests and wetlands and their bird faunas have been in decline ever since the arrival of Europeans five hundred years ago. From the colonial period, when New England's great white pine forests were logged to build British ships, until the westward expansion, when the continent's native cultures and natural heritage were pillaged, the forests suffered tremendously.

Disappearing Habitats in North America
In North America over the last seventy to a hundred years, forest acreage has actually increased as a result of modern natural resource management and the collapse of agriculture in many parts of the Northeast and the Appalachians. Temperate forests have proved to be fairly resilient, able to regenerate after broad-scale logging and clearing. But some forest habitats have been virtually eliminated and others have undergone long-term, perhaps irreversible changes, with profound implications for the migratory birds that depend on them. The most valuable wetlands and shoreline habitats continue to disappear and to be degraded. Estuaries, in particular, continue to be inundated with agricultural runoff, toxins, sewage, and oil from point sources. Consider:

• Less than 5 percent of the wetlands along the coast of Southern California remains undeveloped.

• Vast areas of bottomland forest in the Mississippi Valley have been converted to intensive agriculture.

• Nearly half the population of the United States lives in estuarine areas, such as New York, Los Angeles, San Francisco, Seattle, New Orleans, Anchorage, and Boston.

• Old-growth forest, with its cathedral-like tree stands interspersed with patches of disturbed second growth, has been almost completely logged.

• Large stands of bamboo known as canebrakes have been all but eliminated in the South. Swainson's and Bachman's warblers—two of the rarest wood warblers—may have used canebrake habitats extensively.

• Throughout North America, forests are showing increasing damage from air pollution and acid rain.

• Less than 10 percent of the native woodlands along rivers in the arid Southwest remains, and much of that is damaged by grazing cattle or dominated by exotic vegetation. Riparian woodlands in California's Central Valley have lost most of the Neotropical migratory bird species that were once abundant there.

• Critical coastal refuges for migrant stopovers are rapidly giving way to beachfront development.

• Large portions of the world's populations of certain waterbirds depend on ever-shrinking alkali lakes in the Great Basin. Over 50 percent of Wilson's Phalaropes are thought to feed on the brine shrimp of Great Salt Lake during migration.

• Most softwood forests, which are clear cut for paper production, are managed as large tracts of even-age young second growth, providing poor habitat for most birds.

• Dramatic floristic changes have occurred in the eastern deciduous forests, the most profound being the loss of the majestic American chestnut with its abundant flower and fruit crops. Native dogwoods are now afflicted by a fungus.

• More than 95 percent of the original wetlands in California's Central Valley has been destroyed. These wetlands support nearly two thirds of the waterfowl of the Pacific flyway during the winter, including most of the world's population of Ross's and Tule geese.

• Privately owned forest is being divided into small parcels for suburban and second-home developments. Counties surrounding Washington, D.C., have lost half of their forest cover in the last twenty years. In many areas, the loss of forest to suburbanization is offsetting the forest gained by reversion of farmland to woodland.

The effects go beyond direct habitat loss. Parasitic Brown-headed Cowbirds, open-country birds that once followed the bison herds across the Great Plains, have colonized virtually the entire United States over the last fifty years as modern agriculture and roads have created new open country. Birds that may only rarely have been parasitized in the past are now regular cowbird targets. Worm-eating Warbler nests collected early in this century contained almost no cowbird eggs, but today up to 75 percent of their nests are infested. Cowbirds are particularly devastating to the small populations of migratory birds finding nesting refuge in the remnant riparian forests of western North America.

Perhaps a more critical problem is the increasing amount of edge habitat. Where forest meets field and egg predators like raccoons and Blue Jays abound, there seem to be increasing rates of predation on the nests of forest-living migratory birds. Yet wildlife managers continue to promote the creation of more woodland edges to improve habitat for white-tailed deer and other game.

Loss of Habitat in the Tropics
Throughout the Latin American wintering grounds of migratory birds, the natural landscape is undergoing massive changes at phenomenal rates. By conservative estimates, 1 to 4 percent of forest land is being converted to pasture and farms each year. Furthermore, after large tracts of tropical forest are cleared, the probability of recovery is poor.

Forest loss is greatest in the most important migratory bird areas, such as Mexico and Central America. Some 83 percent of Costa Rica's original forest was destroyed by 1983, for instance, and experts estimate that less than 2 percent remains of the tropical deciduous forest that once blanketed Mexico and Central America. Tropical evergreen forest is essentially gone in Haiti and El Salvador and is headed for elimination in Cuba, the Dominican Republic, and southeastern Mexico. And while vast forest tracts remain in northern South America, deforestation is proceeding rapidly along the Andean slopes preferred by wintering migratory birds.

Shorebird habitat in Latin America is faring relatively well compared with North America because most important estuaries are not sites of major industrial development. However, the productivity of aquatic systems is being threatened by the development of mangrove swamps and toxic runoff from agricultural fields. Farther south, the grasslands and marshes of Argentina are giving way to the sodbusters. It is here, where the true champions of flight—Golden Plovers and Pectoral Sandpipers—find their homes, that tropical-wintering shorebirds are most threatened. Although we know less about them and their winter quarters, the songbirds that fly to tropical grasslands, like the Bobolink, Dickcissel, and Grasshopper Sparrow, face increasing agricultural development on their wintering grounds as well.

Species with geographically restricted wintering ranges and an inability to survive in disturbed or second-growth habitats face the most imminent danger. Swainson's Warblers depend on wet montane or swamp forests found only on Cuba, Jamaica, and the Yucatan Peninsula's Caribbean coast. Cerulean Warblers are confined to mid-elevation forests on the eastern Andean slope of Venezuela, Colombia, Ecuador, and Peru. With all their winter habitat in one disintegrating basket, these and similarly forest-dependent species may be the first to experience serious declines.

Cultivated landscapes may sometimes mimic forest and provide wintering habitat for forest birds. Because coffee and cacao trees require shade, they are grown under a tall "nurse-tree" canopy of native forest or, more often, of fast-growing trees like *Inga*. With their diverse, forestlike structure, coffee plantations attract even forest-dependent migrants. Unfortunately, to combat disease and increase production, researchers are developing new strains of coffee that grow well in the sun, dimming the promise of plantation habitats for birds.

Traditional agricultural practices, such as planting diverse crops in small plots and leaving hedgerows between production fields, also provide living space for birds. In the Mayan highlands, people protect patches of woods for fuel, which they harvest sustainably in long rotation cycles, a practice called "coppicing." Most forest species use disturbed habitat to some degree, so long as it is sufficiently old regrowth to resemble forests or to contain patches of sapling trees. Tropical second-growth may ultimately be the solution for migrating bird populations. Many rural communities depend on secondary forest to protect soil or harvest "minor" forest products like medicinal plants. For all its usefulness to humans and birds, however, this secondary vegetation, which supports many migrants, is being replaced by sterile plantations of more marketable exotics.

Modern mechanized agriculture is replacing traditional, bird-friendly farming. The cotton fields of Central America's Pacific slope and the sugarcane plantations of the Caribbean islands offer little for most migratory birds. Worse is cattle ranching, also a growing industry, which may be the single most destructive land use in its impact on migratory birds and other forest wildlife. What's more, long-term grazing reduces the chances that native forest or even mature second-growth can ever reclaim lost ground.

Agroforestry, coppicing for fuelwood, and maintaining native vegetation in the agricultural landscape would improve the prospects for migratory birds, as well as for resident forest birds, which outnumber migrant species by the hundreds. It is crucial to remember that many resident species also require intact tropical forest for survival and are surprisingly intolerant of disturbance.

The Pesticide Threat

Although still poorly documented, a threat is posed to Neotropical migrants by pesticides, through direct toxicity or severe reductions in food supply. North American forests are commonly sprayed with pesticides that prevent caterpillars and other juvenile insects from molting. Dependent on caterpillars for feeding their young, many species may suffer significantly reduced nesting success as a result. The persistent chlorinated hydrocarbons like DDT, no longer legally sold in the United States, are still generously supplied to farmers in Latin America and the Caribbean, where they enter streams and wash into estuaries that support wintering shorebirds. These pesticides accumulate in the fat of migratory birds, with an understudied but predictable effect: the migrants' rapid burning of fat to fuel long migration trips may inject high concentrations of toxins into the blood at an equally rapid rate. Recent research has revealed that a large variety of agro-chemicals can interfere with normal endocrine function and sperm production in humans. This could be a hidden time bomb in the reproductive tracts of birds and other vertebrates.

Shifting Blame

Scientists continue to debate the causes of declines in migratory bird populations. Is it destruction of wintering habitat in the Neotropics, fragmentation of breeding habitat in North America, or loss of crucial stopover habitat between the two? The complexity of the issue is evident in the plight of the Wood Thrush. Most people agree that Wood Thrush numbers are shrinking at an alarming rate; data from both intensive study plots and broad surveys show declines of several percent a year.

For midwestern Wood Thrushes, Brown-headed Cowbird parasitism seems to be the culprit. Research in isolated Illinois forests, which are little more than tiny islands of Wood Thrush breeding habitat in an agricultural sea of ideal cowbird habitat, reveals phenomenally high rates of parasitism on Wood Thrush nests. The open grain-storage systems currently used in the Midwest further abet the increase of cowbirds by helping them survive the winters. Wood Thrushes seem not to have a chance under these conditions.

In contrast, cowbird numbers are now declining in the East, and Wood Thrushes in isolated forests in Delaware show low, stable, and manageable levels of parasitism. Nonetheless, Wood Thrush numbers there are declining as fewer and fewer adults return from the tropics, suggesting that eastern Wood Thrush populations are suffering from deforestation in the tropics. The forests of the Caribbean lowlands of Mexico and Central America have been devastated in the past two decades, as roads have opened the last frontiers to colonization; and Wood Thrushes wintering in Mexico are largely dependent on these forests. Recent detailed studies, in which scientists radio-tracked Wood Thrushes captured in forest or cut-over areas, bear this out. While the forest-dwelling thrushes lived relatively safely on small territories, those in disturbed habitats were vagabonds that suffered high rates of mortality, probably caused by increased predation.

With habitats degrading at both ends and in the middle, and a large number of species with their own unique habitat requirements, the immediate reasons for species' declines are likely to shift and change. The most prudent action, then, is to protect habitat throughout the Neotropical migratory bird system while scientists unravel the complex chains of causation.

Development that is slowly annexing the last large tracts of habitat in our own communities is a tremendous threat to migratory birds. Many urban areas lack the minimal habitat migrants need for stopovers along their migration routes. Even large tracts of seemingly undeveloped land continue to be poorly managed for migratory birds and other parts of our natural heritage. In addition, we are losing the last large tracts of natural habitats throughout Latin America and the Caribbean.

Underlying these threats to migratory birds are fundamental problems that challenge the future quality of life for humans as well: overpopulation, tremendous inequalities in access to resources and land in developing countries, over-consumption of resources by people in developed countries, poor environmental safeguards for industrial and agroindustrial activities, and war.

It is important to be informed, concerned, and active in addressing these global problems. We include in the resource section of this book a selection of important references. The future of the great migration systems is in doubt as long as land and resources are squandered. However, while dealing with the great problems we face, we must remain optimistic. A good attitude is necessary to tackle the multitude of local battles and personal lifestyle changes needed to improve the environment. In fighting for the well-being of migratory birds, we must avoid becoming cynical or discouraged.

What can you do? What would you be willing to do? Plant native trees and shrubs? Give 1 percent or more of your salary to land protection efforts? Eat less or no beef? Buy foods grown without toxic chemicals? Limit your family to two children? Use public transportation, walk, or bike at least 50 percent of the time? Lobby for laws that protect wildlife and habitat? Work with local planning agencies to promote responsible development that protects open space? Reach out to form partnerships with groups doing similar things in Latin America and the Caribbean?

All these efforts would help ensure future habitat for the millions of birds that cross our skies. What you do will depend on your interest, talents, and time. In the following chapters we provide some guidance for getting started in your work to preserve migratory birds. This book is intended to introduce you to the tools. We encourage you to consult the publications and organizations listed at the end of the book for more in-depth treatment.

2

Make It Count!
Volunteer Opportunities in
Monitoring and Research
Programs

Never doubt that a small group of thoughtful committed citizens can change the world. Indeed, it's the only thing that ever has. —Margaret Mead

Often people call the Smithsonian Migratory Bird Center with seemingly simple questions about migratory birds and their conservation problems, and on many occasions we have to answer, "We don't know." This isn't a result just of our ignorance, but the collective ignorance of all scientists about some very complicated issues. It is humbling that, given the attention ornithology has received compared with other branches of natural history, our understanding of how bird populations respond to the changing world is still rudimentary.

On many conservation issues, we can list certain steps that will improve habitats—we outline some in the following chapters. However, we need to keep improving the information on which we base our plans. Even for such relatively straightforward questions as how many birds there are of a particular species, information may be subjective or just plain wrong. Knowing the population status of a species we are concerned about is a small step toward predicting how different habitat changes could affect that population. As with social planning for human populations, we need to know demographic trends, like rates of births and deaths, emigration and immigration. We also need a clear understanding of the critical resources that affect habitat quality for different species. Finally, we need some concept of how and when bottlenecks are created for different species. This information cannot be gained through one massive research program, like the Human Genome Project, but through the synthesis of many small efforts.

More research is also needed to satisfy our curiosity about migration systems. We have come a long way from the initial theories concerning bird migration (such as the idea that birds changed their species identity or hibernated on pond bottoms). The more we know, the more interesting stories we have about the profound adaptations birds make to survive. Our improved understanding of birds will only increase our interest in their conservation.

AMATEUR ORNITHOLOGISTS
AND THE HISTORY OF VOLUNTEERISM

No other field of science has depended as much on the energy and enthusiasm of amateur volunteers as ornithology. By "amateur" we mean people whose primary income is earned outside the field of ornithology or who have never received formal training in the field. Amateur ornithologists should not be considered less knowledgeable about birds or less likely to make profound scientific contributions than their professional counterparts. The dawn of North American ornithology occurred well before the beginnings of this century. Mark Catesby was studying natural history and painting the birds of North America in the early 1700s. Amateurs were particularly important to the early development of North American ornithology because during the eighteenth and most of the nineteenth centuries there was no recognized professional field of ornithology. However, even today, when science has become increasingly technical and inaccessible to the general public, amateurs continue to make crucial contributions to the science of ornithology.

The Road to Ornithology

Enjoyment of birds in the wild is the paramount characteristic shared by individuals who become amateur ornithologists. The exact number of bird aficionados in North America is difficult to determine, but we know it is very high. Each spring more than twenty thousand people flock to Point Pelee National Park in southern Ontario, one of North America's premier birding locations, to see migratory birds. They are among the more than sixty million people worldwide who are believed to be bird enthusiasts. The twenty million to thirty million bird enthusiasts in North America spend billions of dollars annually on their hobby.

Bird enthusiasts can be roughly divided into two categories: bird-watchers and birders. Bird-watchers are casual bird enthusiasts; they enjoy birds, perhaps use feeders or plants to attract birds to their yards, and may or may not own field guides and binoculars. Birders have turned bird-watching into a competitive sport. They are likely to spend more than $800 a year on birding trips and more than $100 a year on birding equipment, including binoculars, field guides, spotting scopes, tape recorders, and the like. Birders tend to be better educated, have higher incomes, and travel more often than the average North American. To formalize their competitive status, three fourths of these individuals keep track of the birds they encounter, most commonly through lists of species seen in a given year or location and over a lifetime. Some birders drive hundreds of miles in the hope of adding a new species to their annual or life list!

A small subset of the birder and bird-watcher communities seeks to take bird-watching beyond the realms of sports and leisure into science. By applying scientific methodology (discussed later) to their observations and sharing their findings with the scientific community, these individuals often make significant contributions to ornithology.

VOLUNTEER OPPORTUNITIES

To become an amateur ornithologist, the bird-watcher or birder must go beyond merely watching birds and keeping private lists for his or her own pleasure, and collect and share observations with the scientific community. Contributions may be made through information collected on bird behavior, abundance, distribution, and the like. This need not be an intimidating venture. Simple steps, such as contributing unusual observations to a bird magazine or pooling one's checklists with others in a region, will add pieces to the big puzzle of bird distribution.

Further contributions can be made by participating in any one of a variety of surveys, census programs, or research projects. Data from these studies are often used to monitor the status of bird populations and determine environmental factors that may be responsible for an increase or decrease in the number of individuals in a population. In fact, the data used to show declines in the number of Neotropical migratory birds throughout the Western Hemisphere were, for the most part, collected by amateur ornithologists (see Shirley Briggs' essay later in this chapter). Furthermore, research projects that are attempting to determine the causes of these declines and counts that will monitor the phenomenon depend on the energy and enthusiasm of amateurs. The highly motivated and curious amateur can pursue his or her own line of avian research.

The following is a concise listing of the major bird counts and scientific studies in North America that use a primarily amateur volunteer force to obtain data vital to ornithology and, in the long run, to the conservation of birds. Everyone can participate and contribute. All censuses and scientific projects greatly benefit from the continued support of the same individuals playing the same roles from year to year, as variability of results is greatly reduced. So if you plan to volunteer for a project, strongly consider becoming a long-term participant.

Breeding Bird Counts

Breeding Bird Census

Some two thousand amateur and professional volunteers who know local birds by sound and sight participate in the Breeding Bird Census (BBC) annually. The BBC was established in 1937. Originally sponsored by the National Audubon Society, it is now coordinated by the Cornell Laboratory of Ornithology. Volunteers record the number of breeding pairs of birds at particular study sites. The census works on the principle that, in the spring, singing males hold breeding territories; therefore, each singing male represents a pair of breeding birds. The "singing-male method" is not a perfect predictor of the number of breeding birds, since some males may be silent when the census is taking place and some singing males may not have mates. However, it is the best technique available for estimating the actual density of breeding birds. Skill is essential to establish an accurate plot map and to locate male birds by their calls. Each census requires at least eight visits to the same site during a single breeding season to quantify and map birds and vegetation.

An important goal of the BBC is to count birds annually at the same sites over successive years in order to identify and understand local and regional population trends and determine the habitat requirements for breeding birds. Unfortunately, very few censuses have been carried out at the same sites for more than ten years, and sample sizes are very small for all but the most common species. Four major deficiencies exist in the organization of BBCs: (1) habitat types are not equally covered (participants often choose their favorite birding spots); (2) plot sizes are generally inadequate and vary greatly (forty to one hundred acres, or sixteen to forty hectares); (3) individual plots sometimes vary in habitat type; and (4) individual plots tend not to be continuously covered on an annual basis. Nevertheless, the BBC currently provides the best available information on the structure of North American bird communities. For more information on the BBC, contact Cornell Laboratory of Ornithology, 159 Sapsucker Woods Road, Ithaca, NY 14850. You may also contact the Office of Migratory Bird Management, U.S. Fish and Wildlife Service, Laurel, MD 20708.

Breeding Bird Survey

The Breeding Bird Survey (BBS), the most comprehensive nongame monitoring program in North America, is a cooperative venture of the U.S. Fish and Wildlife Service and the Canadian Wildlife Service. The BBS was first conducted in 1965 in the United States and in 1966 in Canada. It was established to determine long-term trends in numbers of birds and to provide a means of monitoring changes in bird populations that might result from environmental factors, such as the use of DDT. Unlike the BBC, which counts birds in individual selected plots,

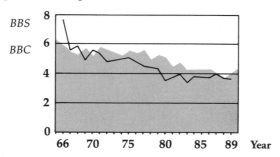

Average number of birds
per transect or plot

The decline in breeding Wood Thrush populations has been tracked through volunteer efforts on Breeding Bird Censuses and Breeding Bird Surveys.

the BBS is based on a continentwide sampling design. During each nesting season (usually in late May or June, when males are the most vocal), volunteers survey one or more of the 1,800 predetermined routes that cover nearly 50,000 miles (80,500 kilometers) of roads and some waterways. Each volunteer (or team) is assigned a 25-mile (40-kilometer) route. Once each spring they follow the route, stopping every .5 mile (.8 kilometer). At each of these fifty points they record all species heard or seen within a three-minute period. Surveys begin one-half hour after sunrise and last approximately four and one-half hours.

The BBS provides adequate population data for more than half of the breeding birds in North America and is perhaps the best example of how numerous amateur volunteers can contribute to a major research program. However, those who interpret BBS data face two major difficulties: First, most birds are counted along roadsides. Roads are likely to go through high ground and disturbed landscapes. Therefore, the BBS does not sample all habitat types equally. Second, the distribution of habitats in North America is continually changing. Since World War II, abandoned farmland has reverted to forest and millions of acres of forestland have been claimed by urban and suburban development. The BBS does not have a built-in habitat classification scheme, so attempts to correlate populations with actual changes in vegetation on the routes must be done by estimation from imagery or maps after the fact. Despite these difficulties, the value of the BBS should not be underestimated. The large sample sizes of the BBS make it more statistically significant and more sensitive to short-term population changes than the BBC. It is the best early warning system that we currently have for detecting precipitous declines in bird populations, including those of Neotropical migrants. Data from the BBS are currently used by the National Biological Service to identify species that may require specific conservation attention before their populations reach critical levels of endangerment. The BBS always needs new volunteers to take over routes or begin new ones. For more information, contact the BBS Coordinator, National Biological Service, 12100 Beech Forest Road, Laurel, MD 20708, or the Migratory Bird Surveys Division, Canadian Wildlife Service, National Wildlife Research Centre, Ottawa ONT K1A 0H3.

Making a Difference   Jimmy Carter

While on a visit to Tanzania to climb Mount Kilimanjaro and visit game pre-serves about five years ago, Rosalynn and I became interested in serious birding. We had always been involved in outdoor activities. As a child in south Georgia, I grew up hunting and fishing on our farm. In fact, I recently wrote a book about those experiences: *An Outdoor Journal.* Since that trip to Tanzania, we have paid far more attention to nongame birds, and have been bird-watching with local experts in a number of countries in Africa, Europe, Latin America, and Asia. We have also listened to tapes of birds in our home area so that now, when we are in the woods, we can pretty well tell what birds are all around us just by listening.

In 1989 I received a letter from Mark Oberle, a doctor with the Centers for Disease Control and Prevention who had been doing the Lacross Breeding Bird Survey (BBS), which happens to cover an area near our home in Plains, Geor-gia. Mark described the changes in bird populations along that BBS route over the last two decades. I asked if we could accompany him on the Breeding Bird Survey, which we have now done for the last five years. The first year we helped Mark and his recorder, Joel Volpi, by keeping time, and also saw ten "life birds." A male and a female Summer Tanager, a Yellow-billed Cuckoo, and a Yellow-breasted Chat were particularly prized sightings. The toughest bird for us to see was a White-eyed Vireo in a river thicket. While Mark did the three-minute bird count at that stop, Joel helped us find the vireo, but only after stepping over an odoriferous dead cow. At the last stop we also saw an Anhinga—a first for that particular BBS route, while two Red-tailed Hawks screamed low overhead.

We enjoy the opportunity to help document changes in bird populations, and we learn a little each time we go into the field. Along the Lacross BBS route there has been a decline in warblers and Northern Bobwhites over the last two decades, which correlates with changes in habitat and farming practices in our area. Some of this decline in songbirds may be attributable to the increasing prevalence of Brown-headed Cowbirds and the alteration of wintering habitat south of our borders.

While I was governor of Georgia and later president, I worked hard to pass conservation legislation, such as the dramatic expansion of our national park system in Alaska. While the political dimensions of those conservation achievements were complicated, the technical dimensions were relatively straightforward. In the case of preserving Neotropical migrants, the exact reason for songbirds' decline may vary from species to species, and the technical solutions may be far from obvious. Habitat destruction in Latin America is intertwined with the problems of unemployment, social injustice, rapid population growth, and political instability that I have been working to help solve there. We share the concerns of biologists and fellow birders for the future of our wild birds and the health of our ecosystem, and we strongly support the efforts of conservation biologists to find workable solutions to these conservation questions.

Former President Jimmy Carter and his wife, Rosalynn, are regular contributors to the Breeding Bird Survey.

Breeding Bird Atlases

The concept of the Breeding Bird Atlas (BBA) originated in Britain in the late 1960s. In North America, BBAs are coordinated through the North American Ornithological Atlas Committee (NORAC) and undertaken by a state, provincial, or territorial conservation organization or agency. Each BBA differs in structure from one location to the next, but is completed over a set period of time, usually five years. In general, each state, province, or territory is divided into several atlas blocks, each consisting of a few square miles. Volunteers take censuses in these blocks several times throughout the breeding season to determine the number of nesting birds in each block. They compile lists of potential, probable, and confirmed breeding birds by species and number. These data are then sent to the coordinator, who edits and analyzes them and returns the results to the sponsoring entity. When an atlas is completed, the state, province, or territory has a reasonably accurate picture of the distribution of its breeding birds that can be cataloged and published in maps to be used for present and future reference.

New York and Ontario have completed two of the most impressive atlases. The sponsors of the New York State Breeding Bird Atlas (Federation of New York State Bird Clubs, N.Y. State Department of Environmental Conservation, and Cornell Laboratory of Ornithology) began planning the project in 1979 and began their fieldwork in 1980. From 1980 to 1985, atlas groups (more than 4,000 volunteers) covered more than 5,300 atlas blocks (each 5 × 5 kilometer, or 3.4 × 3.4 mile) which amounts to 99.8 percent of the state. Data analysis led to the production of species accounts and distribution maps for 238 breeding species. This information has been published in *The Atlas of Breeding Birds in New York State* (1988), edited by R. F. Andrle and J. R. Carroll. Throughout the state, conservationists and managers use a computerized database of atlas-generated information. To date, the New York Breeding Bird Atlas is the most detailed in the world for a land area its size (30 million acres, or 12 million hectares). Ontario, with a landmass of more than 1 million square kilometers (more than 620,000 square miles), has also completed an enormous undertaking. The first atlas to be completed for Canada, *Atlas of Breeding Birds of Ontario* (sponsored by the Federation of Ontario Naturalists and Long Point Bird Observatory), presents the current distribution of the province's nearly 300 breeding species. More than 1,300 volunteers contributed 180,000 hours of fieldwork between 1981 and 1985. By almost every mode of transportation imaginable, nearly every bit of Ontario was combed to collect 400,000 records of breeding birds. For more information on Breeding Bird Atlases, contact the Chairperson, NORAC, Vermont Institute of Natural Sciences, Woodstock, VT 05091.

Migration Counts

Counting birds during migration is advantageous because of the sheer numbers that funnel through particular flyways or rest at stopovers. Some birds, especially raptors, are very dispersed during the breeding and winter seasons. Shorebirds and boreal forest warblers often breed and winter in inaccessible places. Because birds from a large breeding range pass through the migration concentration points, migration counts provide information on regional or global population changes, rather than on local problems on the breeding or wintering grounds.

International Shorebird Survey

Since 1974 the International Shorebird Survey (ISS) has been used to collect information on shorebirds and the wetlands they use during migration. Organized by Manomet Bird Observatory, more than 800 volunteers (two thirds in the United States, the remainder in Central and South America) have contributed by estimating shorebird numbers throughout the spring (April 1 to June 10) and fall (July 11 to October 31). Most of these counts take place east of the Rocky Mountains, primarily along the northeastern and Florida coastlines. In addition, approximately fifty sites have been counted in countries and commonwealths south of the United States. Sites are selected by participants and counted at least three times during key migration periods. The resulting data have helped Manomet Bird Observatory determine the timing of shorebird migration and identify the stopover points and staging sites where shorebirds gather during migration. Early evaluations of the database have indicated that shorebirds concentrate in these areas to such a degree that the loss of one or more of these sites could seriously affect entire populations. This finding resulted in the development of several conservation and management projects, most notably the Western Hemisphere Shorebird Reserve Network (see chapter 6). Although only very large population trends can be detected reliably by the ISS, consistent and alarming declines have been detected for several species. Preliminary analysis of the data for coastal sites has shown declines of 40 to 80 percent over the last two decades for populations of at least three species, Short-billed Dowitcher, Sanderling, and Whimbrel. For more information, contact the ISS Coordinator, Manomet Bird Observatory, P.O. Box 1770, Manomet, MA 02345.

Maritimes Shorebird Survey

Begun in 1974, the Maritimes Shorebird Survey (MSS) was established to identify important sites for shorebirds in eastern Canada and to monitor long-term population trends. Surveys are conducted by volunteers who count shorebirds at regular intervals and specified sites. Because data on distribution and migration can be accumulated over wide geographical areas, the MSS data have been extremely valuable for identifying key shorebird habitat in Canada. For example, the Bay of Fundy is now recognized as the focal point for Semipalmated Sandpiper fall migration and is also important for other species, including Semipalmated Plover, Black-bellied Plover, Dunlin, Least Sandpiper, Sanderling, and Short-billed Dowitcher. To complement its knowledge of shorebird requirements, the Canadian Wildlife Service Latin American Program conducted aerial surveys (1982–1986) to determine the principal wintering areas for shorebirds in South America. This project resulted in the identification of critical wintering sites along some 28,000 kilometers (17,400 miles) of South American coast. For more information on the MSS, contact the MSS Coordinator, Canadian Wildlife Service, National Wildlife Research Centre, Ottawa ON K1A 0H3.

The Pacific Flyway Project

Since 1988 Point Reyes Bird Observatory has conducted the Pacific Flyway Project as a means of collecting data on the importance of western North American wetlands to shorebirds. More than 500 volunteers annually count shorebirds in wetlands during peak periods of use in the spring, fall, and winter in every state west of the Rocky Mountains, as well as areas in Canada and Mexico. Small wetlands are counted by one or more observers. Larger areas are subdivided and surveyed by teams. Wetlands that are too extensive or inaccessible for ground-based counters are surveyed by plane or boat. As of 1992, the Pacific Flyway Project had identified 85 interior and 60 coastal wetland sites that each attract concentrations of more than 1,000 shorebirds, 25 interior and 26 coastal sites that attract more than 10,000 shorebirds, and 3 interior and 9 coastal sites that attract over 100,000 shorebirds. Data from the Pacific Flyway Project enable scientists to describe the species composition and pattern of seasonal use at each wetland. In addition, maps of the geographic distribution patterns for key species can be used to demonstrate links between breeding, staging, stopover, and wintering sites. The Western Hemisphere Shorebird Reserve Network (see chapter 6) has used this information to expand its reserve system and increase public awareness about the need to protect shorebirds through the management and conservation of both coastal and inland wetlands. For more information on the Pacific Flyway Project, contact Point Reyes Bird Observatory, 4990 Shoreline Highway, Stinson Beach, CA 94970.

Hawk Migration Counts

The Hawk Migration Association of North America sponsors Hawk Migration Counts conducted by hawk watchers at known hawk migration lookouts across North America. Where lookouts are not available, roadside surveys are undertaken. The majority of counts are undertaken in the fall as raptors head south. Results are tallied on free, postage-paid data forms that are summarized in the newsletter of the Hawk Migration Association. Forms are stored at Muhlenberg College in Pennsylvania, where they are available to biologists interested in hawk biology and conservation. Data from the migration counts are most appropriate for detecting global or regional population declines, rather than for identifying problems in specific locations at a specific time of the year. Recent data indicate a population decline in the Broad-winged Hawk, a Neotropical migratory raptor. Hawk Migration Counts have also been useful in determining natural areas in need of protection. Data from Hawk Migration Counts influenced decisions by the U.S. Fish and Wildlife Service to acquire forested habitat for inclusion in the National Wildlife Refuge System. For more information on Hawk Migration Counts, write to the Secretary, Hawk Migration Association of North America, P.O. Box 3482, Lynchburg, VA 24503.

The North American Migration Count

Founded in 1992, the North American Migration Count (NAMC) was designed to determine the "shape" of migration for migratory songbirds. Do these songbirds return to North America in the spring en masse, making straight, constant flights across the continent to their various breeding grounds? Do they gather at specific sites to rest and refuel along the way? Do they follow flyways, proceeding like an organized marching band? Or do they fan out chaotically, progressing like schoolchildren released for recess? These questions are important to curious biologists. The data the NAMC will generate are also vital to managers and conservationists. If songbirds follow specific routes or gather at specific sites, then the loss of habitat or the presence of contaminants in these areas may greatly endanger large numbers of migrants. Unlike other surveys, the NAMC is conducted on a single day of the year: the second Saturday in May. Counts, by sight and sound, can be made on foot or by car, boat, bike, or even horseback. No specific routes are defined. Some birders travel long distances to perfect their lists. Bird-watchers may pull up a comfortable chair and count the birds that visit the backyard feeder and woodlot. Data generated by the North American Migration Count may be difficult to interpret as a result of the lack of standardization in size and habitat types for count areas. In addition, the great number of modes of transportation that can be used in the NAMC requires that each be quantified in a different manner. For more information, contact Jim Stasz, NAMC Coordinator, P.O. Box 71, North Beach, MD 20714.

Winter Bird Counts
Christmas Bird Count
The first Christmas Bird Count (CBC) was launched in New York's Central Park in 1900 by Frank M. Chapman and Charles Rogers. That count encouraged birders to compete for the lengthiest species list amassed in a given day, and it was the first attempt to record winter bird populations. Although the CBC does not survey Neotropical migratory birds in North America, it presents a great opportunity for volunteers to develop and hone their bird identification skills. Since the turn of the century, the CBC has been conducted by birding groups (usually bird clubs) at hundreds of locations throughout the United States and Canada. Today nearly sixteen hundred CBCs take place each winter, involving volunteers from every state, each Canadian province, Central and South America, the West Indies, Guam, and Saipan. Through the counts in Central and South America and the West Indies, information is collected on wintering populations of Neotropical migrants.

Each CBC group breaks into teams and spends one day (between mid-December and early January) counting birds by species and number in its local area. Because these counts are conducted by teams, novice bird-watchers have the opportunity to learn from skilled peers. At the end of the day, the teams gather to tally the counts. These tallies are usually associated with festive holiday gatherings that make beginning birders feel all the more welcome and inspired.

The U.S. Fish and Wildlife Service is charged with computerizing the counts and making them easily accessible to researchers. The database constitutes the longest continuous record of bird populations available in North America, and more than two hundred scientific papers utilizing these data have been published in various research journals. However, the data must be interpreted with caution. Because these counts were initially conceived in the name of sport, perhaps more so than science, only minimal efforts have been made to demand precision and observer skill. Vegetational records from count locations are often insufficient or absent. Furthermore, habitat types and environmental conditions in the areas in which the CBCs have been taken are dynamic, having changed continually throughout the past century. For more information, contact National Audubon Society, 950 Third Avenue, New York, NY 10022.

Winter Bird Population Study

Since 1949 the Winter Bird Population Study has been conducted to help biologists gain a better understanding of winter bird populations. The Winter Bird Population Study is carried out much like the BBC, usually at the very same sites. Like the CBC, the Winter Bird Population Study does not provide information on Neotropical migrants, but it is another opportunity for developing bird-watching skills. Beginners can usually find a patient, skilled bird-watcher to help them along. Results from this study are published in the *Journal of Field Ornithology*. For more information, contact the National Biological Service, 12100 Beech Forest Road, Laurel, MD 20708.

Checklist Projects

Many bird-watchers rely on checklists as the simplest and most straightforward record of birds found in a particular place and time. Compilations of checklist data can provide information on avian geographic ranges and the seasonal occurrence of migratory birds. The frequency of birds reported on checklists corresponds nicely to the relative abundance of birds found within the area of checklist coverage. However, most individual checklists languish in desk drawers and filing cabinets without ever being introduced into a larger collection. For this reason, organized checklist projects are now being used to monitor spatial and temporal variations in avian abundance.

In 1948 Quebec established a provincewide checklist program. Volunteers record the number of all bird species seen or heard in a given day at a given site on standardized checklist forms. In addition, they note the date, habitat type, duration of the trip, number of participants, and any remarkable sightings. Since 1978 Quebec checklist data have been computerized in a system known as EPOQ (l'Etude des Populations d'Oiseaux du Quebec, or Studies of Bird Populations in Quebec). The system now contains more than 2.2 million records of observations from 158,000 checklists gathered at 3,600 observation sites. The data are being used to produce maps by season, year, and month, as well as tables and graphs of seasonal or annual fluctuations. In addition, EPOQ data are being used for intensive studies of specific species and communities at given sites. Comparisons of EPOQ and BBS data indicate that most trends are similar, including the dominant trend of declines in many Neotropical migrants. For more information on EPOQ, contact the Biology Department at Sherbrooke University, Sherbrooke, QUE J1K 2R1.

Since 1982, 431 volunteers from the Wisconsin Society of Ornithology, under the direction of Stanley Temple of the University of Wisconsin, have participated in the Wisconsin Checklist Project. Each volunteer keeps careful records by county of bird species encountered throughout each week of the year. Data are recorded on standardized forms that can, with the use of an optical scanner, be quickly loaded onto computers for analysis. The data from the checklist project are being used to determine year-to-year changes in the abundance of birds in Wisconsin. The reported frequency of occurrence for each species in a year or part of a year can be compared among a number of seasons or years. These comparisons have revealed that checklist studies are sensitive enough to detect intrastate trends in bird populations. Results of the Wisconsin checklist program have been published by Stanley Temple and John Cary in *Wisconsin Birds: A Seasonal and Geographic Guide* (University of Wisconsin Press, 1987). For more information on the Wisconsin Checklist Project, contact Dr. Stanley Temple, Department of Wildlife Ecology, University of Wisconsin, Madison, WI 53706. Because of the success of such checklist projects, the National Biological Service is considering a continentwide program.

World Series of Birding

Begun in 1984, the World Series of Birding (WSB) is "the game" for birders. On the second Saturday of every May, teams of high-spirited birders flock to New Jersey to spend twenty-four hours tallying as many species of the state's birds as they can. In the end, every team comes out a winner; by gathering pledges on the number of birds they see, they raise money (from $1,500 to $50,000 a team, $250,000 annually) for their favorite environmental cause. Coveted Urner-Stone, Ed Stearns, and Cape Island cups are awarded to outstanding teams. The WSB is organized and hosted by the New Jersey Audubon Society, but participants come from numerous bird clubs, environmental organizations, and even Fortune 500 corporations.

The WSB has become extremely popular for a number of reasons: it gives birders a chance to test and use their skills for a good cause; it provides a forum in which birders, conservation groups, and businesses that cater to the birding market can interact; it generates hundreds of thousands of dollars for numerous worthy conservation organizations; it focuses media attention on the challenge and adventure of birding, as well as the habitat needs of migrating birds; and it is simply a lot of fun. To learn more or to enter a team (there is a fee), write to the World Series of Birding, New Jersey Audubon Society, P.O. Box 3, Cape May Point, NJ 08212. Foreign teams are encouraged to participate.

Research Projects
Bird Banding Projects
"Banding" is the process of fastening a metal or plastic "anklet" onto the lower portion of a bird's leg. The first bird-banding organization was founded in 1909. By the 1920s the U.S. and Canadian governments had created formal centers for the collection and maintenance of banding data. Since that time, more than forty million birds have been banded in North America and more than one million more are banded each year. Much of the vital information generated by banded birds depends on the recapture of live banded birds or the recovery of deceased banded birds. However, less than 5 percent of all banded birds are ever recaptured or recovered. This figure is even lower for Neotropical migrants.

Nonetheless, the data generated thus far have contributed to our understanding of the timing of migration, migration routes, wintering sites, the longevity of birds, the site fidelity of birds on wintering and breeding grounds, and the reproductive success of localized populations of breeding birds. In addition, banding studies have helped ornithologists establish criteria for sexing and aging birds and for determining breeding condition and molt patterns.

Birds to be banded are caught in a number of ways. Nylon mesh nets, known as "mist nets," are most commonly used. Depending on the size of the mesh, these virtually invisible nets can catch everything from hummingbirds to shorebirds to raptors. Small single- and multicompartment wire traps are baited with seed and used to capture small, ground-feeding birds. Bow-shaped spring traps are often used along with mist nets and a "lure bird" (often a sparrow or a pigeon on a tether) to catch raptors. Waterfowl lured to fields and shorebirds on open beaches are captured with large "cannon nets" that are shot over entire flocks. Each metal bird band is marked with a unique serial number and the abbreviated name and address of the National Biological Service's Bird Banding Lab in Laurel, Maryland, or the Canadian Wildlife Service in Ottawa, Ontario.

For ornithologists to determine the individual identity of a bird from a distance, metal bands are ineffective. Colored plastic bands are commonly used on smaller birds for such studies. A unique pattern of colored bands can be assigned to each bird in a study. Birds then become known by such codes as "right leg—yellow over orange, left leg—green." A variety of markers have been created for larger birds. Long-necked birds may be marked with numbered, colored collars that can be easily read at a distance with the aid of binoculars or a spotting scope. Colored patagial (wing) tags or streamers may be used to identify birds in flight. Bill markers, called "saddles," are attached to either side or bridge the bill of waterfowl (mostly), and held in place harmlessly with a nylon or metal pin through the nostrils.

For studies in which birds need to be individually identified for a short period of time (no longer than one molt), feather marking techniques may be used. Flight feathers may be dyed with bright, sometimes fluorescent, paints. White feathers (often chicken) that have been dyed and patterned with different colors may be cemented to upper tail feathers (coverts). Finally, researchers may strap on or surgically implant transmitters that emit a specific signal that can be tracked with radio telemetry equipment. Radio transmitters are especially effective in instances where birds relocate frequently or when they are present in environments where visibility is low. Data gathered by these studies are collected and computerized by the U.S. and Canadian Wildlife Services.

Ornithologists must have permits from state, provincial, or territorial and federal agencies to carry out their banding, color-marking, and radio-tracking programs. However, many bird banders welcome the assistance of volunteers at banding stations. Although volunteers often do not band the birds themselves, they may assist the program by removing birds from nets or traps. Handling birds is a great way to improve one's bird identification skills. With bird in hand and a field guide for reference, it is much easier to see the distinguishing features of a species. There are three major banding stations that enlist the aid of volunteers: Manomet Observatory (P.O. Box 1770, Manomet, MA 02345), Point Reyes Bird Observatory (4990 Shoreline Highway, Stinson Beach, CA 94970), and Long Point Bird Observatory (P.O. Box 160, Port Rowan, ONT N0E 1M0). In addition, bird clubs often have a number of certified bird banders who run small, local banding stations that are in need of volunteer assistance.

If you find a bird with a leg band or color marking, record the color combination and any numbers that might be present, as well as the bird's sex, age, physical condition, and precise geographic location. If you are not qualified to determine this information, find someone who is. Mail these data (and the band or marker if the bird is dead) to the National Biological Service's Bird Banding Laboratory, Laurel, MD 20708, or the Bird Banding Office, Canadian Wildlife Service, National Wildlife Research Centre, Environment Canada, Ottawa, ONT K1A 0H3. In return for your efforts, you will receive information regarding the locality and date that the bird was originally banded.

Monitoring Avian Productivity and Survivorship

While many of the counts mentioned previously (including the BBS, BBC, and CBC) provide annual estimates of population trends for landbirds, they fail to provide data on demographic (productivity and survivorship) parameters. Without this information, it is virtually impossible to determine the causes for population changes—whether they might be occurring on the wintering ground, breeding ground, in between, or everywhere; and whether they are affecting birth rates, death rates, or both. In an attempt to collect critical long-term population and demographic data for a select group of "indicator" species in North America, the Institute for Bird Populations initiated the Monitoring Avian Productivity and Survivorship (MAPS) program in 1989. MAPS uses standard constant-effort banding and standardized point counts during the breeding season at a continentwide network of stations. The long-term goal of the program is, through the cooperation of bird banders, the establishment and operation of 260 stations across North America. The existence of these stations will greatly increase the opportunities for volunteers to participate in banding and point count efforts. However, this program is new and its ability to produce interpretable indicators of productivity or survivorship is still being tested as a pilot program. For more information, contact the Institute for Bird Populations, P.O. Box 1346, Point Reyes Station, CA 94956-1346.

The National Science Experiment

The National Science Experiment, a project of the Cornell Laboratory of Ornithology (CLO), is one of the newest ornithological projects to enlist the aid of amateur volunteers. Participants in the experiment will engage in a series of coordinated activities aimed at answering specific ornithological questions. One of the most important aspects of the study as far as Neotropical migrants are concerned is the "Project Tanager" segment. Bird club members will monitor each of the four species of tanagers (Summer, Scarlet, Western, and Hepatic) throughout the breeding season. All but the Hepatic are Neotropical migrants believed to be sensitive to forest fragmentation. BBS data indicate that Scarlet Tanager populations have declined significantly over the past ten years. The CLO hopes these studies will help determine the smallest size of forest fragment in which each tanager species can breed. Studies of pigeon behavior and wild bird feeding preferences will be included in the National Science Experiment to attract beginning as well as experienced birders, cover urban and suburban environments, and ensure that some aspect of the program can be carried out throughout the year. For more information, contact Education and Information Services, Cornell Laboratory of Ornithology, 159 Sapsucker Woods Road, Ithaca, NY 14850.

Nest Record Card Program

Founded by the Cornell Laboratory of Ornithology in 1965, the Nest Record Card Program now includes more than three hundred thousand records of individual bird nests. Records include information on the species of nesting bird, nesting materials used, nesting habitat, clutch size, the length of incubation and the overall nesting period, and fledging success. This information has contributed to our understanding of the breeding biology and reproductive success of North America's breeding birds. The data held within this program may be important in clarifying such issues as the role cowbirds play in the reproductive success of Neotropical migratory birds in forest remnants. For more information, contact the Cornell Laboratory of Ornithology, 159 Sapsucker Woods Road, Ithaca, NY 14850.

Project FeederWatch

In 1987 the Cornell Laboratory of Ornithology and Long Point Bird Observatory launched Project FeederWatch, a continentwide survey of birds at bird feeders in private yards. The project grew out of an earlier feeder survey begun in Ontario in 1976 by the Long Point Bird Observatory. Comparisons of several years of feeder survey data with CBC data indicated parallel fluctuations in abundance for a number of birds in each survey. Feeder surveys have the advantage of existing throughout the winter, rather than just as a snapshot around Christmastime. Now more than eight thousand participants throughout North America collect data on the number and kinds of birds that visit their feeders on one or two days every two weeks between November and April. Data are recorded on computerized forms and sent to the Cornell Laboratory of Ornithology, where they are analyzed to answer specific questions. In return for the data, observers receive *FeederWatch News,* a twice-yearly update of data analyses and information on feeding birds. Each participant pays a small fee that covers the cost of the newsletter, forms, and mailing. For more information, write Project Feeder-Watch, Cornell Laboratory of Ornithology, 159 Sapsucker Woods Road, Ithaca, NY 14850, or Project FeederWatch, Long Point Bird Observatory, P.O. Box 160, Port Rowan, ONT N0E 1M0.

Directories of Volunteer Opportunities

In addition to the large, continentwide projects mentioned above, there are numerous state and local projects carried out throughout the Western Hemisphere. The American Birding Association, Inc., publishes an annual listing of volunteer opportunities for bird enthusiasts in its newsletter, *Winging It,* each December. For the most recent directory (there is a small charge), write to ABA Sales, American Birding Association, P.O. Box 6599, Colorado Springs, CO 80934. The Canadian Wildlife Service publishes and distributes *Bird Trends,* a newsletter that provides feedback to volunteers, information on trends in Canadian bird populations, and a menu of volunteer-based ornithological projects in Canada. To subscribe to *Bird Trends* (no charge), write to Nongame Birds and Latin American Program, Canadian Wildlife Service, Ottawa, ONT K1A 0H3.

Be a Great Volunteer
Developing Your Skills
The bird counts and research projects listed previously are only as good as the skill and dedication of the volunteers that undertake them. At the very least, volunteers must be able to identify birds by sight. However, being able to identify birds by sound is critical for studies and counts performed during the breeding season. There are a number of ways you can develop your birding skills and knowledge:

• Take an ornithology course or workshop that emphasizes the field identification of birds. Courses may be found at universities, community colleges, and local nature or recreation areas.

• Join a local bird club or naturalist society. Many such organizations have regularly scheduled weekend field trips. These expeditions present a prime opportunity to tag along with experts and learn your local birds by sight and sound. Make it clear to participants in the outing that you are a beginner interested in developing your bird-watching skills. Ask that knowledgeable peers point out the birds they see and hear, explaining what field marks or vocal characteristics define each species.

• Subscribe to one or more bird or natural history magazines. Many of these magazines regularly have articles intended to help develop the skills of beginners and hone the skills of even the most experienced birders. They also offer information on the natural history and conservation of birds, reviews on birding techniques and equipment, and listings of bird-watching expeditions throughout the world. Visit your library to find out what bird publications exist in your area. These publications often have articles of regional interest, frequently by local amateurs. Suggested national and international magazines include the following:

Audubon Magazine
National Audubon Society
950 Third Avenue
New York, NY 10022

Bird Watcher's Digest
P.O. Box 110
Marietta, OH 45750

Birder's World
720 E 8th Street
Holland, MI 49423

International Wildlife
National Wildlife Federation
8925 Leesburg Pike
Vienna, VA 22184-0001

Living Bird
Cornell Laboratory of
Ornithology
159 Sapsucker Woods Road
Ithaca, NY 14850

National Wildlife
  National Wildlife Federation
  8925 Leesburg Pike
  Vienna, VA 22184-0001

Natural History
  American Museum of Natural
    History
  Central Park West at 79th Street
  New York, NY 10024

Winging It
  American Birding Association
  P.O. Box 6599
  Colorado Springs, CO 80934

• Purchase at least one field guide and a pair of binoculars. Information on the binoculars most appropriate for your needs and financial constraints can be found in the above-mentioned magazines, through local bird-watchers, or at outdoor equipment retail centers. Field guides can be purchased in most bookstores and at many nature centers. We recommend the following field guides for birdwatching in North America: *Field Guide to the Birds of North America* (National Geographic Society, 1987), *A Field Guide to the Birds East of the Rockies* (Peterson, 1980), *Western Birds* (Peterson, 1990). As a companion to your field guide, *The Birder's Handbook* (P. R. Ehrlich et al., 1988) is a must. This extensive handbook summarizes almost everything you might want to know about the natural history of the birds that you encounter and will introduce you to the wonders of bird biology and conservation.

• Listen to cassette tapes of bird vocalizations. Nothing is better than listening to birds in the field where you can actually see them while they are singing. However, when you can't get outside, you can improve your skill by listening to tapes. Narrated bird song cassettes are available in most naturalist shops and through the Crow's Nest Birding Shop, Cornell Laboratory of Ornithology, 159 Sapsucker Woods, Ithaca, NY 14850.

• Learn your local plants and plant communities; it's often as vital as knowing the birds themselves. Participate in classes or workshops about local plants. Join a local garden club or native plant or wildflower society. Visit the nearest library to find field guides appropriate to your region.

Along with identification skills, your ability to accurately record and present your observations is vital to making your efforts useful. Organized counts or projects often distribute specific data sheets for recording observations. In such cases, carefully read and follow the directions. When in doubt as to the methodologies required, consult organizers and experienced participants. When data sheets are not provided or when you want to record data for your personal records, the alternative is to take notes in a field notebook (described later).

Beyond Counting Birds—Natural History

Counting birds can tell you something about the health of populations. However, to understand why a species might be decreasing in number requires knowledge of that species' life history, demography, and ecological requirements. The breeding biology, feeding behavior, social life, and habitat preferences of each species constitute a unique solution to the problem of surviving. Natural history is the study of an animal's or plant's lifestyle. There are numerous accounts of the natural history of North American birds, including *The Birder's Handbook* (Ehrlich et al. 1988) and *American Warblers* (Morse 1989). Alexander Skutch, through such works as *Life of the Pigeon* (1991), *Life of the Tanager* (1989), and *Life of the Woodpecker* (1985), has popularized the natural history of groups of birds throughout the world.

It is not surprising to most people that many of the simplest facts about the natural history of birds in the tropics are poorly known. Many species that migrate to North America to breed lead relatively unknown lives during migration and on their wintering grounds. What most people find surprising is that so little is known about even the most common resident birds in North America. Careful observation of even the most familiar birds can provide new insights. Bird enthusiasts and ornithologists alike need to see more than the bird itself. They must watch birds carefully, over time, with an open and inquiring mind. Herein is where failure often lies.

As an example, we point to the history of our knowledge of the feeding behavior of the Worm-eating Warbler. Although Worm-eating Warblers are not abundant, they are common in oak-hickory woodland and other deciduous forests in the eastern United States, and can be found within driving distance of many of the largest urban areas in the eastern United States. Until recently, almost all popular accounts of the species held that it primarily foraged by walking on the ground. Even more specialized books on wood warbler behavior described the feeding Worm-eating Warbler this way. In fact, recent research has shown that Worm-eating Warblers rarely feed on the ground, but glean (carefully search) leaves above the ground for caterpillars, prying open rolled leaves and hanging on dead leaf clusters suspended from shrubbery. This feeding behavior was first noted in the tropical wintering ground in the nineteenth century. But apparently North American ornithologists and birders were led astray by the accounts of John James Audubon (who was describing a female building a nest) and William Brewster (who attributed the feeding behavior of an Ovenbird to a Worm-eating Warbler).

Careful observation and good note-taking can reveal interesting natural history. Worm-eating Warblers, long thought to be ground feeders, actually feed mainly on insects in dead curled leaves in trees and shrubs.

Why does it matter that Worm-eating Warblers have a foraging specialization more typical of tropical rainforest species? Worm-eating Warblers are declining throughout their range. Failure to understand their unique specialization for feeding out of dead leaves may prevent us from understanding why Worm-eating Warblers live where they do and what must be done to manage their habitat.

Taking Good Field Notes

Clearly, the ability to watch and make accurate and systematic observations of bird behavior can contribute greatly to our knowledge of bird species and their adaptations. The key to making good observations is taking careful field notes. Field notebooks provide a permanent journal of natural observations and encounters. Notebooks may be as informal as loose leaf-paper organized and filed in a three-ring binder, or as sophisticated as files held and sorted in a computerized database. Typically, small pocket notebooks are used when collecting data in the field. To protect against the likelihood of occasional poor weather conditions, notebook paper should be waterproof and acid free. Pencils and permanent marking pens are the most reliable writing instruments.

The type of data recorded in the notebook largely depends on the reason for keeping a field journal. Typically, a field naturalist records the date, time, weather conditions, type of habitat, number of each species encountered (when possible with notations as to age, sex, and physical condition), the exact geographic location of each encounter, and the names of his or her fellow observers. Behavioral observations may also be included. Observations of any kind are most valuable to science when they are quantified. For example, it is more valuable to note that at 7:00 A.M. on a clear morning 200 meters (667 feet) straight out your back door, a Blackpoll Warbler foraged in a nearby oak at a height of 10 meters (34 feet) for 356 seconds, catching two 1.27-centimeter (.5-inch) green caterpillars, which it swallowed in 3 seconds and 4 seconds, than to note that a Blackpoll was seen in a tree eating caterpillars. The former data, when combined with numerous other records, may reveal such information as the weather conditions under which Blackpolls forage, the trees in which they most commonly forage, the height at which they forage, the amount of time they spend foraging, and the number and size of caterpillars they consume in an hour. This will prove to be valuable information in developing management and conservation plans for the Blackpoll Warbler.

Additional information may be conveyed in field notes through the use of sketches and diagrams. As with any other entry, the detail of these illustrations should reflect the intended use of the journal. If you are recording observations for your own pleasure, a quick general sketch may be all you want or need. If you are trying to determine the territory of a given bird, it is important that a mapped location be as accurate as possible. Two special cautions: (1) if you use abbreviations in your notebook, be sure to place a master key somewhere within the pages, and (2) when transcribing data from one location to another, be sure to recheck the information. Mistakes are bound to occur. For further information, see J. V. Remsen, Jr., "On taking field notes," *American Birds,* 31, (1977) 946–953.

Personal Projects

Once you have developed your bird identification and data-recording skills, you are ready to contribute to an organized bird count or science project. However, there is yet another way to make a significant contribution to ornithology—undertake your own project. Though this effort is undoubtedly more tedious and time consuming, it may be exceptionally rewarding if well done. The number of factors that must be taken into consideration when planning and implementing a science project may seem overwhelming. However, amateur volunteers have successfully accomplished such work, making vital contributions to ornithology in the process. For inspiration and ideas, read *Research Is a Passion with Me* (Nice 1976), *Curious Naturalists* (Tinbergen 1958), and *Ravens in Winter* (Heinrich 1989). For additional ideas, read *Beyond Birding: Field Projects for Inquisitive Birders* (Grubb 1986) or consult the Office of Education and Information Services, Cornell Laboratory of Ornithology (159 Sapsucker Woods Road, Ithaca, NY 14850) and refer to the magazines listed earlier. If your findings are significant, you should inform the ornithological community by publishing them in any of a number of ornithological journals.

Whether you are participating as one member in a large count or project or undertaking your own studies, remember to do the following:
- Recognize your skill level and err on the side of caution.
- Follow the guidelines. Precisely follow the directions of standardized counts or projects. Familiarize yourself with laws regarding the study of birds, obtaining permits where required.
- Put the health and safety of the birds first. Data collected at the expense of birds, particularly species whose populations may be in trouble, may be data not worth collecting. If you seem to be bothering the birds, especially during the nesting season, rethink your procedure or stop your work altogether. If birds are extensively disrupted during the nesting season, adults may desert young and eggs may not hatch. In addition, mammalian predators are known to track the scent of humans to bird nests.

Making a Difference   Shirley Briggs

Three of the four longest-running BBCs have been conducted under the auspices of the Audubon Naturalist Society (ANS) in the Washington, D.C., region. As a veteran of these BBCs, I would like to address the factors that have contributed to their durability.

A brief history is in order. Ever since the ANS was founded in 1897, it has exemplified the ornithological tradition of close cooperation between professional and amateur bird enthusiasts. Following World War II, the ANS decided to expand its activities into a full-scale program encompassing all natural history, and emphasizing a broad understanding of the regional environment. As part of this plan, in 1947–1948 two BBC plots were laid out by a professional forester and the first BBC team was instructed by John Aldrich of the U.S. Forest Service (Aldrich had been instructed by the man who devised the official rules for the BBC). The first BBC site was established on Cabin John Island, a floodplain forest island off the Potomac shore just west of Washington, D.C. The second BBC site was in Rock Creek Park in the heart of Washington, D.C., one of the largest natural urban parks in the world.

The third long-term BBC study under ANS's supervision began in 1959 in Glover-Archibold Park, also within metropolitan Washington. At the time, the entire length of the park was threatened with virtual obliteration by a multilane expressway. In an effort to save the park, a BBC, as well as other surveys of other flora and fauna, was conducted to document the diversity and abundance of the wildlife there. More species and individual birds were found in Glover-Archibold Park than in any comparable area under study, and the road was defeated.

Continued encouragement from the ANS and enthusiastic participants perpetuated the Washington, D.C., area BBCs. ANS members have valued the opportunity to contribute to a serious scientific study while becoming familiar with their local environment. Through annual publication of the data, participants have been able to compare their results (whether they participated for one year or ten) with those of other bird enthusiasts. The opportunity to see one's results alongside those of thousands of other BBC participants across the continent has provided a great incentive for participants to continue census work from year to year. New recruits, often inspired by other participants, are introduced to the study and its methods through preview trips (announced in the ANS calendar of events) prior to each BBC season.

In 1978, when the first results of the Washington, D.C., area BBCs were presented at the Wilson Ornithological Meeting, 165 participants contributed their time and energy. All manner of people continue to join the BBC teams, reflecting a city with many professional, government, and embassy people. A few youngsters have helped, with their sharp eyes and keen hearing. To date, more than 200 individuals have participated in one or more of the three BBCs.

The BBC requires two kinds of interest from participants, but not necessarily of the same person. Compilers, long-term participants who supervise the work in each plot, must be dedicated individuals, well-versed in the procedures and attractions of the BBC. These individuals provide year-end summaries, the continuity of consistently high standards, and a long-term vision. People with the skill to make daily census maps are essential to ensure good coverage of the birds seen and heard in the BBC plots. Short-term participants are also useful. These are usually people who enjoy the out-of-doors and follow the annual reports with interest. The final annual reports, now submitted to the Cornell Laboratory of Ornithology before publication, demand individuals with disciplined statistical skills, as well as an aptitude for puzzle solving. The BBC is for people with a continuing concern for birds and habitat, not avid list chasers.

As the Washington, D.C., BBCs have continued over the years, the fascination of following population trends for birds found on the study areas has increased. In the mid-1960s, these studies became landmarks when it was realized they were the first to indicate a strong downswing in eastern-breeding Neotropical migrants. None of the tracts had been altered in major or lasting ways, nor had the same temporary changes happened in all of them. Cabin John Island was more tangled after Hurricane Agnes flooding, and a narrow strip cleared through Glover-Archibold Park for a new sewer line had quickly grown up to compatible flora. Rock Creek Park was subject to less disturbance by horseback riders after the National Park Service cut off trails through the plot. Yet all three places showed losses of the same species of birds, while some year-round residents increased. As inquisitive compilers, Joan Criswell and I began to wonder what explanations might be found in the birds' migration and wintering areas.

Eugene Morton of the Smithsonian Institution, who has studied Neotropical migrants on their wintering grounds, produced data that revealed a close match between the species declining in the Washington, D.C., plots and the loss of their wintering habitats. Morton's own data from the wintering grounds documented a decline in some of the same species of birds. The parallels between the Washington, D.C., figures and those of Central and South America suggested that continental populations were suffering from southern damage. In some cases, there seemed to be fewer birds than viable breeding habitat. People conducting BBCs in other areas also began to notice a decline in Neotropical migrants. Some ascribed the changes to something in their particular summer habitat. Some indicated problems on the wintering grounds. Others indicated that problems existed throughout the range of some species.

As a direct result of these findings, Joan Criswell and I found ourselves giving papers at ornithological meetings and drawn further than expected into professional ornithology. This gave us far more impetus to continue the BBCs, and showed the value of persistent work over many years. Our three complete censuses, and the others we have begun since, reflect the advantages of sponsorship by an organization that can maintain interest and competent participants over the years.

The longest-maintained BBC deserves mention; it is the work of one determined man. A. H. Claugus, following an interest sparked by Boy Scout activities and a professional mentor, has kept a census going since it was organized by the National Audubon Society in 1937. His study area, a Scout camp, has a variety of habitats with consistent use and maintenance. Claugus's many years as a biology teacher contributed to his expertise in assessing the ecology of the area.

A Columbus, Ohio, club concerned with field study and conservation spurred him on. His detailed study of nesting records is especially notable. Though he must now travel 80.5 kilometers (50 miles) from his home to the census tract, he still manages to complete his route at the age of eighty-four!

To maintain long-term bird censuses, you should enlist dogged participants, encourage professional colleagues and organizations to participate, publish the records, and inspire a lasting fascination with the natural history of your area.

Shirley Briggs is Director Emeritus of the Rachel Carson Council. For twenty years she served as editor of the Audubon Naturalist Society's publication, The Atlantic Naturalist. *Through her long-standing involvement with the Audubon Naturalist Society and the Rachel Carson Council, Ms. Briggs has contributed to both the public's and the scientific community's knowledge of the harmful effects of pesticide contamination and the decline of migratory bird populations.*

3

Naturescaping: Saving and Restoring Private Land

A thing is right when it tends to preserve the integrity, stability and beauty of the biotic community. It is wrong when it tends otherwise.
—*Aldo Leopold,* A Sand County Almanac

Of the more than two billion acres (eight hundred million hectares) of land in the United States, almost three fourths is controlled by private landowners: 71 percent of forestlands, 74 percent of wetlands, 64 percent of rangelands, and almost all the agricultural land. East of the Mississippi River, more than 90 percent of the land is privately held. Furthermore, most forest tracts in the eastern United States are small and becoming increasingly so. (In contrast, less than 10 percent of land in Canada is privately owned.) While wilderness in North America and around the world continues to shrink, compromising the health of the planet, garden acreage is increasing. Few private landowners are fortunate enough to have large tracts of undisturbed forest, but many have small groves of trees or a few shrubs in their yards. In light of the scarcity of large forest tracts and healthy, intact wetlands, privately owned habitat remnants have become increasingly significant to migratory bird survival. This is especially true in urban areas, which often lack even the minimal habitat that birds require for stopovers along their migration routes. Private landowners, therefore, play a critical role in our efforts to conserve Neotropical migratory birds.

As land stewards, landowners need to be more than gardeners interested in "beautifying" the landscape. Landowners can be "naturescapers," identifying and incorporating elements of the local, natural environment into gardens that blend into the surrounding native vegetation and serve to restore communities of native plants. Modern gardening is becoming the art of ecological restoration.

Neotropical migrants like this Summer Tanager are vibrant additions to forested yards.

Experienced naturescapers can promote extremely high levels of biodiversity on even the smallest plots. In doing so, they make their lands islands of habitat and hope for migratory birds and other wildlife.

YARD BIRDS

Your own yard is the most logical place for you to start taking responsibility for the care and enhancement of the ecological community, which includes migratory birds and their habitats. The naturescape that is most important to wildlife is that which exists in your region naturally—be it forest, prairie, desert, or mangrove fringe. Your job as a naturescaper is to restore and enhance what nature put there. By concentrating on your own backyard, you won't be able to restore and protect enough habitat to save big mammals, but you may help give plants and smaller (though no less spectacular and important) wildlife a fighting chance. In addition, firsthand knowledge of and experience with the environment will allow you to expand your efforts beyond your property line.

Making a Difference   Emile DeVito

Twenty-five years ago we played whiffle ball in my backyard in New Jersey. The subdivision had been a farm, and the five-year-old landscape was not tall enough to stop home runs from clearing the neighbor's fence. Nor did it attract "cool" birds to the yard. But thanks to my father's efforts and some benign neglect, the seeds had been sown.

My dad had created a floral Noah's ark in our backyard: oak, hemlock, holly, cherry, ash, chestnut, elm, juniper, aspen, dogwood, fir, spruce, maple, cedar, and pine. Within five years these trees were the equivalent of Fenway Park's outfield wall, the Green Monster. The understory of rhododendron, laurel, spicebush, pepperbush, and countless other shrub varieties created a living fence—no galvanized aluminum marked our bounds!

As our "monster" grew, the sparse early-successional suburban fauna of mockingbird, robin, House Sparrow, and Blue Jay was joined by a wondrous variety of migratory birds, especially in the spring and fall. For the last ten years or so, the inchworms found among the needle-leaved giants surrounding the house have attracted Cape May, Blackburnian, Bay-breasted, and Magnolia warblers to an avian feast. American Redstarts are crazy about the "Golden-chain" tree, which leans against the paper birch. Catbirds regularly nest in the hemlock-rhododendron grove on the north side of the house. My journal indicates that an average of twenty-two species of warblers have used our yard each spring for the last five years, and the trend is increasing. Sadly, though, there seem to be fewer individual birds. Something is amiss in the global outfield.

Downy Woodpeckers and Black-capped Chickadees have nested in the stump of the maple, which finally crashed to earth in the last winter storm. Carolina and House wrens constantly remind us of the worth of our waste. A Long-eared Owl has visited the yard each Thanksgiving in recent years. She stays only a few days, perhaps to nab a white-footed mouse when we begin cleaning out the wildflower patch and setting up the armada of winter feeders. Last spring a Cooper's Hawk caught and ate a pigeon as my father and I looked on.

As the late winter snows melt away, I reflect upon my father's foresightedness. I stand peering out the window into the backyard, remembering long-past whiffle-ball games. Anxiously I listen for the chippings of warblers. When the first is heard, I know that the migrants have made it through the turn and are on their final run to the feast that awaits them at home plate.

Emile DeVito, an expert in land preservation and conservation education, is Director of Conservation Biology for the New Jersey Conservation Foundation. He has studied birds for sixteen years.

Assessing Your Property

The first step in developing a garden suited to hosting migratory birds and other wildlife is to assess the present status of the landscape. Here is an easy way to start: On a piece of graph paper, make a scale drawing of your property. Include existing structures such as buildings, fences, paths, and water sources, as well as trees, shrubs, and wildflowers. Record the patterns of sun and shade that move across your property throughout the day.

Does your property offer a constant supply of clean water for birds? Is there protection from harsh weather and predators? Do the plants in your yard produce a constant yet varied food source for migrants? How does your property fit into the larger landscape—from your neighbors' yards to the entire neighborhood?

If you need assistance in identifying plants, refer to field guides, books on gardening for wildlife, or local botanical experts. In addition to identifying your plants, note whether or not they produce flowers or fruit, and at what times of the year. Also determine whether they are native or introduced species.

It's not nature-as-chaos that threatens us, but ignorance of the real natural world.
—Gary Snyder

Some areas have "weed" laws that can make gardening with native plants a bit difficult. It is best to know whether these laws exist in your city or county before you begin to invest in your project. If such laws do exist in your area, see what can be done to change them. A little bit of education can go a long way. Also, be sure to inform your neighbors of your hopes and plans. Many neighbors may be wary of living next to a property where the yard has gone a bit "wild." Assure your neighbors that you intend to produce a "managed" wilderness that will not only attract wildlife but also reduce your need for fertilizers, pesticides, water, and mowing; will increase your home's energy efficiency; and will produce an increased resale value. At the very least, ask that your neighbors respect your efforts. At the very best, persuade them to join in your efforts, treating all the yards as one landscape.

There are a number of ways you can provide resources for migratory birds on your property. Your final decision in this process will be based on the needs of migratory birds, the size of your property, your budget, and your personal preferences. Keep in mind that a wide variety of natural elements will attract and provide resources for the greatest number and variety of birds.

Water

Birds use water from a variety of sources for drinking and bathing. These sources may be as large as a lake or as small as a puddle. If you do not have a natural water supply on your property, there are several simple and inexpensive ways to create a water source for birds. Buy a commercial birdbath (they are available in numerous styles). Place a shallow (less than 2 inches, or 5 centimeters) dish filled with water on a tree stump. Create a small pool by using a preformed fiberglass shell or by digging a hole and lining it with suitable rubberized or plastic liners. If you have the space and are willing to invest some money, hire professionals to create a pond in your landscape.

Whatever type of water supply you choose, there are a few things that you should keep in mind. The water source must be shallow (no more than 2 inches, or 5 centimeters) in at least one area so birds can bathe. A rough surface on the inside of the bath will help birds maintain their footing. The water should always be clean. Regular scrubbing (use white vinegar) is required for heavily used baths. Ponds should be placed in sunny locations and birdbaths in shady ones. Since birds are attracted to running water, you might hang a dripping hose over a shallow dish, conserving water with the aid of a recirculating pump (available at most garden centers). Bathing birds need a nearby sanctuary from predators. Overhanging branches and nearby bushes are usually sufficient.

Food

The type of food migrant birds require varies with the seasonal energy demands of migration, raising young, and molting. Insects, particularly caterpillars, constitute the greatest portion of most songbird diets throughout the spring and summer. Fruits of numerous kinds provide the carbohydrates and fats these birds need to carry them through fall migration.

Providing the variety of foods that birds require is the most fun and challenging aspect of naturescaping for migrants. Choose a wide variety of early- and late-blooming fruiting and flowering plants, so that flowers and fruits will be available to migrants from their arrival in early spring through to their departure in fall. Include plants that attract an array of insects on which migrants feed.

Grow native species whenever possible; they are best adapted to local soils and climates and require less fertilizer, water, and pest control. Native plants also offer the best overall food sources for birds. Moreover, the dispersal of their seeds by avian foragers will help ensure a healthy plant community in the future. If introduced plants already exist on your property, remove potential nuisance varieties (those that spread easily, such as English ivy) as soon as possible.

Maximize your property's resources by choosing native plants that vary in structure, types of foods produced, and times at which foods are available. To ensure that these plants are suited to your property, you can have your soil tested. Consult your local cooperative extension office for assistance.

Hummingbirds present a special feeding challenge. Traditionally hummingbird lovers have relied on feeders alone, but they offer only one source of nourishment: sugar. Flowering plants offer hummingbirds not only food resources, but shelter and nesting sites as well. To attract hummingbirds and encourage them to stay, landscape with numerous plant species that flower from early spring until late fall.

To ensure the health and safety of hummingbirds at supplemental feeders, you should follow some simple guidelines. The sugar-water solution should never be stronger than four parts water to one part sugar. Boil the mixture briefly to dissolve the sugar completely and kill bacteria. Clean the feeder with white vinegar and refill it at least once a week (every few days in hot weather). Never put the

Ruby-throated and other hummingbirds feed eagerly at nectar-producing flowers in gardens.

feeder in direct sunlight. Honey causes a potentially fatal fungus to grow on the tongues of hummingbirds, so don't substitute it for sugar.

Shelter

Birds need shelter to escape predators such as hawks and cats, as well as to survive unpredictable and harsh weather. Quite often songbirds will take refuge in dense thickets of brambles, hollies, and viburnums. Establishing shelter for migratory birds is an easy but vital task. Most shrubs and evergreen trees provide good cover. Use landscaping "scraps" to create a thick brush pile of branches or a meandering rock wall. If your property is large, provide several sources of cover in the yard.

Few species of migratory landbirds find adequate resources for raising young outside of a healthy, intact habitat. However, a good overall backyard habitat may encourage hummingbirds to nest in shrubs, phoebes under the porch eaves, or a sapsucker in the hollow of a dead tree. If you own large tracts of forest or wetland, it is important to protect them from degradation so as to provide adequate nesting habitat for migrants. See later sections on enhancing such landscapes.

One of the most valuable contributions a private landowner can make is the protection and management of trees. Trees are a major source of insect prey for migratory songbirds. They are also the seed banks of our future forests and, thus, future nest sites for birds.

Trees may be damaged by harsh weather, vandalism, neglect, improper pruning, construction, or overbrowsing by deer. They can fall victim to numerous viruses, fungi, and blights, or have their roots damaged by the erosion or compaction of soil. Trees are often among the first organisms to reveal the impact of atmospheric pollution and acid rain. However, not all dead trees are "bad" trees. Snags offer nest sites to a number of cavity-dwelling birds, such as sapsuckers and Tree Swallows, and rotting wood provides insects for numerous other species.

Employ a well-respected tree care company to regularly inspect and manage the trees on your property. Discourage tree vandalism and unchecked populations of deer. Protect your topsoil and the atmosphere.

Getting Started

Return to the graph paper plot of your yard. Place a piece of tracing paper over the map and, with the aid of a pencil, dream away! Reduce the amount of lawn on your property by half or more. Lawns are of little value to wildlife, and in urban areas they are the largest consumer of a yard's water, fertilizers, and pesticides. Design clusters of plantings, mixing plant species and forms. So as not to shade out any plants, always put larger ones in the back, smaller ones in the front.

Take into account the amount of light each plant requires, the size it might

Orchard Orioles are so named because they are often seen in orchards, gardens, and large yards near human settlements.

reach at maturity, and the time needed for it to reach maturity. Create optional designs for your property by sketching each on a separate piece of tracing paper, then decide which you like best and go for it.

Obtaining Plants

Native plants can be obtained through local nurseries or catalogs. Before purchasing, make sure that the plants for sale have not been stolen from the wild. Conservation efforts are defeated if a natural habitat is destroyed to create an artificial, although naturalistic, one. There is one exception. By working with local developers, you may be able to obtain plants at no cost that would otherwise be destroyed. Find out where future development sites are planned in your area and ask the developers for permission to remove unwanted plants prior to their destruction.

The following is a very short list of mail sources of native plants:

Gurney's Seed and Nursery Company
    110 Capitol Street
    Yankton, SD 57078

Mellinger's
    2310 W. South Range Road
    North Lima, OH 44452-9731

National Wildlife Research Center
    2600 FM 973 North
    Austin, TX 78725

Additional sources can be obtained from the Soil and Water Conservation Society's "Sources of Native Seeds and Plants" (7515 Northeast Ankey Road, Ankey, IA 50021).

Completing Your Project

Don't think that your naturescaping efforts must be completed in one day, one week, or even one year. Naturescaping for wildlife is a gradual process, one you may never want to "finish." In fact, you may find the process as enjoyable as the product. Although your native landscape will require considerably less care than a manicured lawn, it will require an initial investment in time and labor and occasional pruning and transplanting as plants grow. Some plants will certainly die, and you may be regularly inspired to add others. You may even consider adding a few benches or a blind.

Dangers in the Garden

Now that you have invited migratory birds into your yard, you have a responsibility to protect them from the hazards they will face because of their close association with humans. Every year countless migratory birds are victims of the predators, reflective windows, and chemicals associated with the human landscape.

Avoid CATastrophe!

The Problem: Domestic cats are not native to North America. They were introduced as early as 1614 and imported into the United States in the early 1800s to control rodent populations in cities. Domestic cats (approximately 60 million in the United States alone), however, do not limit their kills to pest populations of rodents, and have become major predators of many native wildlife species, including migratory birds. Joseph Mitchell and Ruth Beck of Virginia found that free-ranging pet cats killed prey from five of the seven major groups of vertebrates found in the state (no fish or salamanders). Two of the ten species of birds identified in the study were Neotropical migrants (Gray Catbird and Wood Thrush). Mitchell and Beck estimate that as many as 26 million of Virginia's native songbirds are killed by cats annually. This finding supports those of Stanley Temple and John Coleman of the University of Wisconsin, who have estimated that rural cats in Wisconsin kill 19 million songbirds and 140,000 game birds annually. The bird species most preyed on by cats are those that nest or feed on or near the ground. Research by David Wilcove indicates that songbirds nesting on the ground or in low vegetation are subjected to very high levels of predation. In isolated forested tracts in suburban Maryland, Wilcove determined that domestic cats were among the primary predators of migratory songbirds.

Can you solve the problem by putting a bell on your cat's collar? Unfortunately, you cannot. Research has shown that cats either sit and wait for their prey or stalk very slowly. Thus, by the time a cat's bell rings (if it does at all), it is too late for the chosen victim.

The Solution: Although an unpopular solution for cat owners who believe that their pets would not like to have their freedom curtailed, we recommend that cats be confined indoors. Besides directly protecting native wildlife, this greatly reduces the prospects for future generations of unwanted, feral cats. More than 35,000 kittens are born every day in this country, and many are euthanized. A single cat and her offspring, according to calculations of the Humane Society of the United States, can produce 420,000 cats in just seven years! Additional research by the Humane Society has shown that the indoor life may be better for cats. The society has found that the average lifespan for a free-ranging cat is three to five years, while it is not uncommon for an indoor cat to live seventeen years or more. Why the dramatic difference? Free-ranging domestic cats are exposed to numerous diseases (including feline leukemia and rabies, which are rising despite the existence of vaccines) and also to encounters with dogs and automobiles. Keep your own cat inside, and encourage your neighbors to do the same (cats and wildlife don't understand the concept of property lines). Start or support mandatory spaying and neutering policies and feline breeding moratorium initiatives in your area. San Mateo County, California, has begun such a program; according to a city official, it has received a 98 percent positive response from the public (see Sturla's essay in chapter 5).

Nest Predators, Competitors, and Parasites

The Problem: Research has shown that several species of nest predators reach their highest population densities in suburban environments. Jays, grackles, crows, gulls, skunks, raccoons, and gray squirrels (among others) have come to recognize the presence of humans as potential sources of free food. Bird feeders, unsecured garbage cans, open landfills, and deliberate handouts all act to artificially increase the numbers of these predators in a given area. David Wilcove's work indicates that predation rates are significantly higher in suburban woodlots than in forest tracts. This is probably a result of both the increased predator populations and habitat fragmentation, which makes nests more accessible to species such as those listed above.

A number of birds that have been introduced to North America find the human landscape good habitat. Some of these species are well known for their abilities to outcompete our native fauna for food resources and nesting sites. House Sparrows and European Starlings are notorious for taking over cavities that could be occupied by Tree Swallows, Prothonotary Warblers, Great-crested Flycatchers, Purple Martins, and the like. Given the limited number of tree cavities available to birds in many landscapes, introduced nest-site competitors may pose a serious threat to local cavity-nesting migrant populations.

As noted earlier, cowbirds (a species fond of woodland edges and easy grain and seed pickings) lay their eggs in the nests of other birds. Most migratory land birds build open, woven-cup nests, making them particularly vulnerable to cowbird parasitism. Parent birds tend to feed larger, louder nestlings more than their mild-mannered nest mates. Because cowbirds hatch earlier and grow faster than the young of migrants, they get most of the food delivered to the nest. As a result, the true offspring either starve or are crowded out of the nest, to perish on the ground.

The Solution: Avoid providing supplemental sources of food that may attract nest predators, competitors, and parasites. If you feed birds, use feeders that are not accessible to mammalian and avian nest predators and use food that is specific to the type of birds you wish to attract. Refrain from placing food scraps out for wildlife. See that your local landfill covers debris on a daily basis, and ask local farmers to refrain from feeding their livestock in low, open trays.

Reflective Windows

The Problem: Research conducted by Daniel Klem indicates that each year 98 million to 976 million birds, as much as .5 to 5 percent of the estimated continental U.S. bird population after the breeding season, are killed when they strike reflective glass windows. As large as these numbers are, they do not reflect the impact on selected species or the likelihood of increasing rates of impact as new construction adds more windows to the landscape. Project FeederWatch, run by the Cornell Laboratory of Ornithology, has collected data that support Klem's findings, suggesting that 100 million birds die each year as a result of window strikes (this sample is heavily biased toward "feeder species," and therefore may underestimate the deaths of other birds). Together, these data indicate that, with the possible exception of hunting, glass windows kill more birds than any other human-caused avian mortality factor, including the calamities resulting from oil spills, pesticide poisoning, and collisions with vehicles and towers. Findings from controlled experiments and documented collisions indicate that birds are not able to recognized glass windows as a potentially lethal obstacle. Glass is invisible to birds and often reflects images of the natural surroundings. Birds are killed (usually dying from head injuries) by windows of any size or height, in any environment, in any season, and at any time of the day. No birds seem immune to the hazard. Endangered species such as the Kirtland's Warbler (on migration) and Peregrine Falcon (killed by windows near urban reintroduction sites) are known victims. A survey by Klem of window-kills throughout North America suggests that species that generally feed or nest on or near the ground are particularly vulnerable. These include migratory thrushes, wood warblers, and finches. The Ovenbird, a ground-nesting Neotropical migrant already under study because of population declines that are probably the result of habitat fragmentation, was one of Klem's most frequently reported window-kills.

The Solution: To reduce or eliminate window strikes, you must be willing to make a financial investment and live with a partially obstructed view of the out-of-doors. The key is to break up the reflective expanses of glass. This can be accomplished by rubbing soap over the surface to create a dull appearance (a temporary solution in need of repeated applications), installing dark screens or one-way tinting, or hanging streamers, curtains, or other objects over the window. Klem's work indicates that objects should be placed so as to leave no more than five to ten centimeters (two to four inches) of open space between them. This holds true for the falcon silhouettes commonly sold as "the answer" to saving birds from window strikes. Birds are not frightened by the silhouettes, but if enough of them are placed properly, silhouettes (or any other images, for that matter) will sufficiently break up reflective patterns.

Plastic garden protection netting can be mounted on a frame and installed approximately 0.3 meter (1 foot) from the reflective glass surface. Birds that hit the screening will bounce off unharmed. Research is currently being conducted to develop window coverings that would partially or completely cover the glass surface and incorporate pleasing designs. Scientists are also looking into the feasibility of angled windows to meet both bird and human needs. An obvious method of hazard reduction is to refrain from enticing birds into hazardous situations. Placing bird feeders, baths, and vegetation near windows increases the likelihood of bird strikes. Instead, you should lure birds away from the hazardous area. If attractants are used without preventive strike measures, they should be placed within 0.3 meter (1 foot) of the glass surface so that birds leaving the feeder will not build up enough momentum to sustain serious injury.

Pesticides

The Problem: Countless birds die each year from direct or indirect contact with landscape and agricultural chemicals. Direct poisoning occurs when a bird eats a pesticide granule (mistaken for grit or seed) or is sprayed. Indirect poisoning occurs when a bird eats a poisoned insect or other food item.

The Solution: Reduce your dependence on chemical fertilizers and pesticides by planting native species and reducing the amount of lawn on your property. Carefully identify pests and learn about them. Evaluate the potential threat. The problem may go away without your intervention, or the pest may be something you can live with. Physically removing pests may solve the problem. If not, control insect pests by using pest-specific traps, by interplanting species that naturally repel insect pests, and by increasing the numbers of natural insect predators, such as lacewings, ladybird beetles, toads, and, of course, those birds that the garden was intended to attract in the first place. This approach is called "integrated pest management." Use leaf and compost mulches, rather than fertilizers, to add nutrients to the soil. Refer to books on natural organic gardening and let your yard "go wild."

If you are going to use chemicals as a last resort, first try naturally derived compounds, such as insecticidal soaps. If you use synthetic pesticides, choose those that are the least toxic to animals, follow the application directions precisely, and strictly limit the application to the target organism. Your state's Cooperative Extension Service should be able to provide you with information and assistance. However, following the directions and using low-toxicity chemicals does not guarantee that wildlife will be unharmed. The Virginia Department of Game and Inland Fisheries (P.O. Box 11104, Richmond, VA 23230-1104) has an excellent publication on this subject, "Pesticides and Wildlife: A Guide to Reducing Impacts on Animals and Their Habitat" (Publication 420-004). To reduce the potential negative impact on birds, avoid creating puddles of pesticide runoff that might attract birds looking for a place to bathe or drink. Also, avoid using granular pesticides, as birds may mistake the granules for food or grit (for some pesticides, one granule is enough to kill a bird). Do not spray pesticides during the nesting and brood-rearing season, as young birds require a plentiful source of high-protein insects, and avoid spraying when birds are migrating and are already stressed.

Indiscriminant use of pesticides has led to the decline of top predators, such as this Sharp-shinned Hawk.

The following is a brief list of organizations whose primary concerns include the control of toxic chemicals. All can supply you with reference materials.

Greenpeace USA, Inc.
    1436 U Street, NW
    Washington, DC 20009

National Coalition against the Misuse of Pesticides
530 7th Street, SE
Washington, DC 20003

Pesticide Action Network
North American Regional Center
116 New Montgomery, #810
San Francisco, CA 94105

Rachel Carson Council
8940 Jones Mill Road
Chevy Chase, MD 20815

The following is a very short list of merchants that supply integrated pest management or biological pest control products:

Harmony Farm Supply
P.O. Box 460
Graton, CA 95444

The Necessary Trading Company
P.O. Box 305
New Castle, VA 24127

Peaceful Valley Farm Supply
P.O. Box 2209
Grass Valley, CA 95945

Support Organizations

Increasingly home owners, particularly those who dwell in or near urban landscapes, are realizing that their own gardens can provide them the rare opportunity to enjoy a wondrous variety of wildlife, including Neotropical migrants. In response to the growing ranks and enthusiasm of these naturescapers, several environmental organizations have developed educational and technical assistance projects that focus solely on the needs of "backyard wildlife" and its hosts. Two of the most successful programs are described below.

National Wildlife Federation

Organized in 1936, the National Wildlife Federation (NWF) is a nonprofit conservation education organization dedicated to inspiring and encouraging a respect for the resources of the Earth. The NWF runs several conservation education programs, distributes numerous periodicals and educational materials, and litigates environmental disputes in the hope of conserving natural resources.

In 1973 the NWF instituted a Backyard Wildlife Habitat Program to acknowledge the efforts of people who provide and enhance habitat for wildlife on their own properties—from city gardens to suburban woodlots. Because habitat restoration is a critical need for wildlife in the human landscape and almost everyone finds some pleasure in watching wildlife, NWF's program is both conservation-minded and enjoyable. The objectives of the program are (1) to provide individuals with information and direction so they understand the hows and whys of habitat improvement and maintenance; (2) to motivate individuals to create or enhance habitat by providing them with a hands-on process for habitat enhancement on their own properties; (3) to acknowledge the efforts of those who have enhanced habitats through this process by awarding certificates and publicizing their efforts; and (4) to maintain and strengthen the public's commitment to habitat conservation by offering updated information, connections to other program participants, and directions for becoming involved in habitat issues that extend beyond property lines. By 1992, 11,500 participants had created habitats that met the program's criteria, and each participant received a personal certificate and periodic program updates. The NWF has successfully initiated additional certification programs for schoolyard and corporate land habitats. If you are visiting the Washington, D.C., area, be sure to visit the National Wildlife Federation's demonstration Backyard Wildlife Habitat in Vienna, Virginia. For more information, contact the Director of Urban Wildlife Programs, National Wildlife Federation (8925 Leesburg Pike, Vienna, VA 22184-0001).

National Institute for Urban Wildlife

Founded in 1973, the National Institute for Urban Wildlife (NIUW) is a private, nonprofit scientific and educational association that advocates the enhancement of urban wildlife values and habitats and the sustainable use of natural resources. The objectives of the institute are (1) to conduct sound research on relationships between people and wildlife under urban and urbanizing conditions; (2) to discover and disseminate practical procedures for maintaining, enhancing, or controlling wildlife species in urban, suburban, and developing areas; and (3) to increase awareness of urban wildlife issues through community education programs.

Among the active projects of the institute is the Urban Wildlife Sanctuaries Program. The objectives of this program are (1) to enhance urban wildlife habitat; (2) to promote an appreciation and understanding of urban wildlife and its needs; and (3) to give recognition to private and public landowners who dedicate

Even the most urban settings provide habitat for migratory birds. Common Nighthawks often nest on buildings and migrate to a poorly known winter range in South America.

their properties to wildlife uses. The institute, upon request, supplies applications for certification of properties as Urban Wildlife Sanctuaries. Each application includes a list of criteria for the type of property to be certified. The landowner completes and submits the application to the institute for review. If the application demonstrates that the owner has developed and implemented a wildlife management plan that meets the institute's criteria, the property is certified as an Urban Wildlife Sanctuary. In recognition of the landowner's contribution, the Institute awards a certificate, decals, metal signs, how-to publications, and a one-year subscription to *Urban Wildlife News,* the official publication of NIUW. Publicity releases are mailed to local press services, recognition is included in *Urban Wildlife News,* and the property is placed on the National Roster of Urban Wildlife Sanctuaries, which is maintained and published annually by the institute. The institute's staff of urban wildlife biologists is available for consultation.

BEYOND THE BACKYARD

If you are one of those people blessed with property that extends beyond a small front yard or backyard, you have even more to offer birds and, as the land's steward, more responsibility to do so. Even if you own just a few acres, you can provide nest sites and other resources for an array of birds that can't find them in a backyard. If you own a few hundred acres, imagine the possibilities!

The principles that define naturescaping for migrants are always the same, whether for a garden plot, a ten-acre woodlot, or a several-hundred-acre forest patch—you just think on a bigger scale. Bigger scales may seem intimidating, but who said that you had to do it all at once or really had to "do" much at all? Remember the concept of "let it go wild"? And the larger your land, the more assistance there is available to you—informational, technical, and even financial.

Making a Difference   Bill Hilton, Jr.

According to environmental doomsayers, there's little owners of relatively small plots of land can do to counter the decline of Neotropical migrants, but my eleven years of bird observations at Hilton Pond indicate otherwise.

First, a little background information. In late 1981, after I'd spent nearly four years studying Blue Jays in Minnesota, my wife and I decided it was time to return to the warmer climes of South Carolina. We wanted an older farmhouse in reasonably good shape, about five acres, a small pond or active stream, a few blackberry bushes, a magnolia tree to remind us we had returned to the South, and—most importantly—a place where I could continue my pursuit of banding and studying wild birds. Eventually we found a one-story Southern farmhouse with white columns and a big porch, a pond out back, and—amazingly enough—a magnolia tree with a mockingbird on the topmost branch! We fell in love with the place immediately.

As soon as I signed on the dotted line, I went out to explore the three acres of land and adjoining portion of the pond that we now owned. Although there were a few majestic oak, pecan, and hickory trees scattered near the house, most of the property was old field or lawn. The area beyond the pond was covered mainly by grasses, broomsedge, multiflora rose, and Japanese honeysuckle. In addition, the previous owner had cleared so heavily on the gentle slope between the house and the pond that there was almost nothing left except poison ivy and red clay. I didn't mind the unimpeded view of the water, which we quickly dubbed "Hilton Pond," but I quickly resolved to make the whole place more hospitable for birds and other wildlife.

I first built two huge bird feeders and loaded them with black sunflower, cracked corn, and white millet in the hope that wintering birds would start visiting the property after I returned to Minnesota. The feeders were so large (each held twenty-five pounds of seed) that I predicted they might keep the birds happy until I came back for a quick visit in early May.

I also spent a full day surveying the plant life around Hilton Pond, especially noting where there were tree seedlings. In this part of the Piedmont, old field succession starts with broomsedge and is soon followed by goldenrod and blackberry. In about the fourth year of succession, a trio of tree species suddenly appears: sweetgum, winged elm, and red cedar. I was heartened to find many small specimens of all three present in the old field across the pond from the house. I knew such pioneer plants were a sure sign that natural succession was determined to reclaim the land from the farming practices that had denuded it. And I was not about to interfere with succession, in part because I wanted a more natural yard and in part because there was no way I was going to waste long hours on hot summer days cutting four acres of grass!

I wanted to establish permanent nature trails that would give me easy access to all parts of the property, allow me to observe various plants and natural phenomena, take me past those fruit-producing blackberry patches, and provide locations for mist nets that I would be using to capture birds for banding. I decided to limit my mowing to a small patch of lawn adjoining the house, put in three-foot-wide nature trails to meander about the property, and simply sit back and let everywhere else become a model for natural succession.

The benign neglect was difficult, however, when people began referring to the property as the "weed ranch." It is hard to sit back during the first few years of succession and watch a smooth, well-heeled expanse of grass turn into an ever-deepening thicket of unruly vegetation, but that's only because we civilized North Americans have been brainwashed into believing that yards should look like putting greens.

I did do one important thing to enhance succession: I became known as the "Leaf Thief of York" because in autumn I often rode through town with my van and trailer, pilfering leaves that folks had raked from their yards and left for easy picking in plastic bags at curbside. The first few fall seasons we were at Hilton

Pond, I probably scattered a thousand bags of yard rakings in several open plots near the house. Within three years I already had dozens of redbud seedlings, as well as young dogwoods, water and willow oaks, American hollies, miscellaneous pines, and a whole slew of ornamentals that obviously had gone to seed in York residents' yards. I culled the nonnative stuff to maintain the integrity of the land.

After eleven years, things are very different here at Hilton Pond. For one, we've added seven acres to our holdings. It's now impossible to see the house from the road, even though it's less than forty yards away. The token plot of grassy lawn that surrounds the house gets a bit smaller every time I cut, and many trees that sprouted from seeds in the leaf bags have grown to fifteen feet or more and are making their own fruits and nuts.

I've continued to maintain the nature trails (there's more than a mile of them on just eleven acres) and most are shaded by eleven-year-old sweetgums, elms, and cedars, along with a full complement of slower-growing hardwoods that eventually will dominate the more vigorous upstarts. There's a tangle of alders and red maples, of young sycamores and chokecherries. In all, I've cataloged more than forty tree species.

What's most amazing is the diversity of bird life that now occurs on our little homestead. When we bought Hilton Pond, I started a bird list. The first year I listed the expected complement of "field birds"—Northern Bobwhite, Field Sparrow, American Goldfinch, and Eastern Meadowlark, to name a few, and plenty of cotton rats that brought Red-tailed and Red-shouldered hawks. Eastern Bluebirds occupied all six of the nest boxes I put up, but migrant warblers were in short supply, as were many other resident species that required large trees for feeding or nesting. I also started banding that first year and between June and December 1982 had trapped or netted 204 birds from 30 species, most of them either "field birds" or seedeaters that were attracted to feeders.

As vegetative succession has changed the landscape over the past eleven years, there has been a significant increase in the numbers and kinds of birds that visit or breed at Hilton Pond. By May 31, 1993, I had seen 154 kinds of birds on or over the property, including 23 species for which I've found active nests, and I had increased the banding list to 115 species and 24,345 individuals.

There is an indisputable correlation between the increased diversity of vegetation and the greater numbers of bird species that now occur at Hilton Pond. Whereas I was once lucky to band a few Yellow-rumped or Pine warblers as my only parulids each year, I'm now almost guaranteed to handle a dozen or more warblers during any spring or fall migration. At last count, I'd banded 32 different parulids, including three Connecticut Warblers that were only the fourteenth, fifteenth, and sixteenth individuals of that species ever seen in South

Carolina. Common Yellowthroats, Black-and-white Warblers, Yellow-breasted Chats, and Prairie Warblers now nest here every summer, and the breeding population of Gray Catbirds, Indigo Buntings, Northern Cardinals, and Rufous-sided Towhees is increasing by leaps and bounds. Granted, the overgrown fields mean that things aren't quite right anymore for bluebirds, but House Wrens, Tufted Titmice, Carolina Chickadees, and Brown-headed Nuthatches are making good use of the nest boxes.

I think I've encountered most of the arguments against converting private property into wildlife habitat, but I've yet to hear one that really holds water. Some of the more common excuses include the following:

• "But I have only a half-acre lot." Four large hardwood trees and considerable subcanopy vegetation will grow nicely around a house on a half-acre lot. The hardwoods could provide nest sites for several summer residents, to say nothing of foraging areas for hungry migrants.

• "I live in the city (or suburbs), where there are no birds." Even city lots can attract Neotropical migrants, especially if several owners with adjoining homes pool their resources and ideas. (Did I mention that Hilton Pond is only one-quarter mile from the York city limits?)

• "My town has a weed ordinance and I can't let succession take its course." It may be time to join Thoreau as an advocate of civil disobedience. Better yet, get elected to the town council and educate your new colleagues about the substantial benefits of throwing out the weed ordinance.

• "I like a lawn." Mowed grasses are only a tad better than asphalt parking lots when it comes to providing habitat. Lawns provide no shade, produce little oxygen, and take tremendous amounts of time, lawn mower fuel, water, and potentially dangerous chemicals to maintain. Whoever taught us to believe lawns look good performed a great disservice to wildlife and the environment.

• "I don't have time to maintain a wildlife sanctuary." The up-front time it takes to plant trees and shrubs that care for themselves forever is minor compared with the week-in, week-out task of mowing the lawn for the rest of your life. (Letting trees and shrubs "plant themselves" through succession takes even less effort.)

• "I have no stream or pond." It's amazing how attractive a dripping garden hose or simple birdbath is for resident and migratory birds. Water gardens and small ponds are also relatively inexpensive and easily installed, so the lack of natural water is no real shortcoming.

• "My spouse won't let me do anything." Of all the excuses against creating a bird haven, this may be the hardest one to counter. Again, try to beat the uncooperative party with logic, or challenge him or her to join you in your efforts to restore the natural aspects of your yard.

Bill Hilton, Jr., of York, South Carolina, is an ecologist, biology teacher, science education consultant, nature writer, and bird bander. He is author of The Piedmont Naturalist—*a collection of essays about plants, animals, and habitats of the Carolina Piedmont. Hilton's current ornithological research centers on Ruby-throated Hummingbirds in summer and finches in winter. He welcomes visits from fellow environmentalists interested in seeing how Hilton Pond has helped the cause of Neotropical migrant birds.*

Government Support

Landowners who have more than just a backyard to offer wildlife have the opportunity to receive educational, technical, and even financial assistance from a variety of conservation-minded organizations. In general, the larger the property that you are interested in dedicating to wildlife, the greater the number of support programs that are available to you. The following is a brief list and description of some of the many governmental and nongovernmental programs that recognize the importance of private land stewardship to wildlife.

U.S. Fish and Wildlife Service Programs

Our goal as businessmen and stewards of this land is to provide a good living for our families, while having as little impact as possible upon the land and its wildlife. We hope to leave the land and its ecosystem just as we found it, if not better. —Tom Martin, Farmer

Partners for Wildlife. The Partners for Wildlife Program (PWP) seeks to enhance and protect wetland and associated upland habitats through alliances between the U.S. Fish and Wildlife Service (USFWS), state agencies, regional conservation districts, and individuals, while keeping the land under private ownership. Between 1987 and 1991 the PWP entered into more than seven thousand voluntary agreements with private landowners that resulted in the restoration of converted or degraded wetlands on 140,000 acres of private property. Any wetland landowner is eligible to participate in the Partners for Wildlife Program, but priority is given to lands where benefits to threatened, endangered, and other diminishing species can be achieved. Once a biologist meets with the landowner and determines the landowner's goals and objectives for enhancing or protecting fish and wildlife habitat, a legally binding agreement citing the specific conditions for restoration and funding is made between the USFWS and the private landowner. Depending on the type and extent of the habitat under consideration, this agreement may be in effect for ten to thirty years or more.

Funding for this project is provided through the federal government or a cost-sharing program with the landowner and others that might have joined in the alliance. No more than $10,000 in federal support is spent on a landowner's property in any single fiscal year. At least 70 percent of project funds are used for physical, on-the-ground implementation of the restoration activity. Remaining funds are used to provide technical assistance to the landowner. Routine monitoring ensures that the terms of the agreement are being honored.

Those interested in learning more about the PWP should contact the USFWS and ask about the location of demonstration projects and availability of wetland restoration workshops.

U.S. Forest Service Programs

The U.S. Forest Service is divided into three sections: the National Forest System, State and Private Forestry, and Research. Under the Cooperative Forestry Assistance Act of 1978, the State and Private Forestry section offers programs that assist private landowners with forest resource conservation and management, including the protection, improvement, and maintenance of wildlife habitat.

The Forest Stewardship Program. The national goal of this five-year program is to place twenty-five million acres (ten million hectares) of nonindustrial private forest lands under the management of land stewards. Each state, under the direction of the State Forester, has established a State Stewardship Committee with a State Stewardship Coordinator. All nonindustrial private forest lands not currently in management under federal, state, or private-sector financial and technical assistance programs are eligible for the Forest Stewardship Program (FSP). To initiate an FSP, landowners must first decide on their own management objectives (e.g., wildlife conservation, recreation, aesthetics). Once this is accomplished, a professional resource manager prepares a forest stewardship plan based on these objectives and submits it to the State Forester for approval. The plan identifies what actions landowners should take to meet stewardship goals. After the work is completed, landowners are eligible for the prestigious title of land steward and certification of their land as stewardship forests. Contact your State Stewardship Coordinator for more information.

The Stewardship Incentives Program. The Stewardship Incentives Program was designed to assist private landowners with the fulfillment of their stewardship goals through a process of cost-sharing. All private landowners with between ten and one thousand acres (four to four hundred hectares) are eligible for the assistance once they have an approved forest stewardship plan they agree to implement for ten or more years. Each State Stewardship Committee decides what forestry practices will be cost-shared, and at what rate. Funding to each state is based on the total acreage of nonindustrial private forest lands and the number of owners eligible for cost-sharing per state. Contact your State Stewardship Coordinator for more information.

The Forest Legacy Program. The Forest Legacy Program (FLP) was created as part of the 1990 Farm Bill to identify and protect environmentally important private forest lands threatened with destruction or degradation by development. In the pilot stage in the northeastern United States and Washington state, the FLP authorizes the USDA Forest Service to acquire permanent conservation easements from consenting forest landowners. Priority is given to lands that have important ecological, cultural, or aesthetic values and that show the potential for effective protection and management. Landowners who participate in the FLP are required to manage their property according to the terms under which the easement was sold. Contact your State Forester for more information.

America the Beautiful Tree-Planting Initiative. A one-time grant of $25 million has been given to the Tree Trust, a private, nonprofit foundation, for the sole purpose of establishing a network of volunteers to undertake tree planting, improvement, and maintenance. The Trust solicits private-sector funds and oversees the use of contributions in community-based tree-planting projects. Under the stewardship programs (FSP and SIP), America the Beautiful authorizes a rural tree planting and forest management plan, as well as a community tree-planting and improvement program. Contact your state's Urban Forestry Coordinator for more information.

U.S. Department of Agriculture

U.S. Department of Agriculture's (USDA's) Soil Conservation Service (SCS) has three major goals: soil and water conservation, natural resource surveys, and community resource protection and management. Through three thousand locally organized and run conservation districts, the SCS offers a nationwide network of conservation specialists available to help people understand and protect the environment. At the district level, the SCS can provide technical conservation assistance and call on USDA's expertise to solve specific land use problems. The SCS conducts soil surveys; inventories resources; assists in the management of crop, pasture, range, woodlands, water, and recreation areas; restores disturbed sites; conducts environmental education programs; and undertakes research on plant materials.

Through its conservation planning programs, the SCS helps rural landowners establish and improve habitat for a variety of wildlife. Urban residents benefit from SCS's assistance in the selection of shrubs and trees that attract songbirds and other wildlife. To encourage landowners to participate in conservation programs, the USDA offers cost-sharing in addition to its technical assistance.

Private landowners interested in conservation planning can expect a SCS conservationist to take an inventory of existing resources, make soil maps available, outline and discuss different ways to accomplish preestablished goals, help put the plan into operation, and be available for future consultation if questions arise. For more information on SCS programs, contact the U.S. Department of Agriculture, Soil Conservation Service, P.O. Box 2890, Washington, D.C. 20013.

Resource Conservation and Development Areas. In 1962 Congress approved the Resource Conservation and Development (RC&D) Program, for which SCS is responsible. This program is designed to accelerate environmental protection and resource development in areas covered by multicounty jurisdiction. For example, through its RC&D program, SCS has helped many coastal communities protect beaches and dunes with native vegetation and erosion control structures. To participate in the RC&D, local sponsors, with the agreement of the governor and SCS state conservationist, apply to the U.S. Secretary of Agriculture. If the plan is authorized by the USDA and endorsed by the governor, SCS may assign a conservationist to help local sponsors plan an RC&D program. If USDA accepts the plan, technical assistance from SCS (and occasionally other state and federal agencies) and financial assistance will be provided. For more information on SCS programs, contact the U.S. Department of Agriculture, Soil Conservation Service, P.O. Box 2890, Washington, DC 20013.

The Conservation Reserve Program. In response to the need to preserve vegetative cover on highly erodible cropland soils, the USDA began the Conservation Reserve Program (CRP) in 1985 through its office of Agricultural Stabilization and Conservation Service. Vegetative cover reduces soil erosion, improves water quality, and enhances wildlife habitat. CRP offers long-term rental payments and cost-share assistance to establish permanent vegetative cover on cropland that is highly erodible or that is contributing to a serious water quality problem. By 1992, approximately thirty-five million acres had been enrolled in the program. Land eligible for enrollment includes cropland that has been planted to produce an agricultural commodity in two of the five crop years from 1986 to 1990. The land must also be physically and legally capable of continued crop production. For more information, contact the Conservation Reserve Program Administrator, USDA, Agricultural Stabilization and Conservation Service, P.O. Box 2415, Washington, DC 20013.

The Wetlands Reserve Program. The USDA began the Wetlands Reserve Program as a pilot program in 1992 to provide for voluntary restoration and protection of wetlands by agricultural landowners through permanent easements. To be eligible, land must be former cropland, farmed wetlands, or natural wetlands. Land must also have been planted to produce an agricultural commodity in at least one of the crop years from 1986 to 1990. Other land areas, such as upland and riparian buffer zones, are eligible if they affect or link restored wetlands.

The conservation easement is a legal agreement between landowners and the USDA Agricultural Stabilization and Conservation Service (ASCS) to restore and protect wetlands. Bids for permanent easements are given priority over short-term easements. In either case, participating landowners agree to pay 25 percent of the restoration costs and to perform future maintenance and repair on any structures needed to preserve the restored wetlands. To participate in the program, eligible landowners must declare their intent (apply) during a specified enrollment period. They then obtain an approved wetland reserve plan of operation and submit a bid for the total amount acceptable for granting the easement. For more information, contact the Wetlands Reserve Program Administrator, USDA, Agricultural Stabilization and Conservation Service, P.O. Box 2415, Washington, DC 20013.

The Cooperative Extension Service. The Cooperative Extension Service (CES) provides an educational network that involves partnerships between federal, state, and local governments, as well as private citizens. These programs are based on research at land-grant colleges and universities. The educational programs are implemented by respected educators and specialists. With its direct links to USDA, land-grant universities, and a grassroots educational system, the CES can deliver high-quality educational programs. A priority for these programs is increasing public interest in economic, environmental, and social impacts of management and the use of natural resources. The CES plays a significant role in helping landowners and managers reduce soil erosion, improve water resources and quality, protect vulnerable species, broaden sustainable economic opportunities, and address environmental issues and conflict resolution. For more information on fish and wildlife programs, contact the National Program Leader, Fish and Wildlife Management, Extension Service, Rm. 3867 So. Bldg., U.S. Department of Agriculture, Washington, DC 20250-0900. For more information on forestry programs, contact the National Program Leader, Forestry, Natural Resources & Rural Development, Extension Service, Rm. 3869 So. Bldg., U.S. Department of Agriculture, Washington, DC 20250-0900.

State, Provincial, and Territorial Fish and Wildlife Programs

Wildlife conservation at the regional agency level is undergoing a significant evolution in philosophy and practice. Programs that traditionally focused only on game species management ("hook and bullet" programs), have broadened their vision to include nongame wildlife conservation. This change is due in part to the public's growing interest in and concern for nongame wildlife. Bird-watchers, nature photographers, hikers, and other wildlife enthusiasts represent a relatively new and growing constituency for wildlife agencies. Regional agencies have legislative mandates and authority to manage wildlife. For decades, agencies have participated in collaborative efforts with civic and environmental groups, private corporations, private citizens, and other regional and federal natural resource agencies. Primarily through nongame funds, regional agencies have successfully operated research, education, monitoring, and management programs on both agency and private lands. Many such programs benefit Neotropical migrants. In fact, Neotropical migrants are increasingly becoming a focus of regional agency conservation efforts. For more information on the role of regional agencies in Neotropical migrant conservation, contact the International Association of Fish and Wildlife Agencies, 444 North Capitol Street, NW, Suite 544, Washington, DC 20001.

Nongovernmental Support Organizations
Natural Heritage Programs and Conservation Data Centers
To determine what plant and animal species and communities live on your land, consult your state's Natural Heritage Program (often called Conservation Data Centers in Canada). Pioneered by the Nature Conservancy in the 1970s, Natural Heritage Programs gather, store, and manage information on natural ecological diversity at the state level. Typically, these programs inventory plant and animal species and communities in both terrestrial and aquatic habitats, rank them in order of rarity, identify lands where the highest-ranked species and communities occur, set land protection and management priorities based on their rankings, and serve as a baseline for local inventories and conservation actions. Natural Heritage Program staff gather information on both public and private lands without regard to how the land is managed. Both primary (from recent fieldwork) and secondary (from scientific literature, interviews, museums, and herbaria) data are recorded on complete sets of geological survey maps.

"Elements" (identifiable units of species or communities) are defined by committees of scientists that have reviewed the plants and animals of the state and produced a list of declining, rare, or endangered species that should be monitored. All aquatic and plant communities with the state's overall vegetation become elements, as well as specific species. Because the Natural Heritage Programs are concerned with both communities and individual species, they provide both a coarse and fine-filter approach to identifying and monitoring a state's biota. This is extremely important in a world where fragmented ecosystems often produce incomplete communities and individual species often turn up or disappear unexpectedly. The design of heritage programs makes them more valuable as time passes; the quantity and quality of the data changes with each field season, correlating with the dynamics of the landscape and our knowledge and understanding of it. Heritage programs allow for the comparison of like entities based on terms of rarity, endangerment, threats, and vulnerability. For this reason, states are beginning to work together to develop regional strategies for conservation based on biological rather than political boundaries. For more information, contact your state's Natural Heritage Program or your province or territory's Conservation Data Center.

Ducks Unlimited

Ducks Unlimited (DU) is the world's largest private wetlands conservation organization. Founded in 1937, DU attempts to meet the annual needs of North American waterfowl by protecting, enhancing, restoring, and managing important wetlands and associated uplands. Initially DU focused on projects in Canada (where 70 percent of North America's waterfowl breed). This work continues on the upland breeding and nesting sites, as well as shallow ponds. In 1974 DU added Mexican wetland conservation to its agenda. These projects provide secure wintering habitat for waterfowl, allowing the birds to rest and refuel before returning to the United States and Canada to breed. In 1984 DU established wetland conservation projects in the Unites States to provide stopover sites and wintering grounds along migration corridors. By conserving, managing, and restoring wetland habitat, DU has been instrumental in the evolution and success of the North American Waterfowl Management Plan (see chapter 6, International Partnerships). Fundamental projects include the "Farming the Flyways" and "Prairie Care" programs, which assist farmers with habitat restoration and management. Waterfowl are not the only beneficiaries of DU's work. Migratory shorebirds and cranes, as well as numerous other types of wildlife, use wetlands throughout the year. For more information, contact the U.S. or Canadian office: Ducks Unlimited, Inc., One Waterfowl Way, Memphis, TN 38120-2351; Ducks Unlimited Canada, 1750 Courtwood Crescent, Suite 109, Ottawa, ONT K2C 2B5.

Wildlife Habitat Canada

Wildlife Habitat Canada (WHC) was founded in 1984 on the philosophy that healthy landscapes are vital if Canada is to use natural resources on a sustainable basis. It takes a partnership approach to habitat conservation, working with private landowners, other conservation groups, government agencies, and industry to restore, enhance, and protect the entire Canadian landscape. Its programs focus on four areas: agricultural landscapes, forest landscapes, wetlands, and the northern landscape. Wildlife Habitat Canada funds (with proceeds from the Conservation Stamp and Print Program) numerous habitat protection projects throughout Canada, as well as landowner incentive programs. Since 1984, WHC has committed more than $16 million to over 150 habitat conservation initiatives with a total value of more than $550 million. In addition, WHC assesses the impact of legislation, policies, and programs on habitat, stimulating discussion and bringing wildlife concerns to the table in policy debates. For more information, contact Wildlife Habitat Canada, 7 Hinton Avenue, Suite 200, Ottawa, ONT K1Y 4P1.

The Wildlife Management Institute

The Wildlife Management Institute (WMI) is a private, nonprofit, scientific education organization dedicated to the restoration, sound management, and sustainable use of natural resources in North America. The WMI was founded in 1911 and draws its financial support primarily from membership dues. The organization consults federal, state, and local government agencies on wildlife management issues, disseminates information to the public, and publishes a variety of materials related to wildlife management. For more information, contact the Wildlife Management Institute, 1101 14th Street, NW, Suite 725, Washington, DC 20005.

Society for Ecological Restoration

The Society for Ecological Restoration (SER) was organized in 1987 in response to the growing interest in and need for ecological restoration work. Membership in the organization is open to professional and amateur restoration enthusiasts throughout the world. The objectives of SER are to promote research into all areas of ecological restoration and management; facilitate communication among restorationists; promote awareness of the value and limitations of restoration techniques; contribute to public policy in relevant matters; develop grassroots support for restoration of natural areas in the urban, rural, and wilderness landscapes; and recognize individuals and organizations who have made outstanding contributions to the field of ecological restoration. Members (paid subscription) receive the quarterly *SER News* and biannual *Restoration & Management Notes*. The SER holds an annual conference to provide a forum for the exchange of research findings, technique development, and various educational events. It is committed to professional services and public education, and can provide valuable databases of publications, restoration projects, and opportunities. For more information, contact the Society for Ecological Restoration, 1207 Seminole Highway, Madison, WI 53711.

HABITAT CONSERVATION IN THE COMMUNITY

Naturescaping efforts undertaken on your property can teach you a great deal: how to work with nature's processes, rather than against them; how to heal the scars of the earth and prevent further injury; how interconnected life is. Your time and efforts are rewarded with wondrous variety, but you also gain specific knowledge, skills, and experiences that you can share with others.

Before beginning any community-based project, you should read one or more of the following excellent references: *Building an Ark: Tools for the Preservation of Natural Diversity through Land Protection* (Hoose 1981), *Creating Successful Communities* (Mantell, Harper, and Propst 1990), *Making Things Happen: How to Be an Effective Volunteer* (Wolfe 1991), *Land-Saving Action* (Brenneman and Bates 1984), *Organizing for Social Change: A Manual for Activists in the 1990s* (Bobo, Kendall, and Max 1991), *The Simple Act of Planting a Tree: Tree People* (Lipkis 1990), and *How to Save Your Neighborhood, City, or Town* (Lipkis 1993).

The information and suggestions presented below are only an introduction to creative processes. Human, environmental, and financial resources, as well as the political structure, will vary by community. Therefore, every community-based project is unique.

Making a Difference   Robert Horwich

In 1985 an experiment in grassroots conservation began with the initiation of the Community Baboon (howler monkey) Sanctuary along the Belize River in Belize, a small country in Central America. This project was the beginning of community conservation as a movement and as an effective tool for private citizens to begin to become true stewards of their land. In this experiment in grassroots conservation, more than one hundred landowners, mainly subsistence farmers and small ranchers, pledged to manage their lands for the conservation of the Black Howler Monkey. These landowners have since become an inspiration for villagers all over Belize, and the value of what these subsistence farmers have done is beginning to echo throughout the world. But the real magic of this small experiment is that it is a model for any community of landowners to use once they step beyond their own property and join hands with their neighbors to pursue proper management and use of their lands.

Although the Community Baboon Sanctuary targeted the howler monkey for a conservation effort, the complete habitat of the monkey was investigated to determine what was needed to meet the howler's needs in the conservation plan. Since howlers depend on trees for leaves and fruit, the habitat of a wide variety of birds and other animals that depend on the same type of forest were also protected. One third or more of those birds that benefitted from the conservation plan are Neotropical migrants. They spend most of their time wintering in southern countries and coming from or going to breeding grounds in North America. Research in Central America has shown that the lands of the Belizean farmers in the Community Baboon Sanctuary, which are mainly secondary forests, are especially good for these Neotropical migrants. However, destruction of our temperate forests is having an alarming effect on these migrants. Protecting their wintering grounds is doing only half the job.

Just as some Belizeans have learned to become stewards of their lands, so must we in North America protect our lands. You can start with what you have that is most valuable or that most needs protecting. Do you live in a woods or on a prairie? Do you own wetlands? Do you own an eagle roost or an area where box turtles roam? If you choose to target a species, then you need to educate yourself about it—its foods, breeding areas, roosts, nesting needs, total range, and so forth. If it is a large animal, then a large area may be required to meet its needs, even seasonally. If it is a migratory species, your lands might support that species only during certain seasons, but that season may be crucial for it.

Your next step is to develop a conservation plan for the lands you are concerned with. When considering a plan, you must look at the specific area involved and the way it meets or could meet the species' needs. At this point, it is helpful to get or prepare some maps of the area. Government maps, aerial photos, and vegetation and soil maps can reveal what your land is suitable for and whether it can support the species you have targeted or the habitat you are interested in protecting. Once you are ready to formulate a plan, remember to include maps that delineate all properties that must be included in the plan.

Maps give an overall view of the lands involved. They can be generated by computer programs and GIS (geological inventory survey) systems, but the basic principles can be accomplished in low-tech ways as well. You should map as many characteristics of the area as possible or as needed. If you make all maps to the same scale, you can place vegetation maps and property boundary maps against the window or over a light table to see how the boundaries overlap.

You can then make contact with affected neighbors and provide them with education materials. It is best to begin with neighbors who are most likely to be sympathetic to your plan. With luck, these will be your geographically closest neighbors as well. It makes sense to try to maximize your successes in the beginning by aligning with others who share your views. Once momentum begins, social coercion may encourage others to modify their initial objections to your plan.

If support appears likely, you should begin formalizing management plans for individual properties, making sure that they fit together in an overall plan that will most benefit the species or habitats you are seeking to enhance. Ask initially for things landowners would be willing to concede, then gradually expand your conservation goals.

Your neighbors may eventually express an interest in additional outcomes. The initial village in the Community Baboon Sanctuary was interested in tourism, so we worked to get some publicity for the project toward this end. Publicity can have several advantages. Local publicity can inform other neighbors, who might eventually be part of an expanded program. It might stimulate others to begin community conservation projects. If enough neighbors are involved, you might want to publish a project newsletter to keep them abreast of what is happening with the program. Once a strong neighborhood association is formed around a conservation goal, it might function in other ways to create a stronger, safer neighborhood.

Finally, you need a formal structure to keep the program running. If you want the program to evolve and maintain itself successfully, you need a structure by which it can run without you. This may mean the creation of a nonprofit organization or some legal body with a board of directors. If you apply for grants or hire staff, even temporary or part-time workers, you will need a legal entity that can oversee their work. The success of the effort depends on who is involved, what you are trying to protect or conserve, and how you proceed.

If you live near a natural area or a park, your conservation plan can help form a buffer zone. In this case, it is important to contact the park staff and work directly with them. Existing governmental and nongovernmental conservation groups may seem reluctant to embrace what you are trying to do because the concept is new or you lack formal credentials. Work slowly, but maintain contact with the staff. Once park officials see you have neighborhood support and are trying to complement the park's programs, you should have more success.

Suppose you wanted to create a suburban woodland sanctuary to support songbirds. First, you should find a simple way to monitor the breeding bird species and their numbers, followed by yearly censuses of the area to see how well the plan is succeeding. The project goal would be to help natural forest succession slowly take over the neighborhood. Neighbors could be asked to landscape their yards with only vegetation native to the area. Next, you could plant trees within the lawn expanses, allowing enough room for future tree growth. In many cases you need only transplant and nurture seedlings. As the area becomes more shaded, neighbors could be encouraged to cultivate small areas of native flowers and thick groundcovers. Eventually the lawn would be replaced with gravel or woodchip paths meandering through the growing trees and woodland undergrowth.

The main lesson learned from the Community Baboon Sanctuary is that individuals can make a difference. Individuals who take responsibility for their lands and their neighborhoods can sometimes work more effectively and with more success than large public or private organizations. A carefully developed plan, bolstered by self-education and carried out with flexibility and creativity, can be effective and inspire others. Community conservation is an avenue open to anyone.

Robert Horwich is President of Community Conservation Consultants. His interests include research on infant development in birds and primates and the establishment of community sanctuaries. For more information, contact Robert Horwich at Community Conservation Consultants, Howlers Forever, Inc., RD 1, Box 96, Gays Mills, WI 54631.

Land Trusts

Your grand plans for a community migratory bird sanctuary may include properties owned by individuals who do not become involved in the project. They may not have the time or money to invest in naturescaping, they may dislike "group" ventures, or they may simply not share your concern for migratory birds. In such cases (they are bound to arise eventually), your organization should consider the involvement or creation of a land trust.

Today, few North Americans are lucky enough to live close to wilderness. For many people, however, their lives are greatly enhanced by land preserved by land trusts close to home, and at little cost to the public. Land trusts are private, non-profit (local, regional, or statewide) conservation organizations directly involved in land transactions that protect natural, scenic, recreational, agricultural, historic, or cultural property.

Land trusts can own land or hold conservation easements on it and work for the transfer of lands between other conservation groups or agencies. Land trusts are also responsible for managing lands, educating the public, providing technical assistance, influencing public policy on land conservation issues, acting as intermediaries in land disputes, and researching land use and its effects on the environment.

Several types of land trusts are broadly recognized. Multiresource land trusts have more than one resource goal in protecting land. Agricultural and forest land trusts are primarily focused on the conservation of agricultural and forest lands. Community land trusts advocate shared ownership and use of land and its resources. Social and economic goals are met through community-based productive and ecological land-use practices. Other land trusts may function as special interest groups to protect a specific type of habitat or a specific geographic area. Regardless of the title, the preservation of wildlife habitat is the greatest concern of land trusts nationwide.

The formation of land trusts began in the late nineteenth century in the northeastern United States, when concerns about rapid urbanization spawned the creation of "village improvement societies." The movement grew strongly in the 1950s as increased human population pressures, urban sprawl, and land-damaging technologies began to place markedly increasing strains on the environment. Although more than half of the nation's nearly nine hundred land trusts function within single towns or counties, together they protect more than 2,700,000 acres (1,080,000 hectares) of local, regional, and national importance. Collectively, land trusts own 437,000 acres (174,800 hectares); hold conservation easements on 450,000 acres (180,000 hectares); have acquired, protected, and transferred 668,000 acres (267,200 hectares) to other organizations; and used other land acquisition techniques to protect another 1,159,000 acres (463,600 hectares).

Land trusts vary greatly in size. More than half of land trusts are completely staffed by volunteers. Budgets range from less than $10,000 to more than $1 million. Two thirds of the nation's land trusts operate with budgets greater than $100,000. Although independent in nature, land trusts frequently pool their resources and work with other conservation organizations and government agencies to protect and manage lands.

Relevant information on how to form a land trust can be found in S. C. Wilkins and R. E. Koontz, "How to Form a Land Trust," M. R. Fremont-Smith and R. E. Koontz, "Becoming and Remaining a Tax-Exempt Organization" in *Land Saving Action* (Wilkins and Koontz 1984), and *Creating Successful Communities* (Mantell, Harper, and Propst 1990).

The following are a few of the nationally operating land trusts that can provide advice and assistance for local land conservation.

The Land Trust Alliance

Since 1982, the Land Trust Alliance (LTA) has operated as the nonprofit umbrella organization of land trusts and other nonprofit land conservation organizations. Membership includes 450 land trusts, as well as government agencies, concerned citizens, and land-use experts. The LTA provides a variety of services to members, including publications, national conferences, liability insurance, and policy information and guidelines. For more information, contact the Land Trust Alliance at 900 17th Street, NW, Suite 410, Washington, DC 20006.

The Forest Trust

The mission of the Forest Trust is to protect forests and foster productive relationships between human and natural communities; to challenge traditional forest management philosophies; to provide resource protection strategies to grassroots environmental organizations, rural communities, and public agencies; and to provide land stewardship services to owners of private lands of significant conservation value. Created as a project of the Tides Foundation, the Forest Trust conducts programs in national forest planning and policy, forestry development for rural communities, land trust, and land stewardship. Four major outreach programs are carried out by the Forest Trust:

• The Community Forestry Program builds forestry skills and an understanding of forest ecosystems within rural communities through job training, market research, and sustainable business development.

• The National Forest Program protects and restores forest ecosystems in the national forests, and promotes the protection of forests, integration of human activity within sustainable forest ecosystems, and greater citizen participation in forest management decisions.

• The Land Trust Program protects productive forest and range lands through conservation easements, land acquisition, and the application of sound environmental management practices.

• Land Stewardship Services manages private forests and ranches to enhance environmental values.

For more information, contact the Forest Trust, P.O. Box 519, Sante Fe, NM 87501.

The American Farmland Trust

Founded in 1980, the American Farmland Trust (AFT) is designed to protect agricultural resources. The AFT works to halt the loss of productive farmland and to promote farming practices that result in a healthy environment. Membership support is directed to programs offering technical assistance in policy development, public education, and direct farmland protection projects. The AFT also provides consultation services to private farmers for conservation choices in farm estate planning and related subjects. For more information, contact the American Farmland Trust, 1920 N Street, NW, Suite 400, Washington, DC 20036.

Rails to Trails Conservancy

Since 1985, the Rails to Trails Conservancy (RTC) has been working to convert abandoned railroad track lines to public-use hiking trails and recreational areas. Many of the preserved areas also function as wildlife corridors through or around urban environments. Although the RTC does not purchase or hold land in trust, it does carry out technical assistance, public education, advocacy, negotiation, legislation, and regulatory activities regarding land tracts that once served railways. For more information, contact Rails to Trails Conservancy, 1400 16th Street, NW, Suite 300, Washington, DC 20036.

The Nature Conservancy—an International Land Trust

The mission of the Nature Conservancy (TNC) is to preserve plants, animals, and natural communities that represent the diversity of life throughout the world by protecting the lands and water they need to survive. Through its land acquisition programs, TNC has been responsible for the protection of more than 6.3 million acres (2,520,000 hectares) in the United States and Canada. In addition, it has helped partner organizations in Latin America and the Caribbean preserve millions of acres. The Nature Conservancy owns more than 1,300 preserves (more than half received as donations), the largest private system of nature sanctuaries in the world. In addition, it transfers acquired areas to other conservation groups for management. It is a nonprofit organization, and donations are tax deductible. For more information on the Nature Conservancy and programs that it may have in your state, write to the Nature Conservancy, 1815 North Lynne Street, Arlington, VA 22209. If you are interested in donating land, ask for the "Gifts of Land" brochure.

Land Acquisition Techniques

A number of formal and informal techniques are used by land trusts and other land interest groups to acquire or protect property that is of interest to them. These techniques vary greatly in the time and financial commitment required to secure and maintain successful ventures. Several questions should be explored when deciding the most appropriate techniques in a given situation: What is the ecological significance of the property? What elements are currently protected and what are future prospects for protection? What is the price of the property and how much money is available? What is the landowner's attitude toward conservation of the elements on the property? If conservation rights are obtained, who will manage the property, what might it cost, and who will pay?

Be sure to seek the assistance and advice of already established, successful land trusts before you venture out on your own—conservation demands the wise use of resources of time and money, as well as nature. An understanding of the following concepts is essential.

Notification

Notification is the act of informing a landowner that a natural element (e.g., a particular type of tree) identified through a biotic inventory occurs on his or her property, explaining why the element is important, and determining the property owner's attitude to this information. Notification requires only that the landowner listen to or read this information. The facts of the matter alone may convince the landowner to protect or manage for the element in question, as the world's biotic impoverishment is due more to ignorance than to malicious intent. Notification may establish a relationship with the landowner that will eventually lead to permanent protection (in part or entirely) of the property.

Given the sensitivity of private property issues, the success of notification as a conservation measure depends largely on the way the information is presented to the landowner. The best person to do the job may be someone who is already a trusted personal acquaintance. If the landowner is to be approached by a stranger, an informal introductory letter and a phone call are extremely important. The landowner will undoubtedly feel uncomfortable with, and even threatened by, a stranger who wishes to discuss his or her property. The notifier must be able to ease these anxieties. Interactions, therefore, should be brief, to the point, and unbureaucratic. A well-informed, skilled communicator can put the landowner at ease, while briefly but clearly outlining what element is present, why it is valuable, and how the landowner might go about learning more on the subject. A good listener can gather vital information from this brief interaction for future protection strategies. The notifier should try to learn the landowner's current attitude toward the property, current and future needs, and plans to sell or manage the property, and may determine what future measures can be taken to safeguard the biotic elements.

Registration

A registry is a list of properties deserving special attention, based on one or more important characteristics. Membership on this list is obtained through a process of credible evaluation. Some members on the list are ordered on the basis of priority. The registry itself may have no official power, but as a reference source it can be quite an effective tool in land acquisition. The federal Endangered Species Program, National Natural Landmark Program, and Natural Heritage Program/Conservation Data Centers are among many programs whose directives for action come from registries. However, the development of a registry is not limited to government entities; any organization, and even individuals, may create registries.

Registry programs may directly influence development if laws exist that restrict or regulate development on and near an area listed on a registry. Individuals seeking development funds, licenses, or permits may be required to consider their project's effects on registered elements. If conflicts arise, a team of citizens and professional environmentalists may meet with the project director in an attempt to establish a development program that meets his or her approval and is less threatening to the registered element. Pressure from concerned, well-informed citizens may create a very persuasive force for conservation in such cases. However, because both Congress and state legislatures are shying away from open-ended land use regulation policies, it has become increasingly difficult to control development directly through registries.

Many conservation organizations and state agencies are using registries to encourage landowners to volunteer to protect the registered elements that exist on their property. Landowners who have received notification generally agree (in writing) to take measures to conserve the element or elements in question. To persuade landowners to agree to such measures, some of which may require a significant change in land use, those wishing to encourage volunteerism take considerable effort to provide attractive incentives. In recognition of his or her contribution to conservation, the landowner may receive a symbol, perhaps a property sign, certificate, or plaque. Assistance may be offered in the form of management advice or volunteer labor. In some cases, state or local jurisdictions may give the landowner a tax break by reducing the assessed value of the property in return for agreeing not to develop it, at least in part.

Management Agreements

A management agreement is a written contract between a landowner and a conserving party. The management agreement obligates the landowner to manage his or her property in a specific manner for a given period of time. The conserving party may assist the landowner with advice, resources, or labor. Such agreements are especially appropriate conservation measures when a landowner is already conscientiously managing and protecting habitat on his or her property. If a nominal fee (called "consideration") is given to the landowner and the contract is legally recorded, the conserving party has a formal interest in the property and is fully responsible for seeing that the owner fulfills the management agreement.

Leases

A lease on a property works the same way as a lease on an apartment or office space: rent is paid to the owner for the temporary use of the property. Like a management agreement, a lease states the terms of the agreement and the length of time it will last. Unlike management agreements, which are often informal agreements made between individual landowners, leases are formal, legally binding, often standardized documents used by corporations, agencies, and individuals, usually to generate income from their properties. Leases have a political advantage in that they are more often recognized by county recorders, some of whom will not record "management agreements," even though they connote the same exchange of interests as leases.

Rights of First Refusal

The right of first refusal is established when a landowner agrees, often in exchange for a nominal sum, to inform an interested party first if he or she should decide to sell the property. This allows an interested party the opportunity to purchase the property outright or a certain period of time (often thirty days) to match another genuine offer. If the landowner promises to manage the property in the best interests of conservation up to the time of selling, the right of first refusal can be a very powerful tool. Like management agreements and leases, rights of first refusal should be legally recorded in the local courts.

Acquisition of Fee Title and Tax Law

If one considers each right to property ownership (such as the right to live on the land, sell the land, or will the land) to be a stick, then the person who holds all the sticks is said to own "fee title" to the property. Each right, however, can be separated from the bundle and sold, traded, leased, and so forth. If the property must be purchased in full, acquisition of fee title can be very costly. However, the federal tax laws encourage donations. These laws permit individuals and corporations to deduct from their taxable income the value of gifts to many charitable entities, including most conservation organizations. Individuals may give their property by way of an outright donation, bargain sale (sell half and donate half), donation with a reserved life estate (donate the property but can live on it until he or she dies), donation of undivided interest in land (donate a percentage of legal interest in the land, so the land is owned commonly), or donation by will (will the land to an organization). Each mechanism of donation is governed by different tax laws. Each exchange must be recorded by the courts.

Conservation Easements

A conservation easement is a legal contract that a landowner makes with an appropriate third party (such as a land trust or public agency) to control development that might threaten his or her property. Those third parties holding conservation easements can control landowner actions that could threaten the natural elements. The restrictions cited in the contract are tailored to the interests of the landowner and specific to the needs of the property. Conservation easements may be positive (allowing the landowner to do something on the property), negative (prohibiting the landowner from doing something on the property), appurtenant (benefiting a contiguous property), or in gross (benefiting that easement holder, rather than a particular property). A conservation easement demands that the landowner relinquish only a few sticks, rather than the entire bundle required in the exchange of fee title. Therefore, the group that has acquired an easement is said to have gained "less-than-fee" interest in the property. Easements have a conservation advantage in that they may become a permanent fixture on the land (exist "in perpetuity"), requiring all future owners to leave a few sticks out of the bundle. By granting an easement, a landowner can protect his or her land while retaining ownership, often gain a tax deduction, and (if in perpetuity) be assured that no matter who the future landowners are, the land will be protected indefinitely. The donation of a conservation easement to a conservation organization or public agency is considered a tax-deductible charitable gift, provided that the easement is exclusively for conservation purposes and stands in perpetuity. For more information on conservation easements, see the Land Trust Alliance's *Conservation Easement Handbook* (900 Seventh Street, NW, Suite 410, Washington, DC 20006-2596).

Dedication

Dedication is the act of placing natural areas into a legally established, usually state administered and managed, system of nature preserves. When the dedicated land becomes part of a statewide preserve, it is protected against conversion or condemnation. Landowners may donate partial interest in their property or fee title to a state preservation system. A state agency may accept dedicated lands for the state as donations, exchanges, or transfers from other agencies, and may occasionally purchase land. However, in most cases the cost is limited to the cost of managing the property after dedication.

Dedication is a stronger protective measure than acquisition of fee title because nature preserves, by definition, protect properties dedicated to them against conversion or condemnation. By law, county clerks cannot record exchanges by dedication unless they clearly delineate terms for protecting the land against development or modification.

A second form of dedication is known as "trust dedication." In such cases, lands are dedicated to a trust that has been created by law and is administered by an agency. Natural areas become part of the land trust, rather than formal preserve systems. In such cases, final decisions regarding the use of the property are determined in the courts, rather than by the designated administrative agency. In the United States, trust dedications are seldom used.

Negotiating Tips

First impressions count. In the case of land conservation, first impressions may make or break a land acquisition deal. People are likely to have been alerted to your efforts through your own direct mail campaign, the local media, or by word of mouth—all rather impersonal forms of communication. Eventually you must approach landowners face to face. This may be the most critical point in a land conservation effort. Therefore, it is very important to define a plan of action well in advance, review it, and adhere to it. Although everyone's approach will vary and every situation is different, we can offer some pointers that are universally applicable:

1. Write first, or obtain an introduction.
2. Set a time limit (perhaps a half hour for the first meeting).
3. Dress conventionally: your personal appearance does make a difference.
4. Know precisely what you want before you knock on the door. Be prepared to be specific. Exactly what elements do you wish to protect? What do these elements require for survival? What actions might the landowner take to harm or destroy these elements? How might you be able to obtain protective rights to these elements?
5. Do your homework. Try to learn the history of the land and as much about the person you are approaching as possible. Anticipate what the landowner needs and wants.
6. Listen to the landowner. Don't be intimidated by a viewpoint other than your own. Answer questions promptly and appropriately. If you don't know the answer to a question, say so. Then find out and get back to the landowner as soon as possible.
7. Stick to the point. Don't let conversations wander, but be tactful in returning to the topic at hand. Your time with this person is limited, so make the most of it.
8. Don't give in easily. If at first you don't succeed, try, try again. Attempt to get another appointment before you leave. If things have gone well, ask the landowner for his or her assistance when approaching a neighbor.

SEEING THE BIG PICTURE

By naturescaping your own backyard, you won't be able to provide suitable habitat for some wildlife, including forest-nesting Neotropical migrants and large mammals. However, if your lands and those of your neighbors and their neighbors were restored to ecologically sound structure and function, both nature and the human spirit would benefit significantly. Seeing the "big picture" is empowering both for you and for those whose participation you hope to encourage. How does your region compare with others in environmental health? (See the *Green Index* published by Island Press.) Where is your region succeeding or failing? What are the contributing factors? How might these problems hinder your ability to succeed in a regional restoration or migratory bird sanctuary program? Ultimately, consider how all the pieces of the puzzle can come together. The following summarizes one vision of the big picture.

The mission of the Wildlands Project is to help protect and restore the ecological richness and native biodiversity of North America through the establishment of a connected system of reserves.

As a new millennium begins, society approaches a watershed for wildlife and wilderness. The environment of North America is at risk. . . . Healing the land means reconnecting its parts so that vital flows can be renewed. The land has given much to us; now it is time to give something back, to begin to allow nature to come out of hiding and to restore the links that will sustain both wilderness and the spirit for future human generations.

The idea is simple: to stem the disappearance of wildlife and wilderness, we must allow the recovery of whole ecosystems and landscapes in every region of North America. Allowing these systems to recover requires a long-term master plan. . . .

Our vision is simple: we live for the day when . . . vast unbroken forests and flowering plains again thrive and support pre-Columbian populations of plants and animals; when humans dwell with respect, harmony, and affection for the land. . . .

Our vision is continental: . . . we seek to bring together conservationists, ecologists, indigenous peoples, and others to protect and restore . . . biodiversity. We seek to assist other conservation organizations and to develop cooperative relationships with activists and grassroots groups everywhere. . . .

We are called to our task by the failure of existing wilderness areas, parks, and wildlife refuges to adequately protect life in North America. While these areas preserve landscapes of spectacular scenery . . . they are too small [and] isolated, and represent too few types of ecosystems to perpetuate the biodiversity of the continent. Despite the establishment of parks and other reserves from Canada to Central America, true wilderness and wilderness-dependent species are in precipitous decline. . . .

• Populations of many songbirds are crashing and waterfowl and shorebird populations are reaching new lows.

• Native forests have been extensively cleared, leaving only scattered remnants of most forest types. . . .

• Tall Grass and Short Grass Prairies . . . have been almost entirely destroyed or domesticated.

The failure of reserves to prevent [such] losses . . . rests in large part [on] their historic purpose and design: to protect scenery and recreation or to create outdoor zoos. The Wildlands Project, in contrast, calls for reserves established to protect . . . biodiveristy. . . . We reject the notion that wilderness is merely remote, scenic terrain suitable for backpacking. Rather, we see wilderness as the home for unfettered life, free from industrial human intervention.

Wilderness means:

• Extensive areas of native vegetation in various successional stages off-limits to human exploitation. We recognize that most of Earth has been colonized by humans only in the last several thousand years.

• Viable, self-reproducing, genetically diverse populations of all native plant and animal species. . . . Diversity at the genetic, species, ecosystem, and landscape levels is fundamental to the integrity of nature.

• Vast landscapes without roads, dams, motorized vehicles . . . or other artifacts of civilization, where evolutionary and ecological processes that represent 4 billion years of Earth wisdom can continue. Such wilderness is absolutely essential to the comprehensive maintenance of biodiversity. It is not a solution to every ecological problem, but without it the planet will sink further into biological poverty.

We [want] . . . all native species to flourish within the ebb and flow of ecological processes, rather than within the constraints of what industrial civilization is content to leave alone. Present reserves . . . exist as discrete islands of nature in a sea of human-modified landscapes. Building upon those natural areas, we seek to develop a system of large, wild core reserves where biodiversity and ecological processes dominate.

Core reserves would be linked by biological corridors to allow for the natural dispersal of wide-ranging species, for genetic exchange between populations, and for migration of organisms in response to climate change.

Buffers would be established around core reserves and corridors to protect their integrity from disruptive human activities. Only human activity compatible with protection of the core reserves and corridors would be allowed. Buffers would also be managed to restore ecological health, extirpated species, and natural disturbance regimes. Intensive human activity associated with civilization . . . could continue outside the buffers.

Implementation of such a system would take place over many decades. Existing natural areas should be protected immediately. Other areas, already degraded, will be identified and (restored).

The Wildlands Project sets a new agenda for the conservation movement. For the first time a proposal based on the needs of all life . . . will be clearly enunciated. Both conservationists and those who would reduce nature to resources will have to confront the reality of what is required for a healthy, viable, and diverse North America. Citizens, activists, and policymakers will be able to confront the real choices because the choices will be on the agenda. It will no longer be possible to operate in a business-as-usual manner and ignore what is at stake.

For more information, write to The Wildlands Project, PO Box 5365, Tucson, AZ 85703.

Excerpted from Wild Earth, *Special Issue 1992, pp. 3–4, with permission of the Cenozoic Society, Inc. See the Wildlands Project; Land Conservation Strategy, pp. 10–24, for complete details.*

PLAYING POLITICS

To have a broader effect on both immediate and future land use in your area, get involved in local land-use planning and regulation as a citizen representative on a government board or committee. One of the most important processes in which to participate is zoning. Generally defined, zoning is the enactment of ordinances by local governments to designate areas for specific purposes (activities, architectural style, building height, building density). Because local governments are highly variable, local land-use planning has tended to be highly variable. As a result, zoning regulations and applications are very dynamic. Zoning is, nonetheless, a major tool used by local (especially county) governments to protect areas from incompatible land use. Where local wildlife protection is concerned, zoning can be a very powerful land protection tool, particularly if concerned citizens are involved in the land use planning process. (See Bissell et al. 1986 for more information.)

Whether you are formally involved in local government or not, stay abreast of plans for land use in your area. Take a personal stand and rally your community when land use plans threaten the future of vital habitats and the wildlife that depends on them. Never be afraid to stand up for what you believe in and to inspire others to do the same. If you are not comfortable with public speaking, consider taking a course at a local community college. The ability to communicate and the power to persuade are skills that truly define our successes and failures as citizen activists.

Attend "town meetings" on green space issues when they arise. Bring your friends and go empowered with knowledge of the issue at hand. If you have sufficient information, develop a position statement to deliver at the meeting. This statement should explain precisely why you support or are opposed to the project. If you oppose the project, clearly define the impacts of habitat destruction or degradation that are likely to result, as well as the positive reasons for protecting the land. Your statement should consider both human and nonhuman perspectives. Don't be afraid to put some emotion into it. Unfortunately, confrontations are rarely won or lost with facts—remember the power to persuade? Publicize your position statement to empower others.

Seek out and join ranks with others who share your concerns. Become a member of one or more local environmental organizations—a bird club, garden club, naturalist society, whatever. Many such groups now have their own conservation councils or committees. These provide an excellent opportunity to stay informed on issues, to voice concern, to gain support (emotional, financial, tactical) when land use threats arise, and to work constructively toward solutions.

For further advice, see chapters 4 and 5.

Watchdogging: Monitoring Wildlife Conservation Policy

The power of information is magnified by the number of people who have it and use it.   —*Rick Bonney, "Taking Charge,"* Living Bird Quarterly

Migratory birds are an internationally shared, public resource. They know no property lines and are therefore owned by no one. Birds have intrinsic aesthetic value, as well as economic clout, so we look to the government to help protect their populations. Because migratory birds and their conservation problems transcend local political divisions, federal governments and international institutions play an increasingly important role in migratory bird conservation.

Federal governments and their myriad agencies can help or hinder migratory bird conservation efforts. It is up to concerned citizen activists to understand how government policies and their enforcing agencies function and then to keep them on track. Basically, the federal government can influence migratory bird conservation by regulating potentially harmful activities, carefully managing extensive federally owned lands, offering initiatives for sound management, supporting sound research and public education, and entering into international treaty relationships to cooperate with other governments to conserve birds in the Western Hemisphere and the entire world. The various federal agencies play these roles to different degrees.

UNITED STATES AGENCIES

The federal government plays so many different roles in the conservation of migratory birds that it is no wonder that the activities are scattered through numerous agencies and their departments. In this chapter, we will discuss the regulatory and land management roles of these different governmental bodies, beginning with a brief overview of the agencies and their involvement, direct or indirect, with migratory birds.

The U.S. Fish and Wildlife Service

The U.S. Fish and Wildlife Service (USFWS) is the principal agency through which the federal government attempts to conserve wildlife. It manages national wildlife refuges and enforces laws such as the Migratory Bird Treaty and Endangered Species Act. The USFWS has been the lead agency for establishing and managing information on population trends of migratory birds. In addition, it conducts research on questions related to habitat management and the effects of environmental toxins on migratory birds.

The National Park Service

The National Park Service (NPS) manages over 30 million hectares (70 million acres) at 337 areas, including national parks and monuments and the Wild and Scenic Rivers and National Trail systems. The NPS manages lands primarily for the protection of our natural heritage for the enjoyment of park visitors. In this way it is unique among federal land management agencies.

The Bureau of Land Management

The Bureau of Land Management (BLM) oversees more land than all other federal agencies combined—approximately 136 million hectares (336 million acres) of public land. The BLM manages these lands for a variety of uses (fish and wildlife habitat, watershed protection, grazing, timber, and recreation). Most of the land is rangeland that is managed for grazing, but BLM land also includes critical desert and riparian habitats.

The National Biological Service

The National Biological Service (NBS) studies the health, distribution, and abundance of biological resources, with the goals of identifying potential problems before they become intractable, focusing efforts to understand ecosystems, and sharing data with other countries. The NBS draws on the expertise of other agencies in the Department of the Interior, as well as other departments, state agencies, and private organizations (such as the Nature Conservancy, universities, botanical gardens, and museums).

The Smithsonian Institution

The Smithsonian Institution (SI) runs several national museums and the National Zoo. It also has a large, active research staff and functions like a research university. As a quasifederal institution, the SI has no mandate to enforce regulations or manage federal lands. However, it receives considerable support through its research bureaus for ornithologists working on migratory bird research and conservation education. In addition, Congress recently established the Smithsonian Migratory Bird Center to focus attention on the issue of declining songbird populations. The SI runs the Smithsonian Tropical Research Institute, which is the longest-running ecological research institute in the tropics.

The Environmental Protection Agency

The Environmental Protection Agency (EPA) enforces major environmental laws, including the Federal Insecticide, Fungicide, and Rodenticide Act and the Clean Water Act, and conducts research on the causes, effects, and control of environmental problems. Regional offices of the EPA help states comply with environmental laws and develop cases against polluters.

The U.S. Forest Service

The U.S. Forest Service (USFS) manages 156 national forests and 19 national grasslands, which cover 79 million hectares (191 million acres). Its jurisdiction covers timber harvesting, road construction, and mining on these lands, as well as managing lands for recreational use and wilderness protection. The USFS provides technical support and consultation for timber practices.

The Soil Conservation Service

The Soil Conservation Service (SCS) gives technical and financial assistance to farmers, ranchers, and state and local governments in matters regarding soil erosion, flooding, and water conservation, and conducts research to develop plants for many uses. The SCS may be given lead authority for managing wetlands.

The Department of Commerce

The National Oceanic and Atmospheric Administration (NOAA) makes nautical charts and coastal maps, predicts weather, explores oceans, monitors marine pollution, and helps states protect coastlines. NOAA oversees offshore oil developments that are encroaching on critical habitat along the Gulf coast, arctic shores, and the Pacific coast.

The Coast Guard

The Coast Guard administers the oil spill liability section of the Clean Water Act, inspects ships carrying oil and issues certificates of responsibility to operators and owners of vessels liable for oil spills, and acts as the main maritime law enforcement unit.

The Department of Defense

The Department of Defense (DOD) owns and manages large tracts of lands throughout the United States and U.S. protectorates totaling 10 million hectares (25 million acres). The largest bases are in relatively isolated areas, such as the

A number of federal agencies are involved in the management of the wetlands that support Ring-necked Ducks and other waterfowl and shorebird species. Some of the players are the Fish and Wildlife Service, Army Corps of Engineers, Federal Energy Regulatory Commission, Bureau of Reclamation, and the Soil Conservation Service.

southwestern deserts. The DOD is refocusing some of its efforts toward more ecologically sound land management through the Legacy Program, which funds research and inventory work on military installations to improve management of natural resources. In addition, the U.S. Army Corps of Engineers plays a major role in building infrastructure for water reclamation and flood control projects, as well as harbors, and is mainly responsible for Section 404 of the Clean Water Act, which regulates filling and dumping in wetlands.

CANADIAN AGENCIES

At the time this book was written, the Canadian government was proceeding through a series of changes. Bureaus were being renamed and reorganized; their jurisdictions were being redelineated. Rather than exclude Canada from this section on the basis of a lack of definitive information on political organization, we decided to include a brief outline of the current major departments and their roles in wildlife conservation. This section, therefore, should be considered merely a guideline. We suggest that you contact World Wildlife Fund Canada (90 Eglinton Avenue East, Toronto, ONT M45 2Z7) in order to find out what role you can play in affecting conservation policy under the changing government. Stay abreast of government reorganization through the media and through the mailings of conservation organizations.

The Canadian Wildlife Service
The Canadian Wildlife Service (CWS) handles those wildlife matters that are the responsibility of the Canadian government. Such matters include legal responsibility for approximately 220 species of land birds under the Migratory Bird Convention Act. Other responsibilities include endangered species management, control of international trade in endangered species, research on wildlife issues of national importance, and educating the general public on the natural history and conservation of wildlife. The CWS cooperates with provinces, territories, and other federal agencies in wildlife research and management.

Forestry Canada
Forestry Canada makes policy decisions on forest harvesting techniques. In association with the Canadian forest industry, Forestry Canada influences habitat quality over vast areas of Canada: 209 million hectares of commercial forests, 50.7 million hectares of protected forests, and 193.3 million hectares of unharvested forests (453 million hectares total).

Agriculture Canada
Agriculture Canada makes policy decisions on agricultural practices. Such decisions affect migratory birds in terms of available habitat and risk of pesticide poisoning.

Parks Canada
Parks Canada is a significant landowner with a mandate to conserve wildlife and to educate the public on conservation issues. Several of Canada's parks welcome millions of bird-watchers annually.

The Department of National Defense
The Department of National Defense is a large landowner with an interest in maintaining some natural values on its land. For this reason, the Department of

National Defense can have a major influence in the conservation of Neotropical migrants.

STATE AND PROVINCIAL OR TERRITORIAL WILDLIFE AND NATURAL RESOURCE AGENCIES

State, provincial or territorial, and other local agencies play a critical role in the conservation of migratory birds. There are far too many excellent programs in different resource agencies to do justice in this general book. In addition to their traditional jurisdiction over enforcement of game laws and management of land for wildlife, state agencies increasingly play the vanguard in the conservation of all migratory birds. A major trend in the past few years has been the establishment of vigorous programs oriented toward migratory landbirds. Most of the programs involve the establishment of monitoring programs.

One exemplary program has been developed by the Minnesota Department of Natural Resources. In a program entitled "Minnesota's Forest Bird Diversity Initiative," this state agency is overseeing the compilation of information on habitat requirements of its forest migrants, and will integrate the information in the forest management planning process for the state. The Illinois Department of Conservation has supported research on habitat needs of forest migrants, helped identify sites for the Wetlands for the Americas program (the umbrella organization of the Western Hemisphere Shorebird Reserve Network), and developed guidelines for habitat management and enhancement for both forest and grassland birds.

REGULATION AND MANAGEMENT IN THE UNITED STATES

We have already described the range of human activities that can affect migratory birds. It is not surprising, then, that most federal agencies have programs that directly or indirectly affect migratory birds. Migratory birds have played such an integral part in the story of wildlife management that it makes sense to begin with the legislation surrounding the control of hunting and the advent of the agency concerned with management of wildlife.

Conservation of migratory birds has since feudal times focused on the management of game populations for hunting, primarily for the wealthy who controlled the lands. Today the Fish and Wildlife Service still suffers from mandates provided in earlier times. The USFWS and other federal agencies are struggling to broaden their vision of conservation of biological diversity to encompass all populations. Over the past century, the government's approach to the protection of wildlife has evolved in several broad steps.

In 1900 the U.S. federal government took its first tentative step to control wildlife. Concern over the loss of the passenger pigeon and the decimation of other avian species by plume hunters resulted in the Lacey Act. The act was written to take advantage of the power granted to Congress by the Constitution to regulate commerce between states.

The cornerstone for migratory bird protection was set in 1918, when legislation was enacted to implement the landmark Migratory Bird Treaty, signed in 1916 between the United States and Great Britain (on behalf of Canada). Similar treaties followed with Mexico, Japan, and the Soviet Union. The Mexico treaty granted protection to bird species not covered under the Canada treaty, more or less completing the basic legal protection of North American migratory birds.

The Migratory Bird Treaty celebrated its seventy-fifth birthday in 1993 and is still a landmark in conservation legislation. This treaty took a visionary international approach to a common conservation problem and resulted in the recovery of many overhunted populations. However, it fell short of protecting declining waterfowl populations. Ducks, geese, and swans were hit hard by human-caused habitat loss and the drought of the Dust Bowl years. So during the 1930s and 1940s, the attention of bird conservation shifted from hunting regulation to habitat protection.

Endangered species protection and management was the initial focus of most efforts to conserve wildlife that was not hunted for sport. The 1960s and 1970s brought new attention to rescuing imminently threatened populations, most of which were nongame species. The status of these fragile populations was highlighted by the Endangered Species Act (ESA) of 1973. Under the ESA, all federal agencies are required to undertake conservation programs to benefit listed species, and are prohibited from authorizing, funding, or carrying out any action that might jeopardize a listed species or modify its critical habitat (if the listing specifies this habitat). The ESA also made possible cooperative agreements between states, providing matching federal funds for such ventures. In addition, ESA expanded the USFWS's authority to acquire land for species cited under the CITES agreement. The following Neotropical migratory birds are currently listed as threatened or endangered:

Bachman's Warbler, endangered (possibly extinct)
Golden-cheeked Warbler, endangered
Kirtland's Warbler, endangered
Least Tern, endangered
Eskimo Curlew, endangered
Roseate Tern, threatened or endangered

The USFWS identifies candidates for listing as either category 1 or category 2. Category 1 candidates are those for which the USFWS has substantial biological data and relevant information to support listing, and includes the Willow Flycatcher (southwestern). Category 2 candidates are those whose listing may be appropriate but for which the USFWS needs more information. This includes the Black Tern and Common Tern (Great Lakes population). Category 3 includes species removed from the active lists because of extinction, failure to be shown a distinct species or subspecies, or demonstration that they are too abundant for listing. It includes the Long-billed Curlew.

Provisions in a 1978 amendment of the ESA allowed federal agencies to undertake actions that would jeopardize a listed species if the action were exempted by a cabinet-level committee convened specifically for this purpose. To the benefit of species, the amendment also made it possible to designate critical habitat at the time of a species' listing and extended the authority to acquire land within the natural distribution of a listed species.

The act's broad definition of "species" (as "subspecies" or "populations") was restricted to vertebrate populations or subspecies that could be legally defined as species.

Provisions in the 1982 amendments required that decisions on listing be limited to information on biological and trade status, rather than economic or other analysis. The USFWS was directed to make a determination whether to list or not to list a species in response to external petition within a year of receiving the petition. In addition, 1982 amendments made it possible to designate populations of a listed species that might be subject to lessened restrictions on take and implemented provisions of the Western Hemisphere Convention. Further provisions in 1988 amendments required the monitoring of species that were candidates for listing or that had been delisted, allowed emergency listing when evidence warranted it, and required that reports of state and federal expenditures, status lists, and recovery plans be submitted to Congress.

Although the goal of any program involving endangered species is to have the species recover to the point of downlisting or delisting, there are very few examples of such success. Recoveries have generally occurred in only part of a species' range. Unfortunately, more failures (18 listed species have become extinct) than successes have been attributed to endangered species conservation. When the Endangered Species Act was put in place in 1973, fewer than 200 organisms were listed. As of 1990, 554 species had been listed, with an additional 3,650 candidates in line. Some candidates have been "queued up" for a decade; 34 have been declared extinct. Many other species, including the migratory Bachman's Warbler, are likely to be lost in the near future (if not gone already).

The ESA dictates a listing process that targets organisms most likely to become extinct. However, wildlife managers and conservation organizations are more likely to put their limited resources into those species that are most likely to recover for biological reasons or that attract the most funding. It is no wonder that species fall through the cracks.

The most recent steps in the evolution of wildlife policies have been increasing attention toward bird species while they are still common, designing management plans that consider all species, and approaching conservation on the level of the ecosystem. Protecting biodiversity one species at a time is far less efficient and effective than maintaining and restoring entire ecosystems and developing a proactive program that works to conserve organisms while they are still abundant. The earth's ecosystems, from wetlands to forests to deserts, have been afflicted with mass destruction, fragmentation, and degradation in recent time. Many problems, such as habitat alteration, acid rain, and climate change, fundamentally alter the ecological relationships of all organisms. Populations of migratory birds are an indicator of this overall environmental decay.

The evolution of a comprehensive program to conserve all migratory birds has come slowly. Initial efforts have often been mere side effects of habitat management for game birds and animals. The argument that "what is good for game animals is also good for the rest" falls apart when management practices for game animals actually harm many other sensitive populations. For example, shorebirds during migration often benefit when water levels are reduced to expose mudflats and shorelines, but this does not necessarily benefit ducks. Another example is the practice of creating edge habitats to increase deer populations in unfragmented forests. Not only do many forest-breeding migrants have problems reproducing under edge conditions, but large deer populations also tend to browse out the understory plants in which many migrants feed and nest.

Even the monitoring of potential problems for nongame species has had a rocky start. The initial legislation in 1980 that directed the USFWS to monitor all migratory bird populations received no funding for implementation. Until recently, all increases in support have come from annual "add-ons" to the agency's requested budgets. The Breeding Bird Survey (which monitors hundreds of bird species) received approximately the same level of logistical support from the USFWS as a similar survey program aimed at counting only Mourning Doves.

However, there is increasing pressure from the public and the "rank and file" of the agencies to make a good-faith effort to develop conservation programs for all migratory birds. An increase in funding for these programs has been provided to the USFWS, the USFS, and other agencies under the umbrella of "Partners in Flight" (see chapter 6). In addition, the formation of a new National Biological Service bureau reflects, in part, recognition from the highest levels that more needs to be done to protect nongame birds and biodiversity in general.

REGULATIONS AND MANAGEMENT IN CANADA

Traditionally, Canada's wildlife habitat has been protected by designating Crown land for conservation or through the acquisition of private land. The conservation community, however, has recognized that specially designated areas alone cannot save ecosystems and maintain biodiversity—regulations are needed. Migratory birds have been protected in Canada since the 1917 signing of the Migratory Bird Convention Act, and Canadian wildlife in general has had legal protection since the 1973 signing of the Canada Wildlife Act. Provincial and territorial legislators are legally responsible for the management and regulation of wildlife (with the exception of migrant species that cross borders, species on federal lands, or species regulated by international agreements) within their borders. As of 1984 only Ontario, Manitoba, Alberta, British Columbia, the Yukon, and the Northwest Territories had specific regulatory provisions or legislation to protect threatened wildlife. By 1991 conservation provisions had been established in additional provinces, but vulnerable wildlife was still not legally protected everywhere. To encourage the establishment and strengthening of wildlife protection measures, World Wildlife Fund Canada launched the Endangered Spaces Campaign in 1989. Endangered Spaces is a ten-year drive to ensure the protection of the country's biological diversity through a network of protected areas (see chapter 5).

An organization called the Canadian Wildlife Advisory Council coordinates national wildlife conservation efforts. The council is composed of federal, provincial, and territorial governments, as well as several nongovernmental organizations. A committee of the council, the Committee on the Status of Endangered Wildlife in Canada (COSEWIC), is responsible for producing the official Canadian Endangered Species List. In addition to three representatives from nongovernmental conservation organizations, COSEWIC includes federal, provincial, and territorial representation. It commissions scientific status reports on threatened indigenous wildlife, solicits expert opinion on these species, and determines the degree of imperilment for each organism. It does not have the authority to recommend conservation actions. However, after a species has been listed by COSEWIC, appropriate action can be taken by government agencies or nongovernmental organizations. The following Neotropical migrants are listed:

Eskimo Curlew, endangered
Kirtland's Warbler, endangered
Roseate Tern, threatened
Caspian Tern, vulnerable
Long-billed Curlew, vulnerable
Prairie Warbler, vulnerable
Prothonotary Warbler, vulnerable
Louisiana Waterthrush, vulnerable
Cerulean Warbler, vulnerable

It should be noted that at least six of these species are vulnerable only in Canada, which constitutes a small part of their breeding range.

Growing concern over the loss of biodiversity has prompted the Canadian federal, provincial, and territorial governments to organize recovery efforts on a national scale. In 1988 the Council of Canadian Wildlife Ministries established a national strategy for endangered species and an organization to apply it: Recovery of Nationally Endangered Wildlife (RENEW). RENEW is composed of provincial and territorial wildlife directors, the director general of the Canadian Wildlife Service, and representatives from the Canadian Wildlife Federation, the Canadian Nature Federation, and World Wildlife Fund Canada. Work is divided among three subcommittees: Priorities, Recovery Teams and Plans, and Information. Under RENEW, experts develop and implement recovery plans for many endangered species. The efforts of all who wish to help save endangered species—governments, nongovernmental organizations, corporations, and concerned citizens—are effectively coordinated.

Recovery is a free newsletter providing information on Canadian species at risk. To add your name to the mailing list, write to *Recovery,* Canadian Wildlife Service, Environment Canada, Ottawa, ONT K1A 0H3.

MAJOR CONSERVATION POLICIES AT THE FEDERAL LEVEL

The true effectiveness of wildlife policies as protection measures depends not only on strict regulation and compliance, but also on a constant, adequate supply and allocation of funds. Some of the most progressive conservation legislation has been enacted without any appropriations to carry it out. The Fish and Wildlife Conservation Act of 1980, for example, never received base appropriations, and many activities called for are funded by relatively small annual add-ons.

Funds are allocated unevenly to programs so that the management of the fifty-odd species of game birds still receives far more support than the over seven hundred species of nongame birds. Endangered species recovery rightfully receives considerable funding. However, for years financial support for work on individual species has far surpassed the total fund allocation for nonendangered migratory birds (excluding game birds). Even within these programs the funds that are allocated are distributed unevenly, benefiting a select group (often the "warm, fuzzy complex") of species. The Endangered Species Act illustrates the problems species recovery programs face as a result of the way funds are distributed. In 1989 reasonably identifiable expenditures for listed species totaled nearly $44 million. Funds for conservation plans were appropriated to two thirds (345/554) of the listed species. Astoundingly, half the total expenditure was spent on only 12 species (one being the Kirtland's Warbler), and nine tenths was spent on just 60 species!

Just as legislation without sufficient appropriations will produce few tangible results, so appropriations without a specific mandate may produce a relatively weak effort. Recent appropriations for migratory bird conservation under the federal Neotropical Migratory Bird Conservation Initiative are governed by an agreement of participating agencies to cooperate to conserve Neotropical migratory birds. But there is no specific requirement to review agency policies that might affect migratory birds. Except through the watchdog activities of nongovernmental organizations and private citizens, there is currently no way to ensure that the information developed in new research and monitoring programs is applied.

Conventions and Treaties

The following is a brief, annotated list of major conventions, treaties, and statutes that directly relate to the conservation of migratory birds and their habitats in the Western Hemisphere. For detailed information on wildlife policies in the United States see *The Evolution of National Wildlife Law* (Bean, 1983).

• Convention for the Protection of Migratory Birds, 1916; U.S.–Great Britain (on behalf of Canada)

Establishes three groups of migratory birds and provides a species list for each group: migratory game birds, migratory insectivorous birds, other migratory nongame birds; provides year-round protection for migratory nongame birds; establishes hunting season limits for game birds; prohibits taking of nests or eggs of migratory birds, except for scientific or propagating purposes; and authorizes the issuance of permits to kill migratory birds that under exceptional conditions may become agricultural or community pests.

• Convention for the Protection of Migratory Birds and Game Mammals, 1936; U.S.–Mexico

Provides protection similar to the above. Calls for the establishment of refuge zones where no hunting can take place; limits the length of the hunting season to four months for migrants, with permits issued by respective authorities; and allows for nongame migratory birds to be taken with permit only when they become injurious to agriculture and constitute plagues.

• Convention on Nature Protection and Wildlife Preservation in the Western Hemisphere, 1941; Western Hemisphere Convention

Calls for the enactment of domestic wildlife conservation laws, controls on wildlife trade, cooperation in scientific research, and establishment of protected areas by signatory nations. This treaty has been signed by twenty-two countries—but has few mechanisms for sustained funding. Efforts are under way to revitalize this underused convention.

• Convention for the Protection of Migratory Birds and Birds in Danger of Extinction, 1972; U.S.–Japan

Similar to British and Mexican Conventions. Directs parties to take measures to create sanctuaries to preserve, manage, and enhance environments of protected species, including abatement of pollution and cessation of the introduction of exotics to islands; defines no specific dates for hunting, but prohibits it during the nesting seasons to maintain optimum population sizes; and contains very expansive authorization for killing migrants to protect persons and property.

• Convention Concerning the Protection of the World Cultural and Natural Heritage, 1972; World Heritage Convention (administered by United Nations Educational, Scientific, and Cultural Organization, UNESCO)

Intended to preserve both natural areas and cultural monuments of universal value. Assigns the responsibility for designating and protecting natural areas and cultural areas to nations in which they occurred; establishes World Heritage Committee with the power to grant financial assistance to countries designating such areas. Act lacks specific protective measures but provides a means for funding wildlife protection projects in less-developed countries.

• Convention on International Trade in Endangered Species of Wild Fauna and Flora, 1973; CITES or Washington Convention (administered by central secretariat and national authorities of the member states)

Designed to regulate the trade of more than thirty thousand animal and plant species by implementing a system of import and export permits and limitations. Canada became party to CITES when External Affairs signed the treaty in 1975. An existing Export and Import Permits Act was used as the implementing legislation.

• Convention Concerning the Conservation of Migratory Birds and Their Environment, 1976; U.S.–U.S.S.R.

Similar to Japan Convention. Directs parties to identify and protect important breeding, wintering, feeding, and molting areas; prohibits taking of migratory birds, nests, eggs, and the disturbance of nesting colonies; authorizes parties to establish hunting seasons as long as they ensure the preservation and maintenance of stocks of migratory birds; directs parties to establish preserves, protected areas, and facilities for the conservation of migratory birds and to manage areas to preserve and restore natural ecosystems; contains very expansive authorization for killing migratory birds to protect persons or property.

• Convention on Wetlands of International Importance Especially as Waterfowl Habitat, 1986 (U.S. ratification); Ramsar Convention (administered by the International Union for Conservation of Nature and Natural Resources, IUCN)

Encourages the designation and protection of wetlands of unusual importance for waterfowl and other waterbirds; promotes wetland research, training, and coordination of wetlands policies among signatory nations.

Statutory Authorities

- Lacey Act, 1900 (United States)

Makes interstate transport of birds killed in violation of state laws illegal; proclaims that dead animals imported into a state will be treated by law as if they were killed there; prohibits the importation of certain animals (such as European Starlings and House Sparrows); authorizes the Secretary of Agriculture to adopt all measures (subject to the laws of states and territories) necessary for the preservation, distribution, introduction, and restoration of game and other wild birds.

- National Park Service Act, 1916 (United States)

Directs the establishment of national parks for the purpose of conserving wildlife, natural and historic objects, and scenery, and preserving them for future generations.

- Migratory Bird Convention Act, 1917 (Canada)

Enacted to implement the 1916 Migratory Bird Treaty Act (see above). Defines periods and locations of hunting, killing, capturing, and possessing migratory birds and their nests or eggs; grants permits for these activities; determines the number of birds that may be taken and the disposition of the birds; prohibits hunting of migratory insectivorous birds and other migratory nongame birds (except for some by native peoples); declares it unlawful to sell, trade, barter, or buy migratory birds or their eggs, nests, carcasses, or skins without special written permission of the Minister of the Environment; allows lawfully taken feathers to be sold for the manufacture of fishing flies, bedding, or clothing except for ornamental use; prohibits trafficking between Canada and the United States.

- Migratory Bird Treaty Act (as amended), 1918 (United States and Canada)

Implements the provision of international treaties with Great Britain, Mexico, Japan, and the U.S.S.R.; designates migrants as game birds, insectivorous birds, and other nongame birds; provides a season in which birds of each group may not be taken except for scientific or propagating purposes under permits (with minor exceptions for hunting by Native Americans, the closed season on the last two categories is year-round; for migratory game birds, hunting seasons are not to exceed three and a half months); prohibits the taking of nests and eggs of all migratory birds, except for scientific purposes (ends the hobby of oology, or egg collecting); declares penalties for breaking the law to be six months in prison or $500 in fines, or both.

- National Parks Act, 1919 (Canada)

One of Canada's oldest pieces of conservation legislation. Provides for the regulation and acquisition of lands, the use of resources and facilities in parks, fire prevention, and public safety; protects plants, wildlife, soil, water, fossils, natural features, air quality, and cultural, historical, and archaeological resources; allows for the removal or destruction of wildlife only for authorized research, propagation, or management of dangerous or overpopulated species.

• Migratory Bird Convention Act, 1929 (United States)

Establishes a Migratory Bird Convention Commission to review and approve proposals by the Secretary of the Interior to acquire areas as wildlife refuges; expands existing National Wildlife Refuge System; provides authorization for the acquisition of wetlands for waterfowl habitat.

• Migratory Bird Hunting Stamp Act, 1934 (United States)

Ensures a steady source of funding for the National Wildlife Refuge System. Requires every waterfowl hunter over age sixteen to annually purchase and carry a Federal Duck Stamp. Proceeds are earmarked for buying and leasing waterfowl habitat that becomes part of the National Wildlife Refuge System.

• Fish and Wildlife Coordination Act, 1937 (United States)

Authorizes the Secretary of the Interior to assist federal, state, and other agencies in the development and protection of wildlife on federal lands and to study the effects of pollution; requires consultation with USFWS and relevant state agencies on any water modification project by a federal or federally permitted agency for the purpose of determining impacts on wildlife.

• Federal Aid in Wildlife Restoration Act (Pittman-Robertson Act), 1937 (United States)

Provides for federal aid to states for the acquisition, restoration, and maintenance of wildlife habitat, including research, and an excise tax on sporting arms and ammunition to be used for this purpose. Funding is on a matching basis (75 percent federal, 25 percent state). Funds unused by states revert to the USFWS and are used to fund migratory bird research and other programs.

• Sustained-Yield Act, 1960 (United States)

Establishes fish and wildlife management as one of several purposes of national forests, including outdoor recreation, range, timber, and watershed. Fails to indicate how the Forest Service is to reconcile the potentially competing purposes spelled out in the statute.

• Endangered Species Preservation Act, 1966 (United States)

Allows the listing of native animal species as "endangered" and provides some means to protect those listed; assigns responsibility for the protection of listed species and, where appropriate, their habitat to the Departments of Interior, Agriculture, and Defense; authorizes these departments to acquire land as a protection measure.

- Endangered Species Conservation Act, 1969 (United States)

Provides additional protection to species in worldwide danger of extinction; prohibits their importation or sale within the United States.

- National Environmental Policy Act (NEPA), 1969 (United States)

Declares it the responsibility of the U.S. government to restore and maintain environmental quality; requires all federal agencies or organizations receiving public funds to make detailed, *a priori* analyses (environmental impact statements, EISs) of the potential impacts of all major actions significantly affecting the quality of the environment; provides that concerned citizens' groups may sue to halt projects for which these is no adequate EIS.

- Endangered Species Act, 1973 (United States)

First law in the United States to recognize the vital importance of preserving the habitat of an endangered species. Provides for conservation of threatened and endangered species by federal action (regulations to be issued by the Fish and Wildlife Service and National Marine Fisheries Service) and encourages state programs; provides that species or subspecies endangered throughout all or a significant portion of its range be listed with the Secretary of the Interior or Commerce (marine species); requires *a priori* assessment of the impact of any federal actions on the welfare of endangered species; prohibits killing, capturing, importing, exporting, or selling any endangered species, including plants; provides for citizens groups to sue in cases of violation of the act. The 1982 amendment implements the provisions of the Western Hemisphere Convention.

- Canada Wildlife Act, 1973 (Canada)

Empowers the Minister of the Environment to promote wildlife and habitat conservation in Canada through research, conferences, policies, and programs and by acting in an advisory capacity; to protect endangered species; and to acquire and administer public lands assigned to wildlife-related programs. The act allows agreements with provinces regarding the use of public lands within their boundaries, and research and conservation activities carried out in their jurisdictions.

- National Forest Management Act, 1976 (United States)

Directs the USFS to maintain the diversity of plant and animal communities and viable populations of all native vertebrates in national forests and to maintain and improve habitats of management indicator species; declares clear-cutting in national forests illegal; provides increased opportunity for public participation in decision-making; allows for certain receipts from timber sales to be spent for, among other purchases, wildlife habitat.

- Federal Land Policy and Management Act, 1976 (United States)

Directs the BLM to manage lands for multiple use, including wildlife; to designate and protect critical areas for fish and wildlife resources; and to allocate portions of grazing fees for fish and wildlife habitat improvement.

• Forest and Rangeland Renewable Resources Research Act, 1978 (United States)

Directs the USFS to conduct research on endangered and threatened species and on improving fish and wildlife habitat.

• Fish and Wildlife Conservation Act (Non-game Act, Forsythe-Chaffe Act), 1980 (United States)

Strives to encourage conservation programs that benefit both nongame and other wildlife; provides for federal aid to states on a 75 percent federal–25 percent state basis for the conservation of nongame vertebrates and implementation of projects. The 1988 amendment (Mitchell Amendment) directs the U.S. Department of the Interior to monitor populations of migratory nongame birds, identify the effects of environmental change and human activity on species likely to become endangered, and take actions needed to prevent endangerment.

• Canadian Environment Protection Act, 1988 (Canada)

Often considered the most important Canadian action plan. Establishes nationally consistent standards for the control and regulation of toxic substances; expands the scope of federal regulation of environmental impacts on federal lands; establishes an enforcement and compliance regime that authorizes stiff jail terms and fines for polluters.

• North American Wetlands Conservation Act, 1989 (United States)

Provides matching grants to public and private agencies in Canada, Mexico, and the United States to carry out wetland conservation projects that provide habitat (through restoration, enhancement, and acquisition) for a variety of wildlife and plants. Authorizes a $15 million annual appropriation. Additional funds come from fines levied against violators of federal wildlife laws, and the taxes and interest on wildlife- and fisheries-related accounts.

• Coastal Wetlands Planning, Protection, and Restoration Act, 1990 (United States)

Provides for increased federal grants for the acquisition, restoration, management, and enhancement of coastal wetlands of states adjacent to the Atlantic, Gulf of Mexico, Great Lakes, and Pacific. Also included are Puerto Rico, the Virgin Islands, American Samoa, and the Pacific Trust Islands.

• Wild Animal and Plant Protection and Regulation of International and Interprovincial Trade Act, Proposed (Canada)

Prohibits the import and export of wild animals and plants (or their parts and products) according to international agreements, provincial conservation laws, and the conservation laws of other countries; prohibits the import or transport from one province to another of live wild animals and plants; prohibits the transport from one province to another of any wild animals and plants (or parts or products) that have been obtained or removed in contravention of the conservation laws of the province; prohibits the possession of wild animals and plants (or parts and products) that have been imported or transported (or are intended to be) in violation of the act; prohibits the possession of endangered wild animals and plants (or parts and products) if possessed in order to sell or otherwise distribute them.

Making a Difference   Stan Senner

Though the workings of government often seem mysterious and perhaps remote from what happens to bird populations, the connections are real and important to understand. Every day Congress and the administration make decisions that affect birds and their habitats. For example, decisions about land use and protection, funding for agency programs, including for migratory birds, loans for development and agricultural assistance abroad, and grazing fees for livestock on public lands all directly affect birds and their habitats. Even decisions about such things as the closure of military bases or the eradication of drug-related crops have a direct bearing on habitats for migratory birds.

The most effective way to track and influence the many actions affecting birds is through membership in national conservation organizations. Many national organizations monitor bird- and wildlife-related issues, and rely on the informed participation of their members to help them shape the outcomes. Conservation committees of local and regional organizations and chapters of national organizations are an especially good way to share your interest in national issues and to pool resources for effective action.

Although virtually every government decision or action affects birds, the concerned citizen should be aware of several basic laws and processes that bear directly on bird conservation:

The Migratory Bird Treaty Act provides basic protection for nearly all birds that breed in the United States and its trust territories. Nonmigratory game birds such as Northern Bobwhite and ptarmigan are not protected, nor are introduced species, such as House Sparrows and European Starlings. This law was passed by Congress in 1918 to fulfill the United States' obligations under treaties with Canada and later Mexico, Japan, and the former Soviet Union. The law prohibits the "taking" of migratory birds, including shooting or killing the birds themselves (except game birds under lawfully established seasons) and the collecting of their eggs, nests, or feathers. One opportunity for citizens concerned about birds is to work with regional offices of the U.S. Fish and Wildlife Service to ensure that the agency enforces this law, especially with respect to industries whose activities or facilities regularly kill migratory birds (e.g., oil sludge ponds in western states and fish farms in the Southeast).

When the Migratory Bird Treaty Act was passed in 1918, it responded to the major issue of the day, which was the unregulated shooting of waterfowl and wading birds, such as egrets and herons. Today problems in bird conservation are more complicated, and protection of habitat is of overriding importance.

The most recent law focusing on migratory birds is the Fish and Wildlife Conservation Act of 1980, which requires the federal Fish and Wildlife Service to (1) monitor the health of all bird populations, (2) study the effects of environmental change on birds, (3) identify species that are declining, (4) identify conservation measures that would eliminate the need to list species under the Endangered Species Act, and (5) identify habitats that should be protected for the benefit of migratory birds. By focusing on prevention, this law recognizes that the best time to save species is while they are still common. Concerned citizens have the opportunity to work with the Fish and Wildlife Service within their regions to ensure that this law is carried out fully. Accomplished bird-watchers can also assist in fulfilling the law by volunteering to run Breeding Bird Surveys and other monitoring programs.

Because many migratory birds cross international boundaries in their annual flights north and south, it is essential that there be international programs promoting bird conservation. The Convention on Nature Preservation and Wildlife Protection in the Western Hemisphere provides a framework for such programs. This little-known convention, ratified in 1941 during the height of World War II, makes the protection of migratory birds as "shared resources" among the nations of the Western Hemisphere a key goal.

Under the authority of the Western Hemisphere Convention, the United States has cooperated with Costa Rica, Mexico, and other countries to establish university graduate programs to strengthen the training of wildlife biologists and a special course for the training of managers of reserves and other protected areas. These and other education projects are helping build a cadre of trained and committed professionals in wildlife conservation throughout Latin America.

To date, most efforts under the Western Hemisphere Convention have been initiated by the United States. To realize the full potential of the treaty, it is essential that governments of Western Hemisphere nations act jointly to establish a permanent convention office and to meet regularly to discuss how they will work together for the conservation of birds and other wildlife. Concerned citizens can encourage their government to actively implement this important treaty.

Of course, none of these domestic or international programs can succeed without the appropriation of funds by Congress. The appropriations process is one in which all citizens can participate. Each year Congress starts to evaluate budget requests from the president in about February, and in so doing it seeks comments from the public. Citizens can direct letters and telephone calls to representatives and senators expressing concern about adequate funding for migratory bird conservation, such as implementation of the Fish and Wildlife Conservation Act or fulfillment of obligations under the Western Hemisphere Convention. In expressing your concerns, be sure to relate the need back to your locality or state and, if possible, coordinate your efforts with those of others.

Communication with Congress or the administration sometimes may seem like wasted effort, but there is no question that it can and often does help. Government officials will not undertake national and international efforts to conserve birds and their habitats unless they know how important it is to the people they represent.

Stan Senner is Director of Migratory Bird Conservation Program for National Audubon Society.

HOW TO BE A GOOD WATCHDOG

It is the responsibility of concerned citizens to see that elected officials do their jobs. You have the duty, in effect, to be a citizen watchdog. This can be a challenge. However, the more you know, the more effectively you can ensure that an official's responsibilities to the environment are being met. The next section outlines ways the land management policies of federal government can affect Neotropical migrants. Information on how concerned citizens can influence this process can be found in chapter 5.

Being a good watchdog requires an understanding of the legislative process. The following diagrams illustrate the general legislative processes in the United States and Canada. For further information on the U.S. legislative process, see "Making Congress Work for Our Environment" by the National Wildlife Federation (in the federation's "Activist Kit").

The federal governments of the United States and Canada own a considerable amount of land, and so can directly affect migratory bird populations through their resource use and management policies. Most federal land is managed for multiple uses, including economic activities as well as conservation. The policies regulating activities can have a broad impact on bird populations. Much of the federal land is managed for extractive activities, such as grazing, logging, and mining. Each of these activities can have a tremendous impact on populations of migratory birds.

There are a number of ways in which federal agencies can encourage ecologically sound management of government land. Destructive activities can be

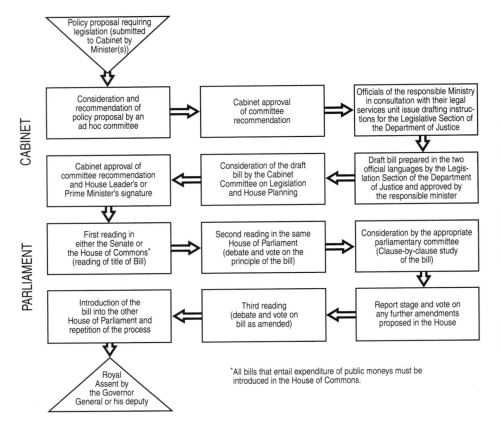

CABINET

Policy proposal requiring legislation (submitted to Cabinet by Minister(s))

| Consideration and recommendation of policy proposal by an ad hoc committee | Cabinet approval of committee recommendation | Officials of the responsible Ministry in consultation with their legal services unit issue drafting instructions for the Legislative Section of the Department of Justice |

| Cabinet approval of committee recommendation and House Leader's or Prime Minister's signature | Consideration of the draft bill by the Cabinet Committee on Legislation and House Planning | Draft bill prepared in the two official languages by the Legislation Section of the Department of Justice and approved by the responsible minister |

PARLIAMENT

| First reading in either the Senate or the House of Commons* (reading of title of Bill) | Second reading in the same House of Parliament (debate and vote on the principle of the bill) | Consideration by the appropriate parliamentary committee (Clause-by-clause study of the bill) |

| Introduction of the bill into the other House of Parliament and repetition of the process | Third reading (debate and vote on bill as amended) | Report stage and vote on any further amendments proposed in the House |

Royal Assent by the Governor General or his deputy

*All bills that entail expenditure of public moneys must be introduced in the House of Commons.

The Canadian Legislative Process

regulated or influenced by altering user fees. In addition, federal agencies can provide advice to other agencies or private landowners.

A major instrument for regulating land management was created by the National Environmental Policy Act (NEPA). NEPA is recognized throughout the world for its rigorous requirements for environmental impact statements (EISs). These statements are required not only for projects on federal lands or those conducted by federal agencies, but whenever a major federal or state action funded by federal money would significantly affect the quality of the human environment. Citizens' groups have the right to sue the government when a project fails to provide an adequate EIS. NEPA has given rise to many state-level "NEPAs" and has served as a model for other countries.

Until recently, Canadian environmental impact assessment (EIA) requirements have been far less rigorous than those of the United States. In 1973 the fed-

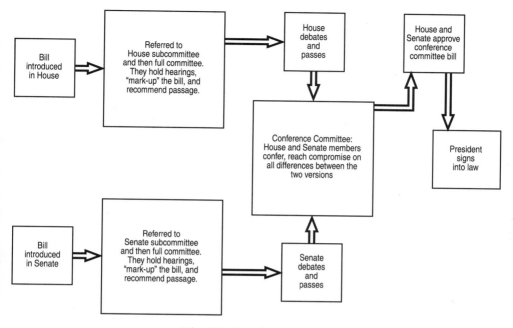

The U.S. Legislative Process

eral Cabinet of Canada established the Environmental Assessment and Review Process (EARP), a process plagued with shortcomings. The EARP process is, however, undergoing profound change. Environmental groups are now using the lack of EIAs as evidence of environmental neglect and winning court cases against the government. If these environmental groups have their way, Canada's EIA policies may become as strong as NEPA.

NEPA has led most U.S. agencies to analyze in writing the potential environmental impact of resource planning actions. More than four hundred formal EISs are performed by U.S. federal agencies each year. Both the Forest Service and the Fish and Wildlife Service undergo periodic reviews of their resource management plans. The management protocols used by these agencies on the lands they oversee have a tremendous impact on breeding populations of Neotropical migratory birds.

MIGRATORY BIRDS AND FEDERAL LAND MANAGEMENT

Since the turn of the century, the conservation community has actively debated the degree to which areas need strict protection or carefully managed sustainable use. The amount of land that is actually excluded from commercial use is very small, so conservation of migratory birds and biological diversity operates predominantly in the realm of used and managed lands. Furthermore, it is increasingly clear that pristine ecosystems cannot simply be protected from human encroachment and left alone. Many ecosystems have evolved under natural disturbance regimes that included human activities, such as regular flooding, fire, and grazing. These and similar disturbances often need to be carefully reintroduced to maintain the natural fauna and flora. The following is a brief review of

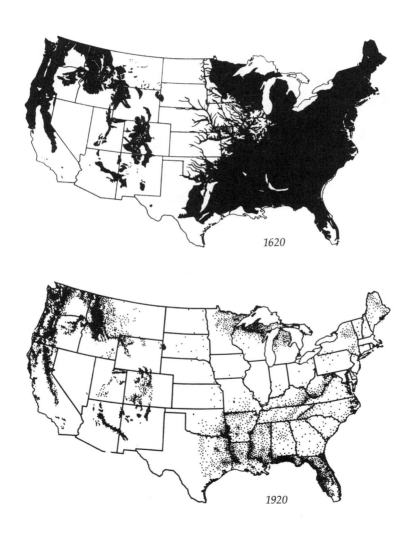

1620

1920

the activities for which public lands in the United States are managed and the ways they can affect migratory birds.

Grazing

The federal government sells grazing rights for much of the public lands, particularly in the West. Although many North American ecosystems are adapted for some level of grazing, much pasture management has been poor, and overgrazing

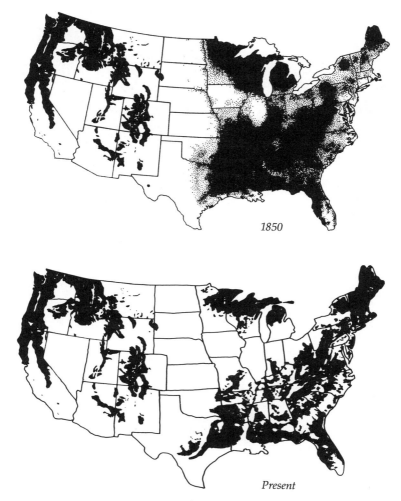

1850

Present

Forests of North America from 1620 to present. After half a century of recovery, forests are again on the decline.

is common. Furthermore, habitats rich in migratory birds are particularly sensitive to grazing. Cattle have a detrimental impact on many species that nest in the riparian corridors along western waterways. These habitats have been hard hit by many changes in land use because they are located on rich floodplains. Cattle disturb the thick understory where many birds nest and alter the long-term composition of plant communities. The impact of cattle on these systems goes far beyond their effect on bird populations. Stream bank erosion and damage to water quality are common results of grazing. Other sensitive habitats include mountain meadows, but all habitats are altered under heavy grazing pressure. A long-term result of persistent grazing is the change in the composition of the plant community and, thus, the birds that can be supported. Millions of hectares of grassy savanna rangeland in the Southwest have been replaced by mesquite- and cactus-dominated thorn scrub. In many areas, particularly the grasslands and savannas of California, grazing has favored the establishment of naturalized Mediterranean grasses and herbs where once native perennial bunchgrasses dominated. In most cases, we have only the most superficial notion of how these massive habitat changes affect the abundance and diversity of migratory birds.

Overgrazing needs to be dealt with, but the issue is often more complex than simply restricting grazing on public lands. Agencies can restrict grazing on sensitive land or can simply raise grazing fees to make them more comparable to free market prices. However, simply raising grazing fees without plans to improve management may have little impact on grazing practices. Furthermore, ranching is a slowly disappearing way of life on western lands. In some areas this may be unfortunate, as ranch lands are replaced by recreational development and building of homes. This often brings large numbers of recreational users to public lands, and human visitors can have as detrimental an impact on land as their cattle predecessors.

Logging
Extracting timber from large tracts of federally owned forest has a large potential impact on bird populations. The impact depends heavily on the management system. Large-scale clear-cutting has the greatest negative impact by creating large areas of homogeneous second growth followed by even-age stands of forests. Even low-level logging can have an impact on some bird species. In addition, logging roads and clearings are a conduit for bringing cowbirds into areas they otherwise might avoid.

An indirect effect of timber exploitation has been the fire exclusion policies that have dominated land management until recently. Many forest habitats are adapted to regular small ground fires. Fire suppression to protect timber and property increases the probability that fewer, larger fires will occur. Further-

The extent of federally managed lands in the United States. Most forests in the eastern United States are privately held; in the western United States much of the forest is federally controlled.

more, numerous small fires create a mosaic of habitats that many bird species depend on.

Water Projects

Water is a highly sought after public resource. Unfortunately, the needs of migratory birds and human development often come into conflict. For example, reservoir creation and channelization along the large rivers of the Midwest have

In addition to facing pollution and commercial exploitation of resources, migratory birds are threatened by poor control of lands used for recreational purposes. Least Terns often nest on beaches used heavily by beachcombers and off-road vehicles.

greatly altered critical wetlands necessary for waterfowl, cranes, least terns, and plovers. These projects often result in an increase in riparian woodlands, where previously a shallow, meandering river maintained a broad zone of sandbars and marshes. While such changes can create habitat for some landbirds, they do so at the expense of shorebirds and waterfowl. The damming of the Colorado River, along with the increase in agricultural development, has greatly altered the riparian woods-wetland systems that bordered the rivers of the arid West.

Recreational Use

The influx of visitors can increase the general appreciation of migratory birds and their natural surroundings. However, visitors can also be highly destructive of critical habitats and disturb sensitive species during the nesting period. This is especially true of beaches, where off-road recreational vehicles can damage the habitat of and disturb shorebirds. Visitors to federal lands are notorious for feeding wildlife, despite the fact that the practice is generally prohibited. It can result in an increase in the population of wildlife that preys on migratory birds, such as raccoons, jays, and crows.

INTERNATIONAL CONSERVATION
AND THE FEDERAL GOVERNMENT

The activities of both the U.S. and Canadian governments affect the people, land, and migratory birds of other countries in the Western Hemisphere. Therefore, it does not make sense for environmentalists to take an isolationist stand. Neither migratory birds nor the federal policies that affect them stop at any border. The policies that are most often intended to conserve migratory bird populations are those implemented under treaties and conventions. However, a wide range of foreign assistance programs affect migratory birds both negatively and positively.

The USFWS Western Hemisphere Program

The United States is a signatory of the Western Hemisphere Convention of 1941, which calls for the protection of wildlife throughout the hemisphere. With increasing awareness of the international scope of conservation problems, Congress funded the Western Hemisphere Program of the U.S. Fish and Wildlife Service. Although the Western Hemisphere Program does not focus exclusively on migratory birds, it supports many international activities of the U.S. Fish and Wildlife Service that are important to migratory bird conservation, particularly the training of wildlife professionals. Core projects include the establishment of long-term training programs with regionally based, master's degree programs in Costa Rica, Brazil, and Venezuela; sponsorship of the local production of environmental education materials (including several bird guides); training workshops; and assistance to local institutions that wish to conduct research and help conserve migratory birds and their habitats.

The USFS Tropical Forestry Program

In 1990 the USFS established the Tropical Forestry Program to promote sustainable use of timber resources overseas, reduce tropical deforestation, assist in the management of biodiversity, and ameliorate possible climate changes caused by forest loss. The program funds projects carried out in cooperation with partner organizations in each of these areas. In addition, the USFS has increased its research program and funding available to others for research on migratory birds in Latin America and the Caribbean. Often this research is the result of partnerships between agencies and nongovernmental organizations in Latin American and regional offices of the USFS. The USFS is developing a "sister forest" program that matches specific forests in the United States with reserves or parks in the tropics.

The USFS work in tropical forestry predates this program through the work of several of its research and consultation units. The Institute for Tropical Forestry in Puerto Rico has a research mandate to study tropical forest dynamics and develop sustainable management practices. In addition, the Forestry Support Program (FSP) provides technical assistance on forestry and natural resource management issues for the Agency for International Development and the Peace Corps.

The Agency for International Development

The U.S. Agency for International Development (USAID) plays a dual role in the conservation of migratory bird habitat. Historically, its projects have often supported the very infrastructure that brings development and colonists into previously pristine areas. USAID continues to support agricultural development that may have a negative impact on migratory birds, such as the modernization of coffee production (converting coffee from a forest interior crop to an agricultural field crop) and the widespread use of pesticides. However, USAID is also the main conduit for federal money to promote the conservation of biodiversity in Latin America. Money is earmarked for park management, migratory bird research, sustainable development research, and restoration of fragile lands. USAID is a decentralized agency, with much of its fieldwork directed from the missions. As in most foreign aid, certain countries receive most of the support. These countries are usually very poor and of strategic importance politically. Certain critical countries for migratory birds, such as Mexico, have had limited involvement with USAID in recent years; however, Mexico now receives funds to support activities that reduce the impact of deforestation on global climate conditions.

The World Bank

The World Bank was founded to provide financing to developing countries primarily to improve their economic infrastructure. Other multinational lending institutions, including the International Monetary Fund and the Inter-American Development Bank, also affect national development in Latin America and hence the conservation of resources and habitat. The United States provides the greatest amount of funding and is the largest shareholder, and therefore has a great deal to say about the policies of the bank. World Bank loans are large and can have a tremendous impact on the economic relationships, social structures, and environment of a region. Following some well-publicized projects that resulted in environmental disasters, increasing pressure has been put on the bank to develop serious environmental policies. Initially, environmental efforts within the bank were extremely small compared with the magnitude of their operations. However, the bank has become increasingly sensitive to public opinion, and several international nongovernmental organizations have formed to monitor the bank's activities. The bank currently has nine environmental policies that govern projects (including wildlands, indigenous peoples, and pesticides). In addition, it has initiated an environmental assessment process for its projects. The World Bank's projects are large and can change the fabric of rural society, creating ripple effects on social relationships and land use. The follow-up assessment of projects is usually short-lived and weak compared with the magnitude of the initial project.

The World Bank is considerably more environmentally sensitive than other multi- or bilateral funding institutions. Driving the World Bank out of projects can have the unintended effect of opening the same project to funding by other institutions, such as Japanese banks and corporations, that are much less open to input from the environmental community.

The Circle of Poisons

When migratory birds winter in or near agricultural habitats in the tropics, they may be exposed to high levels of pesticides and other agrochemicals. Regulation of pesticide use is often less stringent in developing countries. Furthermore, approximately 30 percent of the U.S. pesticides exported are currently illegal for use in the United States (based largely on human health considerations). This figure does not include the many substances that have never been registered in the United States. To date, little research has been conducted on the exposure of migratory birds, particularly songbirds, to this poorly monitored chemical threat. Because of health implications for consumers of imported produce in this country, the issue of how these illegal substances are monitored, either through testing of imported produce or regulations of exports, is a subject of continued debate and revision of policy. Citizens interested in migratory bird populations should follow this issue closely for its broader implications for the health of tropical ecosystems.

Making a Difference   Peter English

Thanks to a Watson Fellowship, I spent two years working with national and local conservation organizations in four Central and South American countries after graduation from college. Eventually I decided that I needed to become involved in conservation efforts in my hometown, Austin, Texas. I found a position with the Texas Center for Policy Studies in Austin that seemed ideal: there had recently been talk of a World Bank forest development project in the northern Mexico states of Chihuahua and Durango, and Mexican environmentalists were concerned about the possible impact of the project. The project involved finding more ways to exploit the dry, mountainous pine-oak forests of this region. The World Bank had decided to fund half of a $90 million project to rehabilitate old logging roads, expand the logging infrastructure (sawmills and pulpmills), and extend credit to those who chose to cut the trees on their property. The bank justified the project by saying that the deforestation already occurring in the area was terribly destructive, and this infusion of cash would improve the situation while increasing the output of the local forestry industry. The region is very complicated biologically and socially, and the World Bank was taking a limited approach to dealing with these complications.

Northern migratory landbirds as well as an endemic species of parrot, an isolated species of trogon, and a race of the goshawk all inhabit this region. This is the only area in the historic southern range of the grizzly bear to still have reports of sightings, and sporadic reports of the near-extinct Imperial Ivorybill Woodpecker still surface in the region every few years. Even the headwaters of the Rio Conchos, the major source of water for the Rio Grande, are within the project area.

In Mexico virtually all rural land is held by cooperatives called *ejidos,* which often have mixed mestizo and indigenous populations and are often dominated by powerful leaders who do not always share the concerns of the majority of the population. In many of the examples that I encountered, the leaders of the community were more affluent mestizos (Mexicans of mixed Spanish and Indian heritage) with little, if any, regard for the traditions and values of the indigenous population sharing the *ejido.* These were the men who had created the original deforestation problems, in concert with a limited number of logging companies, and these were the same men and companies likely to benefit from the huge investment the bank was planning to make in the area.

My job was to find everyone I could who had some professional contact with the area, regardless of their profession, and ask their opinion on the aspect of the bank's project that touched on their expertise. Having had little experience with the World Bank, I was shocked by many things that I discovered. For example, the bank loans money to projects but has no stake in their outcome. When a neighborhood bank lends money to a business that fails, the bank most likely loses its money. By contrast, in the standard operating procedure of the World Bank, the money is lent to a project and regardless of the success or failure of the project, the money is repaid from the general revenues of the country in which the project took place. It was no surprise, then, to find that many of the "facts" cited in the World Bank's Staff Appraisal Report (SAR, a project evaluation) were highly optimistic and contentious opinions. Fundamental issues regarding the sustainability of the forestry project, such as the expected time between cuts on a tended forest plot and the method used to replant the cut areas, were seriously in question.

The best estimates I was able to find from foresters with experience in the region were almost double what the bank was projecting—well over one hundred years between cuts if proper care was taken with the seedlings. The bank's plan proposed that the seedlings would take care of themselves, another issue hotly contested by those who know the Sierra Madre. Still another contested issue was whether the roads being rehabilitated were really old roads or new ones cut into stands of virgin forest, in violation of the SAR requirements. The social issues were equally difficult: the bank's SAR entailed entrusting an agency within the Mexican government with the welfare of the indigenous people in the region, many of whom live in isolated locations and have effectively no political or financial voice. This same agency had recently been boycotted and attacked by indigenous groups for various abuses. Many of its field staff had recently resigned in protest over the agency's mismanagement and policies toward the indigenous population.

Over the course of eight months, I worked full-time on a half-time salary to educate myself on the ways of the World Bank, learning how it picks out individual sentences of a long report or letter and refutes a single piece of evidence in a chapter containing maybe a hundred equally important questions and issues. In the end, with the support of others, we convinced the bank to place this particular project on hold. The deciding factor turned out to be the dubious results of the reports requested by the bank to serve as environmental baseline studies and environmental impact statements. These results were a series of documents that not even the universities that wrote them could defend as accurate or comprehensive. Those who wrote the reports said that both the original set of studies and a recently completed set were all underfunded and, as a result, incomplete. Once copies of these reports were made available to our center and like-minded individuals and groups, there was little hope of the bank's being able to defend the project. Whole sections of the project were months behind schedule, and what was being completed was inadequate. We pooled our findings in a report that we sent to interested parties all over the United States in November 1990, and soon the project was suspended.

The problem, though, is that World Bank projects never seem to die, they only get put on hold. The forestry development project is now being put into action again, this time with a new director and a somewhat more open attitude about input from people concerned about the welfare of the region. Whereas the bank originally did not even recognize the popular tourist destination of Copper Canyon as an important natural resource and potential source of income for the area, it now recognizes its significance and has promised to keep the logging project clear of the canyon. New ideas, such as using a computer-based geographic information system to map the resources of the region, are being incorporated into the plan. Although the basic question of whether this project will help or hurt the region is still unresolved, it is scheduled to begin disbursing funds any time now.

The project has been significantly scaled back as it begins its second life, but there is still debate about the quality of the raw information being used to make the maps of the region. Again, it will be up to the experts and concerned individuals to make sure the project does not harm the region's ecosystem. The original SAR still governs the scale and scope of the project, so it is difficult to gather the precise details of the revised plan.

As huge and imposing an institution as it is, the World Bank is not impervious to rational, well-informed questions raised from outside its system. The bank relies heavily on staff reports for its facts, rather than peer-reviewed literature, so the information it works from is virtually unchecked by outside experts other than those under the contracts and confidentiality agreements of the bank. For this reason, it is important that outsiders become involved in evaluating the bank's projects.

Peter English is a graduate student at the University of Texas. He is currently working on forest bird conservation in Ecuador.

5

Raising Your Voice: Citizen Action

*The race to protect the environment is a marathon and no place for sprinters
who lack staying power.* — *Edward E. Clark, Jr.*

Scientists and birders alike are coming to the realization that most migratory
birds depend on having natural open space protected from development and
pollution. The future of migratory bird populations will depend on how the
balance between economic growth and protection of nature is maintained. The
balance is adjudicated by the government and determined by the political effectiveness of the advocates. Open space and nature cannot speak for themselves;
they need people to advocate their protection. The voice for nature must be
firm and consistent—each conservation victory is only temporary, but a single
victory for inappropriate development can have irreversible effects. In this chapter we outline some of the tools for advancing the cause of habitat conservation
in the political arena.

STAY INFORMED

Suppose you read that numerous birds were found dead after feeding on caterpillars that had been sprayed with a new insecticide. You want to know what
research has been done to determine the environmental impact of this pesticide
and what is being done to control the impact. If you knew the appropriate
agency, you could contact it directly for this information. If you were not certain which U.S. agency (or agencies) was involved, you could contact the Federal Information Center for assistance. (See list of federal agencies and their
jurisdictions in chapter 4.)

It is possible to follow the rule-making processes of all U.S. federal agencies
through the *Federal Register.* Like a daily newspaper on federal agency action,

the *Federal Register* contains official announcements of proposed, interim, and final regulations, as well as executive orders, presidential proclamations, and other documents of public interest. Most federal regulations will be published in the *Federal Register* before they can be implemented. Therefore, if you followed the *Register* on a regular basis, you would be aware of issues concerning the pesticide in question before it reached the market. Your voice is most effective when regulations are still in the proposed stage.

Specific issues can be easily located in the *Register* through the table of contents or index of each issue. Typically, a topic will be briefly described and an address given to which comments may be sent. A calendar of important dates regarding the topic follows. In April and October, the *Federal Register* publishes the long-term plans of all federal agencies, describing what types of issues they will consider and in what order. The *Register* is published Monday through Friday and is available in most libraries.

Other widely available informational resources include local newspapers, daily news broadcasts (radio or television), and publications by various conservation organizations. In almost all cases you must be a paying member of a conservation organization to receive its publications. The magazines and newsletters they produce are written to inform and empower the concerned citizen on issues specifically relevant to the conservation of biological diversity.

The National Audubon Society sends free to its members (on request) a newsletter entitled the *Audubon Activist,* which keeps them informed on policy issues directly related to bird conservation, indicates how they can personally influence the policy process for specific issues, and regularly presents general information on developing and honing the skills needed by all citizen activists. Individuals who are not members of the National Audubon Society may subscribe for a nominal fee.

The National Audubon Society has pooled its materials to create several Audubon Activist Tool Kits that provide information on specific campaigns (Ancient Forests, Wetlands, Endangered Species, and the Birds in the Balance Action Packet). These kits are available through the National Audubon Society at a reasonable fee.

The National Wildlife Federation has produced an Activist Kit and distributes "Action Alerts" to members of its Resource Conservation Alliance. Contact the National Wildlife Federation for information on the most up-to-date publications.

The following publications list organizations involved in the conservation of migratory birds and their habitats: *The Nature Directory* (Lanier-Graham 1991); *Conservation Directory* (National Wildlife Federation); and *The Environmental Sourcebook* (E. C. Stein 1992).

Concern over declining duck populations has fueled efforts for wetland conservation since the 1930s.

The following organizations specialize in migratory bird habitat conservation, primarily in North America:

American Birding Association
    P.O. Box 6599
    Colorado Springs, CO 80934

Audubon Naturalist Society of the
    Central Atlantic States, Inc.
    8940 Jones Mill Road
    Chevy Chase, MD 20815

Canadian Nature Federation
    453 Sussex Drive
    Ottawa, ONT K1N 6Z4

Canadian Wildlife Federation
    2740 Queensview Drive
    Ottawa, ONT K2B 1A2

Cape May Bird Observatory
    Box 3
    Cape May Point, NJ 08212

The Conservation Foundation
    1250 24th Street, NW
    Washington, DC 20037

Defenders of Wildlife
    1244 19th Street, NW
    Washington, DC 20036

Ducks Unlimited, Inc.
    One Waterfowl Way
    Memphis, TN 38120-2351

Ducks Unlimited, Canada
    1190 Waverly Street
    Winnipeg, MAN R3T 2E2

Hawk Mountain Sanctuary
    RR 2, Box 191
    Kempton, PA 19529

Hawk Migration Association of
        North America
    Chairman
    377 Loomis Street
    Southwick, MA 01077

Laboratory of Ornithology
    Cornell University
    159 Sapsucker Woods Road
    Ithaca, NY 14850

Long Point Bird Observatory
    P.O. Box 160
    Port Rowan, ONT N0E 1M0

Manomet Observatory
    P.O. Box 1770
    Manomet, MA 02345

National Audubon Society
    950 Third Avenue
    New York, NY 10022

National Wildlife Federation
    1400 16th Street, NW
    Washington, DC 20036-2266

Point Reyes Bird Observatory
    4990 Shoreline Highway
    Stinson Beach, CA 94970

The Nature Conservancy
    1815 North Lynne Street
    Arlington, VA 22209

The Nature Conservancy/Canada
    794A Broadview Avenue
    Toronto, ONT M4K 2P7

The Peregrine Fund, Inc.
    5666 West Flying Hawk Lane
    Boise, ID 83709

These organizations have an international focus:

Bird Conservation Alliance
        (formerly International
        Council for Bird Preservation)
    (U.S. office) c/o WWF
    1250 24th Street, NW
    Washington, DC 20037

Conservation International
    1015 18th Street, NW
    Suite 1000
    Washington, DC 20036

Rainforest Action Network
301 Broadway, Suite A
San Francisco, CA 94133

Rainforest Alliance
270 Lafayette Street
Suite 512
New York, NY 10012

Rare Center for Tropical Bird
Conservation
19th and the Parkway
Philadelphia, PA 19103

Smithsonian Migratory Bird Center
National Zoological Park
Washington, DC 20008

Wildlife Conservation Society
185th Street and South
Boulevard
Building A
Bronx, NY 10460

World Wildlife Fund
1250 24th Street, NW
Washington, DC 20037

World Wildlife Fund Canada
90 Eglinton Avenue East
Toronto, ONT M45 2Z7

These organizations specialize in environmental policy issues:

Canadian Environmental Law
Association
517 College Street, Suite 401
Toronto, ONT M6G 4A2

Canadian Institute for Environmental Law and Policy
517 College Street, Suite 400
Toronto, ONT M6G 4A2

Environmental Defense Fund
257 Park Avenue
New York, NY 10010

League of Conservation Voters
1707 L Street, NW, Suite 550
Washington, DC 20036

Natural Resources Defense Council
1725 I Street, NW, Suite 600
Washington, DC 20006

Many of these organizations (as well as numerous others) are part of the Partners in Flight—Aves de Las Americas Program (see chapter 6). You can stay up
to date on the migratory bird activities of many nongovernmental organizations,
as well as federal agencies, through the *Partners in Flight Newsletter,* available free

Increased regulation and prohibition of certain pesticides reversed declines in the Osprey; however, increased vigilance throughout the Western Hemisphere is necessary as toxic chemicals banned in the United States and Canada continue to be exported to Latin America.

of charge from the National Fish and Wildlife Foundation, 1120 Connecticut Avenue, NW, Washington, DC 20036.

Many regional and local conservation organizations may also be available in your community. Such organizations provide exceptional opportunities to stay informed on conservation issues (at all levels), to participate in conservation projects, to meet people with similar concerns, and to develop and apply your skills as a citizen activist. Refer to the National Wildlife Federation's *Conservation Directory* (published annually) and your local phone book for listings.

HAVE AN IMPACT

Having up-to-date information on environmental issues is one thing—using this information effectively is another. The three hundred thousand to 1.8 million committed birders and additional 18 million (or more) bird enthusiasts in North America could become a more powerful lobby. If these people were to channel their knowledge, enthusiasm, and commitment into a citizen action campaign, the impact on environmental policy would be phenomenal.

The following sections address the more popular means by which citizen activists can use their knowledge and personal experience to influence policies that affect the environment. These actions are as pertinent to federal policies as they are to local ones. (For this reason, we collectively refer to those who write, declare, implement, or regulate policies as "officials.")

Letter Writing

The power of pen and paper should never be underestimated. Amazingly, few people take advantage of this power. In just a few minutes you can write a letter that may have a tremendous impact on an official's decision. Among other things, letters can inform officials on the specifics of issues about which they are not experts, introduce officials to knowledge and experience on which they can draw to influence others (an official may contact you for assistance), and represent the passions and concerns of the voter (officials want to be reelected). The following is a list of tips for mounting an effective letter-writing campaign:

• Use your own stationery (letterhead preferred) and your own words. A handwritten letter is fine, as long as it is neat and legible.

• Make it timely. An official needs to hear from you while he or she can still affect the policy process. The earlier in the process you write, the better.

• Keep it short and to the point. One page is sufficient, but do write more than just a few sentences.

• Personalize it. Clearly explain how the issue directly affects your life and that of the people and resources around you. These personal notes are often what stick in an official's memory. If you are writing to a federal representative, focus on your own delegation and "take the message home."

• Be crystal clear. Precisely describe the issue, referring to any legislation by official number or popular name. Show that you understand the difference in viewpoint but feel yours is most pertinent. Share your expertise.

• Give a pat on the back. If the official has taken or plans to take stands or measures that support your position, let him or her know that these efforts have been recognized and are appreciated.

• Address one issue at a time. Individual staff members may be directed to handle mail pertaining to specific topics. If you mention more than one issue, your letter may reach only one of the people who need to hear from you, or it may go nowhere at all.

• Request specific action. Ask the official to do something specific in regard to your issue. For example, ask the official to request hearings on a bill, cosponsor a bill, or vote for or against a particular bill.

• Ask for a reply. This is your assurance that your letter has been read by someone and it gives you information on which to base additional action. Don't forget to include your return address. Keep a copy of all correspondence for future reference.

• Follow it up. When the official's reply arrives, take action again. Follow-up letters can be extremely important and more effective than initial letters. If the official agrees with your stand and intends to take action, communicate your appreciation. Many letters, however, will be noncommittal and fail to respond to your specific points. In such cases, write again. Politely name the points that have not been addressed, indicate your continued concern, and ask for another reply. The official will measure your concern accordingly.

• Say "Thank you." When an official takes the stance or action that you request, send a letter of thanks. Praise is always welcome and often inspires further action.

Here are some don'ts:

• Avoid using form letters or postcards. They have considerably less impact because many officials consider them part of "pressure mail" campaigns. Some conservation organizations send form letters or postcards to their members, encouraging them to sign and mail them. Although this tactic may be better than nothing, your message will be more effective if you use these mailings as the basis for personal letters. Be wary of publications that contain form letters on various topics and insist you can solve major issues by photocopying (or tearing out), signing, and mailing the letters. If you care about an issue, don't take shortcuts—officials can see right through them.

• Don't cut off your nose to spite your face. Avoid being unnecessarily critical and never threaten or personally insult an official. Negative correspondence can do more harm than good, and may actually encourage an official to support the other side.

• Don't be a pen pal. If you write in on every issue, officials won't know when to take your concerns seriously.

Telephone Calls

Telephone calls made directly to officials or members of their staff can be very effective as part of a last-minute campaign strategy. A phone call often takes less time (both to make and to be received) than a letter and is cost effective. Moreover, phone calls let officials know that an issue is important enough for you to take the time and spend the money to reach them. This is impressive. Check the government pages of your phone book or reference section in your library for listings of local officials. A few calling tips:

• Give your name and location, state your business, and politely ask to speak to the official of choice. If this official is not available, ask to speak to the staff member who specializes in the topic of concern.

• Keep it short, organized, and polite. Clearly present your issue, expressing your personal concerns and expertise. Consider writing an outline or informal script in advance, but be careful not to sound as if you are reading from a document.

• Ask for action. State specifically what you want (by bill name or number). Ask that relevant materials on the issue be mailed to you.

• Take notes. The information you glean from this interaction may be of great value in the future. Write down the name and title of the person you talk to, as well as the date and time of the call.

• Send a follow-up letter that thanks the individual for his or her time and any action that might have been taken on behalf of your concerns.

Telegrams

Telegrams may be shorter and faster, and communicate a higher degree of concern than letters. They are, however, more costly for you. Unlike telephone calls, telegrams may get "lost in the pile," but they put the message in writing. As an additional or alternative means of contacting officials in a critical, brief time period, telegrams can be especially effective. Refer to your phone book for a telegraph office near you.

One on One

Nothing impresses your concerns on an official more than a personal meeting. You make a statement by just crossing the threshold. In fact, personal meetings can be more effective than a swarm of professional lobbyists beating down doors in the nation's capital. Congressional representatives can be approached when they return to their home districts (on weekends or for a recess) or when you visit Washington. To make an appointment, call the official's state or D.C. office and tell the staff member you would like to meet with your representative. Local officials may have regular schedules for citizen meetings. If you don't know the appropriate phone numbers, check in the reference section of your library.

Think strategically. Decide which other people should be in the meeting (a coalition representing a few organizations can be effective) and who should be the spokesperson. A practice session is often appropriate. Prepare any graphic materials and handouts, including fact sheets, that can clearly make your point. Plan to dress in business attire.

At the meeting, the spokesperson should introduce those in attendance (including their organizational titles or affiliations). The rest of the strategy follows that of letter writing and phone calling. When you follow up with a thank-you letter, don't forget the staff that assisted you in setting up the meeting.

If you are unable to obtain a personal meeting, ask the relevant staff member if town meetings or public forums are planned. By attending, you can at least get in a question regarding your concern and, in doing so, alert others in attendance to the issue.

Town Meetings

Town meetings on specific topics are generally scheduled by congressional representatives during a recess. If you can communicate your specific interests, an official's office should be able to give you a schedule of relevant meetings. If no meetings are scheduled, you can attempt to establish one. This is, of course, considerably more work, but it also means that you are in control. Decide which officials should be invited and contact their staff members. State the specific purpose of the meeting and the kind and size of audience you expect, and suggest several possible dates and an appropriate location. Once a commitment has been secured, put the information in writing and send it to the officials for their records. Publicize the event. In setting up the event, make communication easy for everyone in attendance (consider chair arrangements and the number and placement of microphones) and allow ample time for questions, answers, and discussion.

Making a Difference   Gene Morton

It happens all the time: a forest you thought would be there forever is targeted for a housing project. It is the last forest in your community, the rest gone to lawns, houses, and subsidized predators (pets). Surely, you think, the county will rescue the last of its kind? Nope. Most lawyers, developers, and county planning and zoning personnel have long treated land as a commodity and care nothing about birds, environmental quality, or anything other than making a buck.

An adjacent landowner has decided to appeal the decision to allow the forest's destruction. You join forces, using the lists of complete communities of breeding birds, copperheads, and old-growth trees to illustrate to county officials the value of preserving this portion of the 353-acre Arnold Forest. You point out that some Neotropical migrants recently breeding there will certainly be lost: Blue-gray Gnatcatcher, Yellow-throated Vireo, Black-and-white Warbler, Worm-eating Warbler, Northern Parula, Ovenbird, Louisiana Waterthrush, Kentucky Warbler, Hooded Warbler, and American Redstart.

County authorities take your point seriously. You make one mistake, however. You recommend that county officials contact a respected colleague to explain the presence or absence of breeding birds as an indication of the forest's value. You didn't realize that the recommended authority on birds was committed to the "island biogeography" theory. (Island biogeography suggests that an island that is small and far out to sea will have fewer species on it than an island that is larger and closer to a mainland source of colonizing species. Forest fragmentation on land is suggested to operate in the same way for birds. It is true that fewer breeding birds are found in smaller forest fragments, but whether this is a direct result of size or other factors is not known.)

The outside expert, having no firsthand knowledge of the area, draws on his understanding of island biogeographic theory and provides just the opinion the developer wants to hear. The developer sums it up: "As you recall in our meeting with the expert ornithologist . . . adequate breeding habitat size for the species of birds mentioned by Dr. Morton is more realistically two thousand to three thousand acres. The outside consultant also stated that as a result of past (within the last twelve years) habitat fragmentation, this area is marginal habitat for those species, and not the pristine habitat that Dr. Morton observed. He feels that sensitive species (birds sensitive to habitat disturbance) are not there." This misapplication of biological theory stops the local conservation effort cold. The appeal of the issuance of the county's permit is denied and the housing project, already on the county maps before the case ended, starts bulldozers.

Since the project began, one bulldozer operator has been bitten by a copperhead. Only a handful of luxury homes have been built. The builder ran off with some of the down payments and skipped town. Many of the lots have still not been sold. The forest is gone. The birds are gone. Hardly anybody or anything wants to live there.

Remarkably, something good came of this. The county, realizing a mistake was made, began to take birds seriously and decided to incorporate breeding birds as part of its definition of "forest" for the Chesapeake Bay Critical Area Commission. In May 1986, five ornithologists, including myself, met at the Smithsonian Environmental Research Center to discuss protection of "forest

Forest-Dwelling Bird Species
Afforded Protection in Maryland's Critical Areas Program

Common Name	Habitat Type	
	Upland	*Riparian*
Chuck-will's-widow	☐	
Creeper, Brown		☐
Flycatcher, Acadian	☐	
Hawk, Broad-winged*	☐	
Hawk, Cooper's*	☐	
Hawk, Red-shouldered		☐
Ovenbird	☐	
Owl, Barred*	☐	☐
Redstart, American*	☐	☐
Tanager, Scarlet	☐	
Vireo, Red-eyed	☐	
Vireo, Yellow-throated	☐	
Warbler, Black-and-white	☐	
Warbler, Hooded*	☐	
Warbler, Kentucky	☐	
Warbler, Northern Parula		☐
Warbler, Prothonotary		☐
Warbler, Swainson's*	☐	☐
Warbler, Worm-eating*	☐	
Waterthrush, Louisiana	☐	☐
Whip-poor-will	☐	
Wood Duck		☐
Woodpecker, Hairy	☐	
Woodpecker, Pileated	☐	

*sensitive species

interior–dwelling birds." We came up with a list of species that show a high degree of association with forests adjacent to the Chesapeake Bay and that are restricted to, or depend on, large upland forests or riparian forests for breeding.

We determined that the "presence" of birds, as used in the criteria, should be related to the overall habitat quality afforded by a given area for interior dwelling birds. Accordingly, we suggested the following guideline: In upland forests of approximately one hundred acres or more in extent, and in riparian forest of approximately three hundred feet or more in width, protection measures for interior dwelling birds are necessary when it has been determined, based on surveys conducted using standard biological survey techniques, that such species are present as follows:

• Four of the species listed in the accompanying table are found, based on breeding criteria described in the Maryland Breeding Bird Atlas Handbook, to be "probable" or "confirmed" breeders in the forest; or

• One of the sensitive species listed in the table is found, according to the same criteria.

Although Arnold Forest was lost to the bulldozer, by introducing birds into the equation that determines sites for protection, we gained a valuable input to the Chesapeake Bay Critical Area Commission Criteria for Local Critical Area Program Development. Documentation of breeding birds with on-site surveys using standard biological survey techniques is now required by law. The sheer size of a forest is no longer considered the only reason to preserve habitat. Zoning officials have come to understand that what species are present in a specific habitat also counts. More generally, patches of forest are viewed in a larger geographic scale, and the value of remnant forests to birds migrating through a landscape, as well as to the breeders, is considered of vital importance.

Concerned citizens everywhere are confronted by the problems Maryland residents faced in trying to save the Arnold Forest for future generations to enjoy and learn from. I encourage the use of birds to define and protect forests, and hope that the Maryland example will stimulate similar efforts.

Gene Morton is Research Zoologist for the National Zoological Park, Smithsonian Institution, where he has conducted pioneering research on the ecology and behavior of migratory birds.

Making a Difference   Kim Sturla

The companion cat population is estimated at 49 million in the United States, and the estimated feral cat population is 30 million to 60 million! Eighty-one percent of all cats entering shelters in the United Stated are euthanized, which computes to approximately 5.7 million to 9.5 million cats. Less than 2 percent of lost cats are claimed by their guardians.

Clearly, cats are out of control.

Interest in solving the cat overpopulation problem is shared by many. Government officials have a financial interest—it cost California taxpayers $100 million to operate animal control services in 1991. Health departments and animal control agencies have a public health interest—cats are becoming the number one domestic animal to test positive for rabies. Humane societies have a deep personal interest—they face the grisly task of killing millions of cats each year. Animal rights organizations have an ethical concern—managing the "surplus" cat problem by killing them is not a humane solution when more can be done to prevent births. Environmental groups have a wildlife concern—millions of birds, small mammals, reptiles, and amphibians are preyed on by cats each year.

Adoption promotion campaigns, low-fee spay-and-neuter clinics, and humane education programs have reduced the number of surplus animals, but we have not even come close to solving the crisis. More innovative and aggressive approaches are obviously necessary.

We need laws on the books that regulate the breeding of animals until we no longer have a surplus. During the past several years, dozens of communities have passed breeding control legislation. Some ordinances mandate spaying and neutering unless a guardian purchases a breeding permit. Others impose a substantially higher licensing fee for unaltered animals. Still others call for a complete breeding moratorium. All these ordinances have one common denominator—they provide a financial incentive for people to sterilize their animals.

For the sake of wildlife, we also need laws that curtail the domestic cat's ability to prey on native animals. Research findings indicate that even well-fed companion cats kill wildlife. Laws that prohibit cats from being outside altogether or that allow them out only on leash are most effective. Such laws also benefit cats—they are less likely to be exposed to disease, dogs, and traffic hazards.

California has required shelters to either spay and neuter all dogs and cats or take a sterilization deposit at the time of adoption. Although this has helped, it was not sufficient. In 1990, therefore, I wrote and helped pass the first mandatory spay-or-neuter ordinance for San Mateo County. And in 1993 I put together a coalition to sponsor state legislation, dubbed the Feline Fix Bill, that would require all outdoor cats to be sterilized. Failure to comply would result in an infraction. More than 120 animal protection and conservation groups endorsed the bill, including the Audubon Society, the California Veterinary Medical Association, the California Animal Control Director's Association, the State Humane Association, Alley Cat Allies, and the Fund for Animals. But the bill has not yet passed.

To initiate domestic cat control ordinances in your community or state, you should establish an alliance with other individuals and groups who share your concern for wildlife and domestic animals. Focus not on your differences, but on your common ground. Wildlife and companion cats both need protection.

Kim Sturla is Western Director of the Fund for Animals. She has seventeen years of experience in animal shelter and animal rights work and believes all animals, domestic and wild, deserve respect and protection.

USE THE MEDIA

You awake on a crisp spring morning to find the dawn choir has just begun to take up its first notes of the day. Quickly, you travel to your favorite birding spot, anticipating tanagers, grosbeaks, thrushes, and a variety of warblers. You wonder whether the early blooming wildflowers along the streambed will open today. They won't.

You arrive to find spray-painted red crosses on all but a few trees. It is, to your eyes, a deadly brand. The gentle, leaf-carpeted trail on which you have traveled so many a morning has been gouged by the jaws of bulldozers. You are shocked, angered, distraught, but not powerless.

Later that morning, through phone calls made to city officials, you learn that the forested watershed has been slated for development. The city has leased the land to a developer specializing in the construction of upscale malls. No community hearings were held or are scheduled. No environmental impact report has been filed. City officials and the developer will not accept phone calls or take appointments.

You know that the area is of vital importance to Neotropical migratory birds. Hundreds of species funnel through the corridor every spring and fall. Other species, some of which have been declining elsewhere, nest there in the summer. Moreover, the watershed is valuable to other forms of wildlife. Because you have kept complete and accurate field notes, you have the data to support these facts. You have what you need to take your concerns to the media and inspire other concerned citizens to help protect the watershed.

There are many approaches that can be taken when using the media to communicate the need for citizen action. Below, we briefly summarize the most common options. In determining which are most appropriate for communicating your message, consider a short- and long-term strategic plan. What do you hope to accomplish? In what time frame? What resources (human, financial, technical) will you require? In all cases, approach reporters with respect. Be prompt and courteous, even if the reporter has another viewpoint. Arm yourself with facts and contacts. Think pictures and sound bites (short, catchy, to-the-point statements); you may have very limited space or only a few seconds in which to communicate your message. Familiarize yourself with media deadlines. Expect both good and bad luck to play a role. If a natural disaster occurs on the day your story is to be released, it may be scrapped completely. If it is a slow news day, you may make the front page. Call reporters early in the day and plan activities for them to cover on a weekday.

Press Releases

The press release is not in itself a media option. It is a tool ("the hook") that will help convince the media to run your story. Occasionally reporters will use a press release verbatim, so it is important to make it as informative as possible, without losing the inspirational edge.

The following are basic rules for producing a successful press release:

• Print the release on good-quality, standard 8½-by-11 stationery. If you have a formal letterhead, use it. Although you may use colored stock, avoid dark tones that make reading the text difficult.

• Keep the release to one page if possible. If additional pages are required, type "MORE" on the bottom of all but the last page. At the bottom of the final page, type "END," "-30-," or "###" to mark the end.

• Type the release double-spaced. Leave a three-inch margin at the top of the first page. Leave margins on each side wide enough for a reporter to write notes.

• Type the source (name, address, telephone number of contact person) of the release in the upper lefthand corner.

• Type the date, in capital letters, just below the source information, on the right side of the page.

• Summarize the issue addressed in the release in a headline (typed in capital letters).

• The text should be brief and to the point (who, what, when, where, why, and how), yet catchy enough to inspire a reporter who might receive more than a dozen press releases a day. Use brief, quotable passages.

• Establish and maintain an up-to-date mailing list for your press releases. Each release should be addressed to a specific, appropriate individual.

• Distribute the press release two to four days before an event and—very important—make follow-up calls to ensure that the release reached the right person and was read. Attempt to set up a personal meeting.

Press releases are especially effective when they are part of a press kit. Press kits are commonly two-pocket folders that contain resources aimed at making a reporter's job easier and inspiring interest in the story. Typical resources in a press kit (in addition to the press release) include fact sheets, photographs (black-and-white), related stories, organizational newsletters, lists of contact persons with titles, addresses, and phone numbers, and a calendar of events. In addition, press kits may include a videotape that contains a brief (a few minutes at most) snapshot of relevant footage that can be aired on television. The press kit should be well organized, colorful, and catchy.

A press kit or press release should be given to every reporter you meet or call. Send new releases whenever you have a specific activity planned.

Media Events

A media event centers around some kind of action, such as a demonstration or accountability session in which real, specific demands are made. To bring the issue to light, demonstrators might picket in front of a developer's or official's office or stand in front of bulldozers with signs reading, "Save Warbler Watershed," "Demand an Environmental Impact Statement," or "Migrants, Not Malls!" When planning a media event, identify a spokesperson who is knowledgeable on the issues, comfortable with addressing the media, well-spoken, and cool-headed. Efforts must be made to keep the action from turning into a free-for-all. An audience misses the point when it sees adults attacking each other or exchanging caustic language. Because they are action oriented, media events are most appropriate for attracting television coverage, but this does not mean that radio and newspaper reporters should be excluded from your mailing list!

Press Conferences

Unlike media events, press conferences generally involve no action other than discussion of the issues. The media are invited to hear one spokesperson or several speakers address a single, timely issue. In conferences in which several speakers are involved, everyone should recognize and strictly adhere to time limits. It is wise to have speakers who are experts on the issues and represent a variety of interest groups. This gives credibility to your cause and encourages others to become involved (the "lemming phenomenon"). Television or radio reporters may use clips from your conference. Newspaper reporters and other journalists may use the conference to gather background information for their stories.

Letters to the Editor

With the exception of the front page, and perhaps the comics, the most widely read section of the newspaper is letters to the editor. Your ability to reach concerned citizens and to alert editors and journalists through this section should not be underestimated. Letters should be short (250 words maximum) and to the point. The issue addressed should be timely and of local interest. Any actions that you demand and the persons who should take them should be clearly outlined.

Conclude with information on how the audience can learn more and become involved with your efforts. Type and double-space the letter for submission. If you are representing an organization, be sure to include its name and any title you may hold in it when signing the letter.

News Stories

News stories not only call attention to your issue but give it credibility. If you don't know a good newspaper reporter personally, look through the newspaper to find one who covers environmental issues. Reporters for radio stations can be reached through the station's news director. When trying to locate the appropriate reporter at a television station, ask the assignment editor. Call the reporter, introduce yourself, clearly explain your issue, and ask for an appointment. A radio station reporter may ask to tape your interview and air parts of it later. If the issue is timely and important to others in the community, the reporter is likely to take an interest. Before leaving the meeting, make sure the reporter knows how to reach you for further information.

Feature Stories

Unlike news stories, feature stories are not "hard" news. What they lack in news value, however, they can make up for in depth. Realistically, few issues are decided by facts. An inspirational, emotional, persuasive story often has more impact on the human psyche. If you expect an issue to be relevant for several months, find out whether any of the media have related features already scheduled. Encourage the feature reporter to work your issue into his or her outline.

Editorials

Editorials are a very important part of any environmental campaign because they garner the attention of public officials and community leaders who are trying to stay in step with community concerns. There are two ways to work your story into newspaper editorials. First, you can write your own editorial. Such articles, called op-ed pieces, appear on the page facing the editorial page. Familiarize yourself with editorial style by reading the editorials and op-ed pieces of several papers. Keep your op-ed piece short and to the point. One page is sufficient. Submit the piece (typed, double-spaced) with a cover letter that presents some background on the issue and explains your personal involvement. If you plan to submit an article to the op-ed section, consider having a public official or other recognizable individual write (or at least sign) it for you; you have a better chance of getting it published and the name gives credibility to your cause.

Your second option is to persuade an editor to write an editorial. Small papers have one editor; large ones have editorial boards. Get to know editors personally. When meeting with an editor to discuss your issue, include experts who support your position. This can help convince the editor that you are a credible person with a credible mission.

If an editor decides to air your issue, he or she will either support or oppose your position. Unlike the newspaper, if the radio or television editor sides with the opposition, you can request time for a rebuttal. Some radio and television programs will permit you to write a letter that a spokesperson reads verbatim over the air.

Public Opinion Messages

Many publications and radio stations offer free community bulletin boards. These provide an excellent opportunity to reach concerned citizens, community leaders, and public officials with announcements of specific meetings, hearings, actions, and projects. They also present a means by which you can make a plea for specific support or action. Some radio stations will allow you to tape a brief speech that presents your concerns and opinions. If you send a tape to the station with a cover letter that convincingly explains your position, the tape may be aired. Expect the station to also air any responsible replies to your tape, whether for or against it.

Talk Shows

Radio and television talk shows may take considerable planning, but they often pay off in effectiveness. Make an initial contact with the station by phone, describing your issue and your position. Once you have a contact person, follow up with a letter that again defines your position and hopes. In securing a talk show appearance, get to know the producer and the assistants. Communicate your expertise and your ability to use your personal contacts to line up guests and define material. If the producer finds you both knowledgeable and credible, you may be contacted as the citizen respondent to related issues. Whenever you appear on television, consider using visual aids to make your point. In all cases, have facts, figures, and examples handy. Be prepared for call-in questions. Have a colleague play devil's advocate in advance to prepare yourself to answer difficult, sometimes emotional, questions.

OTHER WAYS TO INFLUENCE CONSERVATION POLICY

The more time you devote to citizen activism, the more opportunities to effect positive change in environmental policies will become apparent to you. Inspiration and creativity are powerful tools; use them to your benefit. The following is a brief list of actions that you can take immediately. While many of these actions are locally based, they can have wide-ranging implications for the conservation of migratory birds and other wildlife. If you are already a citizen activist, consider adding new actions listed below to your campaign. If you have never before been a citizen activist, consider these actions for your starting point.

The Color of Money

While a general increase in the public's interest in wildlife conservation has resulted in an increase in funding, financial resources remain low for most programs. In addition to writing to federal representatives and encouraging them to appropriate funds for programs you consider of vital importance, you can allocate your own funds to conservation projects. Even the change that lies beneath your couch cushions can make a significant impact when it is donated through a program that combines it with donations from thousands of other concerned citizens.

Nongame Programs—Check Them Off!

In many states you can contribute to nongame research, management, restoration, and habitat acquisition programs by placing a check mark in a box on your state income tax form. By checking this box, you donate your state tax refund to the state's nongame program. State nongame initiatives, often desperate for money, have significantly benefited from checkoff programs. If your state or province does not have a checkoff program, contact your nongame department and inquire about initiating one.

Stamp Out Habitat Destruction

In 1934 the U.S. Migratory Bird Hunting Stamp Act was passed to provide the funds needed to buy land for the 1929 Migratory Bird Conservation Act. The Stamp Act requires every waterfowl hunter over the age of sixteen to annually purchase and carry a Federal Duck Stamp. Ninety-eight cents of every Duck Stamp dollar goes directly toward the purchase of wetlands.

The Duck Stamp program met with immediate success. Since 1934, the price of Duck Stamps has increased as the availability of wetlands has decreased. A collector who purchased each of the fifty-nine stamps issued by 1992 (at issue price) would have spent $242. Today the investment would be worth over $4,000. All stamps not sold are destroyed three years after issue.

The Federal Duck Stamp program has proved to be one of the most successful conservation programs ever initiated. Duck Stamp dollars have preserved about four million acres (1.6 million hectares) of wetland in the National Wildlife Refuge System. The success of the program has expanded into other conservation efforts, including youth education programs. The Duck Stamp also aids wildlife other than waterfowl, as one third of the nation's endangered or threatened species live in wetlands secured under the program. The preservation of these wetlands also helps maintain groundwater supplies, water quality, and shorelines. Possession of the most recent stamp also provides free admission to all U.S. National Wildlife Refuges.

In 1985 the Canadian Wildlife Service, Canadian Post Corporation, and Wildlife Habitat Canada launched the Canada Conservation Stamp Program, modeled after the U.S. Duck Stamp Program. Canadian hunters must purchase a conservation stamp to validate their migratory game bird hunting permits. To take advantage of the rising popularity of wildlife art and stamp collecting, Wildlife Habitat Canada releases limited edition, signed and numbered prints and lapel pins, along with a new stamp design, each August. When new designs are released, the previous year's prints and stamps are canceled. Between 1985 and 1990 Wildlife Habitat Canada raised more than $18 million through the stamp and print program. These proceeds were used to fund over 140 habitat protection (primarily wetland) initiatives. Buy your stamps today.

Participating in the Environmental Planning Process
Although Environmental Impact Statements and Assessments (EIS/EIA) are written by biologists, economists, and other experts, the public has many chances to participate in the process. When you learn that an EIS/EIA is being prepared, hold an informal meeting with those preparing the document. You may be able to provide them with valuable information (such as migratory bird use of the land in question). Federal agencies hold public meetings several times throughout the EIS process. Speak at these meetings and voice your concerns about the project. Ask to be placed on the mailing list for the EIS/EIAs. When a draft document is issued, send your comments to the appropriate agency. Agencies must respond in writing and consider all reasonable alternatives to their plans. Alert the media to your concerns, especially if project plans will put the health of the environment at risk.

The process that determines the environmental impact of U.S. Forest Service (USFS), Bureau of Land Management (BLM), and U.S. Fish and Wildlife Service (USFWS) actions and makes adjustments to their management plans is open to the public. As a concerned citizen, your role in this process is a vital one. However, your concerns should not be put aside when the planning process is complete and a formal document is produced. It is important that you continually watch plan implementers, making sure that the documented plan is strictly adhered to. It is also important to monitor and record how a management plan affects the environment (paying close attention to migratory birds, of course). The information you gather as a citizen watchdog can be a critical part of the evaluation and redirection process when a plan is again up for review.

National Forest Planning Process

The U.S. Forest Service has been criticized for maximizing timber production at the expense of most wildlife, including migratory songbirds. It must operate all national forests under a comprehensive management plan, and each forest must periodically go through a planning cycle with opportunities for public hearings and comment. Although the Forest Service is developing its own program to protect migratory birds, the management plans used in many national forests are, as of yet, far from adequate in meeting the long-term needs of migratory species. Contact the superintendents of national forests that you are familiar with and ask to be placed on the management plan mailing list. You should then receive all notices of public meetings and all documents relevant to the management plans of those forests in which you are interested. Join conservation organizations that closely follow the management plans of national forests. Review, comment, and provide written as well as oral testimony for the management plans that you follow, demanding that land managers address the needs of migratory birds.

Refuges 2003

The National Wildlife Refuge System (NWRS) is the only U.S. network of federal lands established primarily for wildlife. The USFWS manages the NWRS and has been criticized for overemphasizing the management of waterfowl and other game birds at the expense of nongame wildlife. As a result, the USFWS is preparing a new programmatic EIS and management plan called "Refuges 2003." A Fish and Wildlife Service manual and other documents related to Refuges 2003 are expected to be completed, and available to the public, by early 1995. Under the new guidelines, each existing national wildlife refuge will have to go through a replanning of management practices. Each refuge added to the system will need a comprehensive management plan that adheres to the new standards within two years. To receive all documents and notices relevant to refuge management practices, contact the director of national wildlife refuges with which you are familiar or the Chief of the Division of Refuges (USFWS, 4401 N. Fairfax Drive, Room 670, Arlington, VA 22203) and ask to be placed on the mailing list. Join a conservation organization that closely monitors the management of local refuges. Review, comment, and provide formal testimony for refuges with which you are familiar. Suggest that refuge managers consider the long-term needs of all Neotropical migratory birds, not just waterfowl.

Bureau of Land Management

Giving input into the management of BLM land can best be approached at the district level. Although there are a number of important national policies on reducing overgrazing and protection of critical riparian zones, most land use planning is done at the local level. *How Not to Be Cowed,* an excellent citizens' guide to becoming involved in BLM land use decisions, can be obtained from the Natural Resource Defense Council (1350 New York, Ave., NW, Washington, DC 20005).

Making a Difference   Edward E. Clark, Jr.

For those of us who really love birds—and for that matter, even for those who don't—the Bald Eagle is a beautiful and compelling symbol of all that is wild and free. Unfortunately, in recent years the Bald Eagle has also come to be a symbol of endangered wildlife in the United States. Most people rarely see this spectacular bird, and even more rarely experience its penetrating gaze at close range.

The first Bald Eagle I ever saw was on the arm of Roy Geiger, a naturalist with the National Wildlife Federation who was traveling the United States in 1982 with a live eagle, helping the nation celebrate the two-hundredth anniversary of the eagle's selection as the symbol of the United States. I will never forget the experience. As the newly elected president and executive director of the Wildlife Center of Virginia, a hospital for native wildlife, I was in the front row. I had never seen anything more moving than that eagle's stare. In the words of one audience member, "That bird looked at you hard enough to leave a scar!"

Three years later I saw my second eagle at close range. A disabled Bald Eagle had been found in a field along the James River near Richmond and was brought to the Wildlife Center of Virginia.

The once proud and defiant eagle could barely stand. Its head hung down in what seemed a pitiful surrender to an unseen force. The fierce stare was reduced to a vacant gaze from eyes that could not focus. The Wildlife Center's veterinarian determined that the eagle had been poisoned. State wildlife biologists found that this eagle had been brought to the brink of death by a granular insecticide called carbofuran, sold under the trade name Furadan 15-G.

Fortunately for the poisoned eagle, my colleagues administered antidotes in time to save its life and eventually return it to the wild. However, just as my first memories of a Bald Eagle left me changed forever, so, too, did the haunting image of this innocent victim.

Over the next year and a half, granular carbofuran was identified in the fatal poisonings of five more eagles in the Chesapeake Bay area alone. Yet in spite of absolute proof that the chemical was killing endangered species, neither state nor federal officials did anything.

Finally, after months of repeated inquiries, the U.S. Environmental Protection Agency (EPA) decided to undertake a special review of granular carbofuran. A special review is a process through which the agency decides whether to suspend the registration of a product. The EPA promised a decision within eighteen to twenty-four months. However, as time passed, the body count continued to rise. Soon it became clear that the agency had no intention of acting at all. Virginia's state agriculture officials responded to the eagle deaths with comments about the value of pesticides for modern agriculture.

Since working within the system produced no results, we took our case to the public. The EPA defended the delays as allowing time for additional analysis. Veteran observers labeled the delays classic "stonewalling." Soon word was received from within the EPA that employees supporting a cancellation of the registration of granular carbofuran were being subjected to intense pressure to change their position. The company that produced carbofuran was using every tactic in the book to buy time for its deadly but highly profitable product. Among the tactics used were calling for more field testing of their product, asking the EPA to delay its decision on carbofuran until all granular pesticides could be evaluated and regulated at once, and actively organizing farmers and farm organizations to oppose the attempts of environmentalists to "ban all pesticides."

Fortunately, few things make the media respond more quickly than evidence that government agencies have failed in their responsibility to protect the public from predictable dangers. Our complaints about the lack of response to the string of Bald Eagle deaths led one reporter to spend several months investigating the Virginia Department of Agriculture and Consumer Service's Office of Pesticide Programs. The result was a five-day series of articles that painted an alarming picture of ineffective oversight and inappropriate relationships between state officials and the companies they regulated. Our concern for the birds led to the discovery that neither wildlife nor humans were being adequately protected.

As a veteran of many public policy battles over environmental issues, I know that the same basic principles apply, regardless of the specific battle. One of the most common factors is the apparent imbalance of power—with wildlife and the environment usually on the short end of the stick. Another given is that "the system" is not going to change just because it is not working. It takes overwhelming pressure, either from the public or from the key people with the power to force the change. To exert this pressure requires credibility, and that means you must have your facts straight and be able to back up your claims. Above all, any meaningful change takes time. The race to protect the environment is a marathon, and no place for sprinters who lack staying power.

With these principles firmly in mind, we set out to rid the environment of granular carbofuran. To do so, we needed information, attention, and allies—in that order.

Most of the information we needed about carbofuran came straight from the EPA's files, but not just from the public statements. Armed with the Freedom of Information Act, we demanded to see the entire carbofuran file, which contained thousands of pages. We learned that government scientists suspected that granular carbofuran, registered to control insects in the soil, was also responsible for the deaths of as many as two million birds each year, including many endangered species. Why, then, was the product still on the market? We also learned that in its first twenty years, the EPA had never banned any pesticides purely for environmental reasons. All actions, including the ban on DDT, had been based on the products' effects on human health.

A steady stream of information was supplied to the media. Each time another eagle was found killed or poisoned, we renewed our calls for action and called both state and federal representatives to help force the agencies to do their jobs. We went so far as to offer draft letters of inquiry for Virginia's congressional delegation to send to the EPA. Every time the Wildlife Center presented education programs to school or civic groups, the story of carbofuran was told. Every major conservation group in the state was asked to pass resolutions calling for a ban on carbofuran. National environmental organizations were visited and recruited as well.

Finally in 1988, four years after the carbofuran battle began, the governor of Virginia was convinced that the state's pesticide program was not working and ordered a study of ways the program could be made more effective. In the meantime, the EPA was still reviewing the evidence.

Not surprisingly, the study showed the problems with pesticide regulation to be severe. However, it was the state legislature that was responsible for the adoption of a new law. The law, passed as a result of the study, created a new regulatory body in Virginia called the Pesticide Control Board. This was an important victory, but still far from the final goal. The board had to write the new regulations and get itself organized before any action against carbofuran could be taken. This took another year.

In 1990 the carbofuran issue finally came before the new state board. To take our frustration to a new high, the board decided to accept the pesticide manufacturer's assurance that it could prove that its product was safe if one additional year of field study was allowed. While this was a setback, we did get the new board to accept independent monitoring of the test by a state wildlife biologist. The EPA was still reviewing the data.

In the spring of 1991, granular carbofuran was applied with the special involvement of the manufacturer and under the watchful eye of conservationists. In the long run, this was the best thing that could have happened. Bird kills occurred in every single field to which carbofuran was applied. We made sure the whole world knew it.

Faced with such powerful evidence gathered at its own direction, the Virginia Pesticide Control Board enacted an emergency ban on the use of granular carbofuran and canceled its registration in Virginia. Six years had passed since the first Bald Eagle was known to have been poisoned in the state. Three days after Virginia's action, the EPA announced that it had reached a negotiated agreement with the manufacturer, which agreed to surrender the registration on its product. While this might seem like a total victory, by "volunteering" to stop selling the product, the manufacturer avoided a legal ban and therefore could continue to sell its products overseas, often killing the same migratory birds we sought to protect. Still, through perseverance, we have managed to remove one major threat to the resident birds of the United States.

Effective activism requires the belief that improvement is possible. It requires a vision of the future. It requires a willingness to learn how, where, and by whom decisions are made. Ultimately, the most important thing required is a willingness to take the first step to get involved. A single person can make a difference, especially if he or she takes the time to recruit others. Movements are made up of individual people who care.

Edward E. Clark, Jr., is President of the Wildlife Center of Virginia, the leading veterinary and research hospital for wildlife in the United States. A specialist in grassroots organization, his efforts have influenced state and national environmental policy for more than twenty years.

Secure a Place for Endangered Spaces

To date, only 4.6 percent of Canada is secure as protected natural areas. This figure falls far behind the United Nation's recommendation that countries protect at least 12 percent of their territories. Launched by the World Wildlife Fund in 1989, the Endangered Spaces campaign is a ten-year drive to ensure that a sample of each of Canada's 340 natural regions is saved as a park or other protected area by the year 2000. To meet this goal, federal, provincial, and territorial governments must design a protected areas system in a manner that properly represents the natural diversity within their boundaries. Achieving the Endangered Spaces goal will be a step towards ensuring protection for Canada's unique biological diversity, including the nesting habitats of many migratory birds.

Thus far, Endangered Spaces progress has been encouraging. Between 1991 and 1992, one hundred thousand square kilometers were protected. Eighty-seven of Canada's natural regions are now represented by protected areas. Still, Canadian wilderness disappears at an alarming rate every day.

With more than 90 percent of Canada held as public lands, Canadians are in a position to demand that more protected areas be included in land use planning. You can become a part of the Endangered Spaces campaign by doing the following:

• Sign the Wilderness Charter, the mission statement of the campaign. Have your friends and associates sign it, too. Contact the World Wildlife Fund (90 Eglinton Avenue East, Suite 504, Toronto, ONT M4P 2Z7) to add your name to this vital petition.

• Write to your member of Parliament and member of the Legislative Assembly and ask them to sign the Wilderness Charter. Encourage them to press their respective ministers and governments to complete protected areas networks.

• Become a Wilderness Crusader. The Wilderness Crusader program invites concerned citizens to raise funds and public awareness for the Endangered Spaces campaign. Contact WWF for Crusader information.

Go Green

As members of a relatively affluent society, how we spend our money has tremendous implications for the environment. Although the damage certain products can do to the local environment or the overall ecological health of the United States and Canada is obvious, environmentalists are now beginning to realize the global impact of their weekend shopping sprees.

One of the first products to raise an alarm was beef. In the mid-1980s, conservationists became alarmed by the vast amounts of tropical rainforest habitat that were being destroyed for large-scale cattle ranching to produce, in part, cheap beef for fast-food restaurants and dog food in the United States and Canada. Christopher Uhl and Geoffery Parker calculated that about a half ton (or 6¼ square meters) of rainforest was lost for every hamburger ultimately produced. The lost habitat meant the destruction and disturbance of many species, as well as ecological processes (e.g., water cycling). To reduce this threat to biological diversity, citizen activists and conservation organizations ran an aggressive campaign against some of the largest, best-known fast-food chains. The campaign strategy was simple—to encourage the public to boycott fast-food chains that bought "rainforest beef." The campaign was successful, hitting the restaurant chains in their most sensitive spot—the pocket. This boycott resulted in some striking successes. For example, Burger King announced it would no longer serve Central American beef. More important, many fast-food chains have attempted to be more environmentally sensitive throughout their operations. However, it is unclear whether this had a significant effect on the conversion of tropical forests to pasture. Boycotts are a blunt instrument for effecting improvements in pasture management and sustainability. And such a campaign can create bad feelings among nationals of targeted countries, even those not involved in raising beef cattle.

A more positive approach to green consumerism has been adopted by many groups. Commodities that are produced in a relatively sustainable and ecologically friendly manner are promoted. Every day you consume products of tropical lands: fruits, nuts, medicines, herbs, spices, and the like. Some of these products benefit tropical conservation by promoting sustainable development. The development of these export industries opens many questions regarding the equitability of trade and the degree to which profits are returned to the people producing the commodities. Organizations that import such products with an eye on social justice issues include Equal Exchange (101 Tosca Drive, Stoughton, MA 02072) and Pueblo to People (2105 S. Iber Road, Suite 131, Houston, TX 77055).

There are many examples of small efforts to promote new products. Every morning many of us consume a classic example of a potentially "ecologically friendly" product: coffee. Coffee and cacao (chocolate) have traditionally been grown under shade canopies. In some areas this includes the understory of natural forests. Coffee, in particular, provides a refuge for forest-loving migratory birds in regions of fertile soils where little native vegetation remains. However, this situation is rapidly changing for the worse as coffee is increasingly grown without shade on large agroindustrial holdings. The consumer can choose to purchase organically grown coffee (which is usually shade coffee) and demand that coffee distributors start selling "green" coffee (coffee purchased from growers using shade plantations.)

Positive marketing reinforcement is also being used to decrease the negative impact of other damaging crops. Banana production is an important industry throughout the low-lying areas of Central America and the Caribbean. Many communities are dependent on the jobs, investments, and foreign exchange provided by banana production. However, there is a growing worldwide concern about serious environmental issues related to banana farming, such as the use of large amounts of pesticides and fertilizers, conversion of lowland tropics to monocultures, displacement of wildlife, disposal of organic wastes, sedimentation and chemical contamination of rivers, and physical disruption of stream systems.

Some consumers in North America and Europe are calling for a banana boycott. However, the Rainforest Alliance has developed a plan that will keep local people employed while reforming the banana industry. The "ECO-OK Banana Project" is based on cooperation between Costa Rican banana growers, scientists, environmentalists, government officials, and other interested parties. Together, they have developed a new environmental code of ethics for the banana business. Companies that abide by this code may market their bananas with an ECO-

OK "seal of approval." The Rainforest Alliance hopes that the success of the program in Costa Rica will transform banana production throughout the tropics. ECO-OK bananas have been marketed mainly in Europe but will soon be available in the U.S. For more information on the ECO-OK Banana Project, contact the Rainforest Alliance, 65 Bleeker Street, New York, NY 10012-2420.

We have singled out tropical crops because many people might not realize how faraway areas are affected by the items that fill their shopping carts. Many agricultural and industrial practices in the United States and Canada also must undergo a "green reformation" if they are to be environmentally sound. You can keep yourself informed on issues related to consumerism and conservation through Co-op America, a nonprofit organization with the goal of economic sustainability. Publications such as *Shopping for a Better World* describe ways to align buying and investing habits with such issues as environmental protection and peace. For more information, contact Co-op America, 2100 M Street, NW, Suite 403, Washington, DC 20063.

Mark Your Calendar for International Migratory Bird Day!

In 1993 the Smithsonian Migratory Bird Center in cooperation with the Partners in Flight Program (see chapter 6) declared the second Saturday in May "International Migratory Bird Day" (IMBD). On IMBD, individuals and organizations throughout the Western Hemisphere participate in activities dedicated to the conservation of all migratory birds—songbirds, shorebirds, raptors, and waterfowl. IMBD provides a platform for the numerous conservation efforts already under way through the Partners in Flight Program and inspires others into action. The concern of scientists is taken to the media, the public, and legislators. Grassroots organizations in North America join forces with their counterparts in Latin America and the Caribbean.

As an individual or a member of a conservation organization, you can join the effort. The following is a brief list of ideas for IMBD activities. In deciding what to plan for IMBD, be creative and pay close attention to local, timely issues that affect Neotropical migratory birds in your community.

• Set up educational displays in libraries, shopping malls, and school cafeterias.

• Participate in the North American Migration Count (see chapter 2). Bring a child, neighbor, or local official along.

• Hold a town meeting to discuss the conservation of green space. Dedicate a community sanctuary or expand one that already exists (see chapter 3).

• Ask your state, provincial, or territorial official to declare the second Saturday in May International Migratory Bird Day.

- Plant native trees and shrubs—lots of them.
- Remove introduced plant species such as kudzu (East) and salt cedar (West).
- Hold a fundraiser. Use the money to purchase land needing protection or give funds to (or buy supplies for) a conservation organization in Latin America in need of assistance (see chapter 6).
- Organize a beach cleanup and discourage off-road vehicles on beaches in order to protect nesting shorebirds.
- Establish a training course for hunters, emphasizing the ecological value of migratory raptors and their need for protection.

For further information about IMBD, contact the Smithsonian Migratory Bird Center, c/o The National Zoo, Washington, DC 20008 or the U.S. Fish and Wildlife Service, Office of Migratory Bird Management, 4401 North Fairfax Drive, Room 634, Arlington, VA 22203.

Making a Difference   Jamie K. Reaser

It is not every morning that I get up at 5:00 A.M. OK. Volunteer list, VIP list, press list, staff list, camera, tape, markers, water, sunscreen . . . binoculars. Where are the binoculars?! Huh? Oh, yeah . . . my neck. Ready to go.

At 6:00 A.M. the bird-watchers began to arrive. They came separately, but once parked, flocked together like dull-eyed blackbirds, groggy and not quite ready to leave the roost. I don't think a one noticed the Rufous-sided Towee just a few feet away, scratching in the leaves, demanding, "Drink your tea!" Maybe they were all thinking, "I want my coffee!"

The press came, too. They had had their coffee—several cups. "Where's Roger Tory Peterson?" "You must introduce me to our host, Dr. Lovejoy!" "Will the Clintons really be here this afternoon?" "How many birds will we see?" "What kind?" "Excuse me . . . Neotropical whats?" "Spell that, please."

At 6:30 we flushed all of them into a charter bus and two vans for the short ride to Theodore Roosevelt Island, the living monument just across the Potomac from Georgetown. It was the appropriate place to go. Under Theodore Roosevelt's administration, more than 234 million acres were reserved for conservation. The U.S. Forest Service, five national parks, fifty-one bird refuges, and four game refuges were established.

Sometime during the short trip from the National Zoological Park or soon after their arrival, everyone woke up. Cognizance was rewarded with the melody of late-dawn songsters. It would turn out to be one of the best mornings of 1993 for migration in the District of Columbia. Eighty-some bird-watchers saw and/or heard eighty species: thirty-six Neotropical migrants, twenty or so warblers. Reporters were enthralled by a reminiscent Roger Tory Peterson. The first International Migratory Bird Day couldn't have taken off any better.

The Clinton women were among the zoo's fifteen-thousand-plus visitors later that day. At the Kids' Tent, Chelsea and her classmates educated the public on the wonders of the rainforest, winter home to many Neotropical migrants. Staff from the U.S. Fish and Wildlife Service entertained visitors with a lively introduction to avian biology and research. A Broad-winged Hawk and Gyrfalcon from the Wildlife Center of Virginia made meeting a migrant an up-close-and-personal venture. Children gathered around crayon-strewn tables, drawing migrants for unknown peers in Latin America. They, in turn, received a letter from a Mayan child appealing for help to save migratory birds.

Elsewhere in the park, local experts, videos, displays, and slide shows expounded on various aspects of migratory bird biology, decline, and conservation. Teachers participated in a workshop on birds. Zoo visitors took time out from viewing animals to help create an exhibit for wildlife, the Migratory Bird Garden. Dirt-clad children and muscle-sore adults planted more than 150 native plants donated by nurseries and individuals. Before the day ended, a pair of Gray Catbirds claimed as their own the new fern-edged stream that runs from dripping faucet to frog-rimmed pond.

No, it is not every morning that I get up at 5:00 A.M. For the life of me, I can't figure out why not.

Jamie K. Reaser is a former Bird Conservation Specialist for the Smithsonian Migratory Bird Center. Currently, she is a doctoral candidate in biology at Stanford University, where she is investigating issues relevant to the global decline of amphibian populations.

6

International Partnerships

Listen, friend. I don't want you killing birds. . . . You must love them because many of them come from far away and they are tired, hungry, and thirsty.
—*Abigail Yam Coh, age 11*

Destruction and degradation of habitats throughout the Americas threaten many migrant species. Because of their seasonal movements between breeding grounds in North America and wintering grounds in the tropics, migratory birds constitute an international resource that demands shared responsibility. International approaches to conservation are thus necessary to stem the tide of declining migratory bird populations.

Although Neotropical migrants are but one member of threatened ecosystems, they can serve as ambassadors for a hemisphere-wide conservation agenda that seeks to conserve various forms of wildlife, including nonmigratory birds. Conservation organizations, federal governments, and concerned citizens can use Neotropical migrants as a point of common ground. By working together to conserve migrants, these groups can learn to communicate across political, economic, and cultural boundaries to the benefit of all species.

MAJOR INTERNATIONAL PROGRAMS

Three major, hemisphere-wide initiatives focus on migratory bird conservation. International in scope, these programs have enlisted the support of governmental and nongovernmental organizations, industry, and concerned citizens throughout the Americas. Although individually the programs focus on one group of migrants—landbirds, shorebirds, or waterfowl—taken together they provide a comprehensive program for Neotropical migrants, as well as for much of the wildlife that shares migrant ecosystems.

The North American Waterfowl Management Plan

Initiated in 1986, the North American Waterfowl Management Plan (NAWMP) was the first international initiative to address the issue of wetland conservation for waterfowl by the cooperative action of federal and state, provincial, and territorial agencies, as well as private groups. NAWMP is a $1.5-billion, fifteen-year program to protect 2.4 million hectares (6 million acres) of wetlands and restore waterfowl populations to 62 million breeding individuals. The program focuses on conservation of nine initiative areas, including prairie potholes, Atlantic and Pacific coast marshes, California's Central Valley, southern bottomlands, and Great Lakes region wetlands, as well as the arctic areas where waterfowl breed. NAWMP is primarily governmental, with agreements between the United States, Canada, and Mexico. Most financial support for NAWMP has come from the United States, a smaller amount from Canada, and about 5 percent from the private sector. An implementation board for the program brings together a diverse group of international private organizations. The plan calls for some governmental acquisition of land, but relies heavily upon joint ventures between government and private landowners. One such joint effort is on the U.S. Gulf Coast, where activities range from changing the timing of rice field flooding, modifying logging practices of bottomland hardwoods, and developing educational materials showing farmers and ranchers how wetland management can be integrated into farm operations. For more general information and a listing of the specific joint efforts, write the U.S. Department of Interior, Fish and Wildlife Service, Arlington Square-NAWMP, 1849 C Street, N.S., Washington, DC 20240 or Environment Canada, CWS-NAWMP Implementation Branch, Ottawa, ONT K1A 0H3.

The Western Hemisphere Shorebird Reserve Network

Since its establishment in 1985, the Western Hemisphere Shorebird Reserve Network (WHSRN) (now under the umbrella organization Wetlands for the Americas) has concentrated its efforts on identifying critical habitat for shorebirds and establishing cooperative programs to conserve these sites. In 1992 the mandate was broadened to conserve healthy wetlands throughout the Western Hemisphere. WHSRN has identified approximately twenty-one critical sites in seven countries on which to focus cooperative conservation effort. In addition to on-the-ground conservation, WHSRN has helped develop multilingual educational and training materials. Many of its programs involve the establishment of local networks and programs to work on wetland conservation within the international context. For example, WHSRN has worked with both governmental and nongovernmental groups in Peru to establish a wetlands conservation countrywide program. Wetlands for the Americas publishes a newsletter; write to P.O. Box 1770, Manomet, MA 02345.

The Neotropical Migratory Bird Conservation Initiative—Partners in Flight

The most recent and most ambitious program is the Neotropical Migratory Bird Conservation Initiative, or "Partners in Flight-Aves de las Americas" (PIF) program. Founded in 1991, this program brings together federal and state, provincial, and territorial agencies, industry, nongovernmental organizations, and concerned citizens from countries throughout the Western Hemisphere. The goal of PIF is to develop a program to halt the decline of migratory birds. The program consists of a loose amalgamation of working groups that communicate through international, regional, state, provincial, and territorial or subject-matter-specific working groups. Working groups vary in their approaches. Some have made considerable progress in establishing prioritization systems that focus conservation efforts of the participating groups. PIF members coordinate International Migratory Bird Day activities (see chapter 5). PIF produces a free newsletter that is available through the National Fish and Wildlife Foundation, 1120 Connecticut Avenue, NW, Washington, DC 20036.

BECOME A PARTNER

One of the simplest ways that U.S. and Canadian citizens can influence international conservation is to financially support a North American–based organization that works to promote conservation in Latin America and the Caribbean. A small listing of such organizations can be found in chapter 5. When considering which of many organizations to support, remember that not all conservation groups have the same goals or use money in the same way. Write to the organizations that interest you and ask for information on their programs, specifically those activities your funds would support. Examples include the following:

- Strictly preserve large, intact forest ecosystems.
- Protect critical wetlands and estuaries.
- Manage forest fragments, hedgerows, and shelter belts in agricultural landscapes for birds and human use.
- Develop agroforestry techniques that integrate valuable native trees in agricultural systems.
- Reduce the use of exported pesticides through the use of integrated pest management.

Some migratory birds traverse large distances through Latin America and the Caribbean. These Eastern Kingbirds are feeding on fruit in Mexico en route to Bolivia.

• Establish small, community forest reserves for public education, for the harvest of minor forest products, and for the protection of soils.

• Promote the sustainable, nondestructive use of existing unprotected forest land.

• Obtain scientifically sound information on critical habitats and food resources for migratory birds.

One of the most direct ways U.S. and Canadian citizen activists and grass-roots organizations can participate in international conservation is to establish formal partnerships with conservation groups in Latin America and the Caribbean.

The following section outlines a proven process for establishing international partnerships. The information presented here assumes that the partnership is between two grassroots organizations, because organizations often provide the best forum for amassing resources, such as creativity and funds, and guaranteeing a long-term commitment to a project. By no means, however, do we want to discourage individual citizens from establishing partnerships if they can do so. To assist U.S. and Canadian citizens or groups in locating partner organizations, we have included an international directory (indexed by geographic area and by individual country) that lists approximately forty Latin American– and Caribbean-based organizations involved in protecting migratory birds and critical habitats.

Many birds wander over large areas of the tropics in search of seasonal foods. Red-legged Honeycreepers move to find new crops of flowers.

Be creative when establishing your international linkage. Even a small, focused effort can affect international conservation in a big way. The Smithsonian Migratory Bird Center and Bird Conservation Alliance, for example, have joined forces to initiate the "Migrant Exchange," a pen-pal program between schools in the United States and Latin America and the Caribbean. Through letters and artwork, students exchange information and impressions that focus on the social, cultural, and biological aspects of Neotropical migratory bird conservation. By prompting communication about a shared resource, this exchange program emphasizes the interconnections between the lives of people throughout the Western Hemisphere. Teachers interested in learning how to set up a pen-pal exchange may contact the Smithsonian Migratory Bird Center, c/o The National Zoo, Washington, DC 20008.

Laying the Groundwork for Successful Partnerships

A successful partnership with an organization in another country will depend on broad interest and support for international conservation within your group. Here are some ways to raise interest in and awareness of international conservation issues, particularly those associated with migratory birds:

• Host conservation programs that stress how international issues relate to environmental problems in your community.

• Host educational programs on migratory birds that breed in your region and winter in Latin America and the Caribbean. Use the bird biographies of this book to identify relevant information.

• Publicize in your organization's newsletter the work and needs of conservation groups from other countries and highlight in the local media your partnership efforts (see "Using the Media" in chapter 5).

Plan for Action

Your program should begin with focused and achievable goals. Establish a realistic long-range strategy and short-term objectives. Inventory the resources in your group, for example:

• Who is fluent in Spanish, French, or Portuguese?
• What are your financial resources?
• How much time can individuals commit?
• Has anyone lived or worked in Latin America or the Caribbean?

The resources of your group are likely to be well beyond those of groups in other countries.

Here are some questions to help focus goals and objectives for your international partnership:

• What are your organization's interests and what is its defined mission (education, recreation, conservation, etc.)? How will a partnership with an international organization match your interests and fulfill your mission?

• What resources can your organization offer: information, supplies, technical or volunteer support, fund-raising expertise?

• What specific partner organizations do you hope to work with? See the international directory for assistance.

• What are the needs of this partner organization?

• What resources exist within your organization, and what additional public and private resources are available to meet these needs?

• What additional preparation is needed to enable your group to take effective action?

• Can other organizations and individuals in the community participate in the project, and if so, how?

• What does your organization hope to gain from the partnership?

• How long do you intend to maintain the partnership?

Using the Directory to Identify an International Partner

Each entry in the directory that follows has three parts:

1. The organization's title, address, and the name of a contact person
2. An organizational abstract
3. A brief listing of the organization's needs from international partners

North American contact organizations are indicated for some of the foreign organizations. North American contacts are listed to assist in gathering more information about the programs found in the directory, to offer creative advice and logistical support to ensure the success of partnerships, and to minimize the number of queries made to each foreign organization. The position title of the contact person and an appropriate address are given at the beginning of the listing.

Begin by writing to the North American contact person and discussing the best first step. The contact person will know, or can find out, what the partner group needs—books, field guides, equipment, money—and what opportunities exist for visits and volunteering. The North American contact can also assist you with the logistics of how and where to transport materials, supplies, or equipment.

Next you should develop a tangible project. Use the following efforts as the anchor for a strong link between your organizations.

• Establish a newsletter exchange with your partner group. This newsletter should inform each group of the other's mission, activities, and goals. It should also indicate what each group can offer and needs from the other.

• Exchange information with your partner organization on migratory bird species found in your area. Share lists of species, distribution, frequency, and habitat types.

• Adopt a particular migratory bird species with your partner group. The adopted species should be one that breeds in or near your community and winters near your partner's region. You can then develop monitoring activities and educational materials on this species, including information on its particular habitat needs (on the breeding and wintering grounds and along migration routes).

• Share descriptions of local habitat conservation projects, indicating how they benefit migratory birds.

• Develop a joint fund-raising project, education exchange, or conservation program.

To expand your project, locate other groups in your community with shared interests (such as local teacher associations) and help connect them to your international partner.

Sending Materials and Money to Other Countries
Transporting Equipment
Discuss with your North American contact person the best means for transporting supplies and equipment. A variety of channels exist, and some are better than others under certain circumstances. Your contact will know the best option.

Another means of donating equipment or funds to a variety of organizations and projects is through the Birder's Exchange, a program sponsored by the Manomet Observatory. The Birder's Exchange was formed in 1990 to provide birders in Latin America and the Caribbean with basic field equipment, such as binoculars, spotting scopes, and field guides, most of which are either not available or prohibitively expensive in Latin America and the Caribbean. The Birder's Exchange is eager to work with groups and individuals from across the United States and Canada who are interested in helping efforts in the tropics to preserve birds and their habitats. To make a donation, contact the Birder's Exchange, Manomet Observatory, P.O. Box 1770, Manomet, MA 02345.

Sending Funds
For individuals and organizations that wish to receive a U.S. tax deduction, all checks must be made payable to a U.S. organization. The following list names those U.S. organizations able to act as "pass-throughs" for contributions to organizations listed in the directory. Make checks payable to one of the U.S. organizations affiliated with your project via the North American contact person. This will ensure that your contribution is forwarded to the specified program and that you or your organization benefits from the tax deduction.

INTERNATIONAL DIRECTORY

NORTH AMERICAN CONTACTS

National Audubon Society
  Attn: Southwest Regional
    Representative
  Southwest Regional Office
  2525 Wallingwood Road
  Suite 1505
  Austin, TX 78746

The Nature Conservancy
  Attn: Protected Areas Specialist
  Latin American Science
    Program
  1815 North Lynne Street
  Arlington, VA 22209

Bird Conservation Alliance (for-
    merly International Council
    for Bird Preservation)
  1250 24th Street, NW
  Suite 220
  Washington, DC 20037

Wetlands for the Americas
  c/o Manomet Observatory
  Attn: Executive Director
  P.O. Box 1770
  Manomet, MA 02345

American Museum of Natural
    History
  Attn: Ornithology Department
  Central Park West at 79th Street
  New York, NY 10024

MEXICO AND CENTRAL AMERICA

Mexico

San Miguel de Allende Audubon Society, Apartado No. 559, San Miguel de Allende, GTO, 37700, Mexico. Attn: Robert Haas. U.S. contact organization: National Audubon Society.

Abstract: San Miguel de Allende Audubon Society conducts environmental education programs for the people of San Miguel de Allende and works to protect central Mexico's 150,000-acre Santa Rosa Forest, an important Neotropical migratory bird corridor. The Audubon chapter owns a tree nursery that provides interested residents with trees for reforestation.

Needs: Funds to support expansion of the tree nursery.

PRONATURA Peninsula de Yucatan, Calle 13, No. 203-A, García Gineres, Merida, Yucatan, 97070, Mexico. Attn: Joann Andrews, President. Contact organization: The Nature Conservancy.

Abstract: PRONATURA Peninsula de Yucatan is a private, nonprofit organization established to promote and support protection of critical areas of the Yucatan peninsula. PRONATURA Yucatan has three staff ornithologists who conduct research and monitoring projects throughout the Yucatan peninsula. Two researchers are conducting scientific investigations on birds in the Calakmul Biosphere Reserve. PRONATURA Yucatan is also working with Mexican government officials to manage the reserve at Calakmul. Calakmul shares a border with the Maya Biosphere Reserve in Guatemala and the Rio Bravo in Belize. Together these three protected areas represent over five million acres (two million hectares) of forest habitat vital to Neotropical migratory birds.

Needs: Various types of equipment, including field guides (*Birds of Mexico*, Peterson's Spanish edition), binoculars, spotting scopes, mist nets, Coleman lamps and headlights; funds to purchase a pickup truck and to provide adequate enforcement for resource protection at the Calakmul Reserve, the Maya Biosphere Reserve (managed by the Consejo Nacional de Areas Protegidas [CONAP], Guatemala), and the Rio Bravo (managed by the Programme for Belize, Belize).

Belize

The Belize Zoo and Tropical Education Center, P.O. Box 474, Belize City, Belize, Central America. Attn: Sharon Matola.

Abstract: The Belize Zoo and Tropical Education Center's primary goals are to educate Belizean citizens about their country's natural resources and conservation opportunities. The zoo houses a modest collection of Belizean fauna, and the center conducts on-site and outreach environmental education programs. Research projects include an ongoing study on distribution and ecology of wintering American Redstarts and a study of critical habitats, accompanied by workshops for resource managers.

Needs: Funding to continue these projects; field guides, sleeping mats, two-person tents, electric typewriters, and binoculars (7 × 35 or 8 × 40).

Belize Audubon Society, P.O. Box 1001, Belize City, Belize, Central America. Attn: Janet Gibson. Contact organization: National Audubon Society.

Abstract: The Belize Audubon Society serves as the official managing agency for several of Belize's national parks and reserves, including Half Moon Caye,

Belize's first national park, and Cockscomb Basin, with the highest recorded jaguar population in the region. Member Janet Gibson received the Goldman Environmental Prize in 1990 for her work to protect Hol Chan Marine Reserve, a coral reef island and sanctuary. Plans are currently under way to expand a reserve for howler monkeys created by local landowners, called the Community Baboon Sanctuary.

Needs: Funds for expansion and management of the protected areas.

Guatemala

Guatemala Audubon Society (GAS), 10 Avenida 2-44 Zoná 14, Guatemala City, Guatemala América Central. Attn: Frederico Fohsen. Contact organization: National Audubon Society.

Abstract: The hundred-member Guatemala Audubon Society works to protect the spectacular rainforest and cloud forest ecosystems of the mountains of Guatemala. Guatemala's mountainous zone contains one of the largest examples of wildlife diversity in the Western Hemisphere, including jaguar, Great Anteater, Harpy Eagle, Solitary Eagle, and the Resplendent Quetzal. The chapter recently obtained nearly one thousand hectares of tropical forest in Alta Verpaz, Guatemala. GAS supports a captive breeding program designed to help sustain the population of one of Guatemala's rarest birds, the Horned Guan, and has campaigned successfully against illegal fishing and bird trafficking. It is also negotiating with landowners to establish a voluntary system of wildlife sanctuaries.

Needs: Funds to continue stewardship programs on wildlife reserves near the Sarstoon River and Rio Dulce, and to carry out the group's Jovenes de Audubon, or Junior Audubon, environmental education programs.

Consejo Nacional de Areas Protegidas (CONAP)-Guatemala, 2 Avenida 0-69-Zona 3, Guatemala City, Guatemala, América Central. Contact organization: The Nature Conservancy.

Abstract: CONAP manages the Maya Biosphere Reserve, which is connected to the Rio Bravo Reserve in Belize and the Calakmul Reserve in Mexico. Together they represent over five million acres (two million hectares) of contiguous forest habitat for Neotropical migrants and indigenous species.

Needs: Funds for management of the reserve.

Honduras

Universidad Nacional Autónoma de Honduras, Ciudad Universitaria, Tegucigalpa, Honduras, América Central. Attn: Sherry Thorn, Departamento de Biología CUEG-UNAH. Contact organization: Bird Conservation Alliance.

Abstract: Sherry Thorn, of the Universidad Nacional Autónoma de Honduras and BCA representative for Honduras, has conducted weekend workshops on the birds of Honduras for many years. She and her colleagues average two workshops a month, including instruction and fieldwork on bird migration and conservation. These programs are held in all parts of the country. Several students from the university are currently conducting inventories of resident and migratory birds in protected areas around the country.

Needs: Funds to meet increasing costs for travel and materials—binoculars, bird books, display cabinets, and waterproof notebooks for university courses in ornithology (these are courses with a proven track record of producing well-trained, enthusiastic graduates, some of whom have subsequently embarked on research and conservation studies in Honduras).

Costa Rica

Escuela de Biología, Universidad de Costa Rica, Ciudad Universitaria Rodrigo Facio, San Pedro, San José, Costa Rica, América Central. Attn: Gilberto Barrantes, Profesor de Ornitología.

Abstract: This group of teachers, researchers, and students of the School of Biology, University of Costa Rica, is working to protect areas known to be important for Neotropical migrants.

Needs: Mist nets, three-to-four-person tents, and 10 × 35 binoculars.

Asociación Tsuli Tsuli (Audubon) de Costa Rica, Apartado 4910-1000, San José 1000, Costa Rica, América Central. Attn: Rafael Celis. Contact organization: National Audubon Society.

Abstract: The Tsuli Tsuli de Costa Rica chapter promotes ecologically sustainable development, biodiversity preservation, rational energy use, and population planning. It directs an ecotourism program to educate tourists and tour guides about the positive and negative impacts of tourism. An environmental education and management program at Manuel Antonio National Park provides visitors with information about the area's ecology. Tsuli Tsuli is involved in two reforestation projects and supports the expansion of Tortuguero National Park. The Asociación is starting its own television station, which will produce only environmental programming and will reach all of Costa Rica.

Needs: Funding for bilingual education materials and broadcasting equipment at the television station.

Monteverde Conservation League (Asociación Conservacionista de Monteverde), Apartado 10581-1000, San José, Costa Rica, América Central. Attn: Omar Coto Loria, Executive Director.

Abstract: The Monteverde Conservation League is a private, nonprofit group dedicated to the preservation, conservation, and rehabilitation of tropical ecosystems. The league owns and manages Bosque Eterno de los Niños, the first international children's rainforest, and works with surrounding communities in reforestation, environmental education, and small sustainable development projects to ensure long-term rainforest protection. In addition to buying forestland to protect habitat, efforts include helping farmers protect their patches of remaining forest and connecting patches to form corridors for wildlife (focusing especially on altitudinal migrants, such as the Resplendent Quetzal and Three-wattled Bellbird).

Needs: Funding for teacher workshops on environmental education, equipment and salaries for forest guards, natural history publications for children, and materials and equipment for an education center in the children's rainforest.

Panama

Asociación Nacional para la Conservación de la Naturaleza (ANCON), Apartado 1387, Panama 1, República de Panamá, América Central. Attn: Juan Carlos Navarro, Executive Director. Contact organization: The Nature Conservancy.

Abstract: In 1985 a group of prominent scientists and business and community leaders established ANCON, a nonprofit organization dedicated to the protection and conservation of Panama's natural resources. ANCON, working in partnership with other public and private organizations in Panama and abroad, provides administrative and technical support for national parks in Panama. They currently support management activities at five large nature reserves in Panama: Darien National Park (an over-1.5 million-acre, or 600,000-hectare, rainforest preserve), Soberania National Park (a 50,000-acre, or 20,000-hectare, park), Chagres National Park (which protects the Alajuela Lake watershed and the upper Chagres River), La Amistad International Park (extensive highland park), and the Bastimentos Island National Park (35,000 acres, or 14,000 hectares, of coral reefs, mangroves, and lagoons). In addition, the organization's science division administers a geographic database that lists the characteristics, numbers, protection status, location, and distribution of Panamanian flora and fauna and identifies natural areas that require immediate protection. The database already contains 894 avian species identified through census activities in four of the five parks.

Needs: Funding for research, equipment, administrative personnel, and technical courses in bird banding; binoculars, books, banding equipment, and photographic equipment.

Circulo de Estudios Cientificos Aplicados-Panama (CECA), Apartado 303, Chitre, Herrera, Chitre, Panama, América Central. Attn: Ing. Cecilio Cigarruista.

Abstract: At the Estación Alejandro von Humboldt, CECA has begun a project of banding migratory birds and a program of environmental education directed at young people in primary and secondary schools. It is involved in the conservation of the Reserva Biológica Ciénaga de las Macanas, which has been under pressure from hunters and pesticides.

Needs: Funds to purchase equipment and for management; binoculars (7 × 50), field guides (birds and insects), and 35mm cameras.

Panama Audubon Society, Box 2026, Balboa, the Republic of Panama, Central America. Attn: Gary Vaucher. Contact organization: The National Audubon Society.

Abstract: Established in 1968, the Panama Audubon Society is actively involved in monitoring and protecting birds and bird habitat throughout Panama. The chapter leads regular birding trips, maintains extensive records, and conducts the number-one-rated Christmas Bird Count. In addition, it is sponsoring the Spanish translation of *Birds of Panama* and conducts various conservation projects designed to protect remaining habitat.

Needs: Funds to support its ecotourism and tropical forest conservation projects.

WEST INDIES AND THE CARIBBEAN

Barbados

Caribbean Conservation Association, Savannah Lodge, the Garrison, St. Michael, Barbados. Attn: Calvin Howell, Executive Director; Embert Charles, President.

Abstract: The Caribbean Conservation Association (CCA) is a nongovernmental organization with a track record of twenty-five years of advocacy work in the promotion of environmental management and sustainable development.

The CCA, which retains a regional focus, is dedicated to promoting policies and practices that contribute to the conservation, protection, and wise use of natural and cultural resources. It often establishes partnerships with organizations and groups that share its objective of proactively enhancing the quality of life for present and future generations. CCA's five major program areas are (1) the formulation and promotion of environmental policies and strategies; (2) information collection and dissemination services; (3) promotion of public awareness through environmental education activities; (4) research on, support for, and implementation of natural resource management projects to foster sustainable development; and (5) assistance for cultural patrimony programs.

Needs: Contact the association to determine assistance needs.

Bermuda

Bermuda Audubon Society, P.O. Box 1328 Hamilton HM FX, Bermuda. Attn: Andrew Dobson. Contact organization: National Audubon Society.

Abstract: The Bermuda Audubon Society has three hundred members and owns ten reserves. It exists to protect and restore Bermuda's scarce wetland habitat and is closely involved in the protection of the Cahow (Bermuda Petrel).

Needs: Funds for further land acquisition, improvement of existing reserves, and the Cahow project.

Montserrat

Montserrat National Trust, Parliament Street, Plymouth, Montserrat, West Indies. Attn: Dorothy Greenway, Director.

Abstract: The Montserrat National Trust is the only nongovernmental organization on the island dedicated to the conservation, preservation, and enhancement of Montserrat's natural and historical beauty. The trust manages several areas on the island, including the Foxes Bay Bird Sanctuary, which is situated in one of the two wetlands on the island. This sanctuary is the main nesting area for many resident birds and provides shelter to migratory birds, such as Belted Kingfishers and Yellow-billed Cuckoos.

Needs: Funds and volunteers to develop interpretive trails and educational materials.

Jamaica

Jamaica Conservation and Development Trust (JCDT), P.O. Box 1225, Kingston 8, Jamaica, West Indies. Attn: David Smith, Executive Director. Contact organization: The Nature Conservancy.

Abstract: The Jamaica Conservation and Development Trust works on habitat protection, environmental education, research in sustainable development, and environmental policy. It is collaborating with the government of Jamaica on a national park protection program at the Blue Mountain/John Crow Mountain National Park in eastern Jamaica. The Blue Mountains and John Crow Mountains include 193,290 acres (78,500 hectares), which constitute the largest area of unaltered forest and contain the highest level of biodiversity in Jamaica. Thirty-two species of North American migrants winter in the Blue Mountain region, as do most of Jamaica's endemic species.

Needs: Equipment, including field guides, *Birds of Jamaica,* binoculars, and spotting scopes; funds to provide adequate protection and management for the John Crow and Blue Mountain parks.

Gosse Bird Club, P.O. Box 1002, Kingston 8, Jamaica, West Indies. Attn: Catherine Levy, Secretary.

Abstract: The Gosse Bird Club is the only Jamaican organization dedicated entirely to birds. It has been collecting information and publishing a semiannual journal on Jamaican birds since 1963. Club leaders lobby for conservation of Jamaica's birds and habitats, conduct field trips for members and other interested people, and present education programs, including illustrated talks, to schools and other groups. Major research projects include monitoring bird populations in the Old Harbor Bay area and studying the use of wetlands by resident and migratory birds.

Needs: Funding, banding equipment, binoculars, telescopes, reference books, identification manuals, educational programs on conservation, and training in the use of cannon-type nets.

Society of Caribbean Ornithology, c/o 2 Starlight Avenue, Kingston 6, Jamaica, West Indies. Attn: Catherine Levy, President. Contact organization: Bird Conservation Alliance.

Abstract: The Society of Caribbean Ornithology is a nonprofit organization whose goals are to promote the scientific study and conservation of Caribbean birds and their habitats, to provide a link among island ornithologists and those elsewhere, to provide a written forum for researchers in the region through the publication of a refereed journal entitled *Ornitologia Caribena,* and to provide data or technical aid to conservation groups in the Caribbean. In 1992 the society formed a Neotropical Migrant Bird Working Group to facilitate the exchange of information regarding this category of birds in the Caribbean.

Needs: Funds; the society encourages persons interested in Caribbean avifauna and habitat conservation to become members.

Dominican Republic

Instituto Dominicano de Investigaciónes Biológicas (IDIBIO), Josefa Perdomo No. 7 Gazcue, Santo Domingo, Dominican Republic. Attn: Francisco A. Nunez, Presidente.

Abstract: IDIBIO members are biology professors dedicated to the research and protection of the Dominican Republic's flora and fauna. Their goals include promoting educational activities with other conservation groups, performing research on the protection of critical ecosystems, and preserving the country's forests and wildlife. IDIBIO is currently evaluating bird population trends in the Dominican Republic and other Caribbean islands (Puerto Rico, Cuba, U.S. Virgin Islands, and Trinidad).

Needs: Networking with other interested groups.

Grupo Jaragua, Inc., Leonardo da Vinci #122, Urbanizacion Real, Santo Domingo, Dominican Republic; or Dirección Nacional de Parques, Apartado #2487, Santo Domingo, Dominican Republic. Attn: Sixto Inchaustegui, President. Contact organization: The Nature Conservancy.

Abstract: The Grupo Jaragua was formed in 1986 to work with the national government on the protection and management of Jaragua National Park. This park, located in southwestern Dominican Republic, is the largest protected area in the country. The Grupo Jaragua is made up of scientists who conduct research studies at Jaragua Park, provide public education on park values, and help the area. The Grupo Jaragua is currently conducting research on the 60 percent of the country's bird species that occur in the park.

Needs: Equipment, including field guides, binoculars, and spotting scopes; funds to provide adequate protection and management for the park.

St. Lucia

St. Lucia Naturalists' Society (SLNS), P.O. Box 783, Castries, St. Lucia, West Indies. Attn: Mr. Crispin d'Auvergne, Chairman.

Abstract: SLNS is a nonprofit, nongovernmental organization founded to study, protect, and preserve the flora and fauna of the island. The society has been instrumental in helping to save an endangered species of parrot from extinction. SLNS society also assists the Department of Fisheries in monitoring turtle nesting beaches and has been involved in bird counts conducted by the Department of Forest and Lands.

Needs: Funds that would allow the purchase of equipment such as binoculars, TV/VCR, tents, and backpacks. Funds are also needed to cover the costs of printing the quarterly newsletter and other educational materials.

SOUTH AMERICA

Venezuela

FUDENA, Fundacion para la Defensa de la Naturaleza, Avenida. Ppol. Los Cortijos de Lourdes c/2da. Transv., Edificio Centro, Empresarial Senderos, Piso 6, Officio 611-612, Caracas, Venezuela. Attn: Diego Diaz Martin, Coord. de Proyectos.

Abstract: FUDENA conducts extensive research and environmental education programs with the goal of protecting Venezuela's environment. Previous programs have included the identification of floral and faunal species in Venezuela, promotion of the conservation of endangered animals and plants, and identification of nonprotected but ecologically significant critical areas. FUDENA educates citizens about the rapidly degrading environment, with particular emphasis on sharing responsibility among all citizens for protecting the environment. It also researches the Aves Island ecosystem, which includes resident and migratory birds. This research, which has been ongoing for eleven years, has generated several publications. Studies are being conducted on diurnal birds of prey in the Llanos of Venezuela, with preliminary work done on population densities, reproductive habits and behavior, and raptor communities.

Needs: Funding, books, binoculars, Zodiac-style rubber boats, environmental education equipment, access to courses on modern methodology of field studies, mist nets, tents, cages, and trapping equipment.

Sociedad Conservacionista Audubon de Venezuela (SCAV), Apartado 80450, Caracas, 1080-A, Venezuela. Attn: Miguel Lentino or Alejandro Luy. Contact organization: National Audubon Society.

Abstract: The Venezuela Audubon Society, a nonprofit, independent Audubon chapter, works to conserve and protect Venezuela's diverse natural resources. It has helped protect Venezuela's estuaries from harmful mining, agricultural, and industrial activities. SCAV has an active excursion and travel program for both members and foreign visitors to the country. It operates a bookshop, publishes a Spanish newsletter, and holds monthly conferences on nature and conservation topics. It also publishes *Birding in Venezuela,* a booklet designed to help North American and European visitors find the best observation spots in the country. SCAV is conducting migratory and resident bird banding projects and intensive rainforest and coastal wetlands inventories.

Needs: Funding for expansion of the projects, mist nets, scales, banding pliers, rulers, spotting scopes, and binoculars.

The Phelps Ornithological Collection, Apartado 2009, Caracas 1010-A, Venezuela. Attn: Kathleen Phelps, President; Miguel Lentino, Curator. Contact Organization: American Museum of Natural History.

Abstract: The Phelps Collection, founded in 1938, is the first and most complete ornithological collection in Venezuela and one of the best in Latin America. Work is directed toward conducting inventories and establishing the distribution and systematics of Neotropical birds.

Needs: Publications on the topics related to its work.

BIOMA, La Fundación Venezolana para la Conservación de la Diversidad Biologia-Venezuela. Edificio Camara de Comercio de Caracas, Piso 4, Avenida Este 2, Los Caobos. Apartado 1968, Caracas 1010-A, Venezuela.

Abstract: BIOMA seeks to protect the remaining natural ecosystems of the Paraguana Peninsula in the northwestern section of Venezuela, which has been heavily eroded by development activities. In collaboration with the Venezuelan government, it has created three biological reserves of approximately two thousand hectares in size. The BIOMA Reserve program created and manages a biological reserve (about 5,000 hectares, or 12,500 acres) in high tropical montane habitat. The group is monitoring the impact of extensive cattle ranching on endangered species, conducting agricultural production courses, and building a visitor's center and manager's office.

Needs: Binoculars, books (field guides and library reference books), satellite images of the reserve, and project and building funds.

Colombia

Fundación Pro-Sierra Nevada de Santa Marta, Calle 74 No. 2-86, Apartado Aero 5000, Bogota, Colombia. Attn: Juan Mayr, Executive Director. Contact organization: The Nature Conservancy.

Abstract: The Fundación Pro-Sierra Nevada de Santa Marta is a nonprofit, nongovernmental organization devoted to research, conservation, protection, and sustainable development of the ecological and cultural heritage of the Sierra Nevada de Santa Marta. This work is conducted in close collaboration with regional and national government agencies, local community groups, and other conservation organizations. The Sierra Nevada de Santa Marta is the highest coastal mountain in the world and supports a rich ecological mosaic that includes numerous endemic species. The mountain region is also an important site for Neotropical migrants that winter in the Andes. Research is being conducted in the park on birds, including migrant and endemic species. The foundation plans to install scientific research centers in the Sierra Nevada.

Needs: Equipment, including field guides, binoculars, and spotting scopes; funds are also needed to provide adequate protection and management for the park.

Bogota Ornithology Group, AA 250842, Bogota, Colombia. Attn: Loreta Rosselli. Contact organization: Bird Conservation Alliance.

Abstract: This new, energetic group links a flourishing network of conservation organizations and universities in Bogota. It organizes surveys of important habitats close to the city, including the wetlands of the Sabana de Bogota and forest tracts in the eastern Andes that provide important wintering sites for migrants. Members are developing a variety of educational projects, including a children's bird-watching course, for which funds are urgently needed. They also hope to design and build attractive displays about birds and conservation for the Natural History Museum at the National University, produce a popular conservation-oriented guide entitled *The Birds of Bogota and Surrounding Areas,* and publish a newsletter on conservation activities in Bogota.

Needs: Funding and binoculars.

Fundación Herencia Verde, A.A 32802, Cali, Colombia. Contact organization: Bird Conservation Alliance.

Abstract: La Fundación Herencia Verde exists to study and conserve the high degree of biological diversity that characterizes Colombia. It seeks to achieve its objectives by promoting sustainable development techniques, educating the public, and acquiring and managing natural reserves. The organization offers support to several research projects, including a study of the role fruit-eating birds play in forest regeneration.

Needs: Funds for the support and expansion of projects.

Fundación Natura, Avenida 13, No. 87-43, A.A. 55402, Bogota, Colombia. Attn: Elsa Escobar, Assistant Director. Contact organization: The Nature Conservancy.

Abstract: Fundación Natura promotes the conservation and protection of Colombian natural resources through the establishment and management of reserves, the study and monitoring of the biodiversity that lies within these reserves, public education, and the development of techniques for sustainable use of natural resources. It emphasizes the role of local communities in all conservation strategies.

Needs: Funds for the hiring and training of park rangers, the promotion of environmental education campaigns, and the expansion of management and sustainable development projects.

Ecuador

Fundación Maquipucuna, P.O. Box 17-12-167, Quito, Ecuador. Attn: Rodrigo Ontaneda.

Abstract: Fundacion Maquipucuna is a nonprofit organization founded in 1988 to promote sustainable development while maintaining biological diversity. It focuses on the management and conservation of the Maquipucuna Reserve and the protection of the cloud forest of the Rio Guayllabamba. Over 210 avian species have been identified so far in the Maquipucuna Reserve. The group has initiated a project to assist in the management of a 41,000-acre (16,600-hectare) protected forest, and a 7,000-acre (2,800-hectare) private biosphere reserve. Additionally, it has been working in the buffer zone of the 300,000-acre (122,000-hectare) Podocarpus National Park in southeastern Ecuador. The organization offers environmental education programs in forestry and sustainable management and conducts scientific research on the preservation of biodiversity.

Needs: Funding for taxonomic and ecological research; environmental education projects; specialized books on ornithology, tropical biology, and forest management; field guides, binoculars and other basic avian research equipment, camping equipment, and a laser printer.

Fundacion Natura, Casilla #253, Quito, Ecuador. Attn: Ruth Elena Ruiz. Contact organization: The Nature Conservancy.

Abstract: The Fundacion Natura is a nonprofit, nongovernmental organization created in 1978 to promote the conservation of the natural environment in Ecuador. The organization has three regional chapters in Quito, Guayaquil, and Azogues. It is working on environmental education and community awareness, scientific research in biodiversity and development, and land protection.

Together with the government of Ecuador, Natura is helping to protect eight natural reserves. One of these reserves, Podocarpus National Park, is the only protected area in the southern Andean region of Ecuador. It is extremely diverse biologically and is a critical area for the Neotropical migrants that overwinter in the Andes. Scientists from around the world have conducted studies on the diverse plant and bird life in the park. International pressure is needed to help protect this important habitat from the threat of gold mining, colonization, deforestation, and trafficking in wild species.

Needs: Field guides, binoculars, and spotting scopes; funds to provide adequate protection and management for the park.

Consejo Ecuatoriano para la Conservación y Investigación des Aves (CECIA), Casilla 9068 S.7 Quito, Ecuador. Attn: Nancy Hilgert de Benauides. Contact organization: Bird Conservation Alliance.

Abstract: CECIA is the only ornithological group in Ecuador. It conducts a wide range of educational activities, and has published the *Action Guide for Bird Conservation* in mainland Ecuador. Workshops designed for children, teenagers, and adults explain the importance of birds as indicators of environmental health, their role in the ecosystem, and the importance of conservation.

Needs: Funds to maintain and enhance the educational program.

Tierra Viva, Gran Colombia 5-20, Casilla 01.05.1891, Cuenca, Ecuador. Attn: Franklin Abad.

Abstract: Tierra Viva is a nonprofit, nongovernmental organization that works to preserve the native forests of Ecuador through the promotion of proper agroforestry methods and environmental education.

Needs: Funds are needed for the expansion of projects.

Peru

Asociación Peruana para la Conservación de la Naturaleza (APECO), Parque José de Acoste. 187-Lima 17-Peru.

Abstract: APECO conducts research on the distribution and conservation of migratory birds in the Paracas National Reserve of Peru. Researchers are analyzing the impacts of tourism and recreational use on the reserve, and the effects of marine contamination on the survival of bird populations. APECO is also developing educational programs directed at local communities.

Needs: Funding and equipment such as mist nets, bird bands, binoculars, and field guides are needed for the continued study of migratory birds and for educational programs.

Argentina

Humedales para las Americas (Wetlands for the Americas), Monroe 2142, 1428 Capital Federal, Argentina. Attn: Pablo Canevari, South American Director. Contact organization: Wetlands for the Americas.

Abstract: Wetlands for the Americas is an international organization devoted to the conservation and sustainable use of wetlands in the Americas. One important program of this organization is the Western Hemisphere Shorebird Reserve Network (WHSRN). WHSRN was formed in 1985 to address the factors behind the decline of many species of shorebirds. WHSRN, a voluntary collaboration of private and government organizations, gives international recognition to critical shorebird habitats and promotes their cooperative management and protection. Currently, the network consists of twenty-two sites from Alaska to Tierra del Fuego. Wetlands for the Americas has an extensive network of contacts across Latin America and can put prospective donors in direct contact with local groups.

Needs: Field equipment and funds for education and research projects.

Asociacion Ornitologica del Plata, 25 de Mayo 749, 2 Piso, (1002) Buenos Aires, Argentina. Attn: Diego Gallegos Luque, Director. Contact organization: Bird Conservation Alliance.

Abstract: Founded in 1916, the Asociacion Ornitologica del Plata (AOP) was the first environmental nongovernmental organization in Argentina. Its focus is the study and protection of the birds of Argentina and neighboring countries. Among its many educational activities, the association offers an introductory bird-watching course for the general public and, in collaboration with BCA Argentina and the Asociación Natura, a two-year course for naturalists. AOP manages a library, publishes two journals, and in 1991 created its first private reserve. AOP is also involved in the international effort to protect the Eskimo Curlew.

Needs: Funds to purchase a computer; assistance in fund-raising.

Fundación Vida Silvestre Argentina, Defensa 245/51-P6, Buenos Aires, 1065 Argentina. Attn: Christian Ostrosky, Conservation Assistant.

Abstract: Fundación Vida Silvestre Argentina (FVSA) seeks to promote the conservation and wise use of natural resources through public education; the establishment, management, and protection of reserves; and scientific study.

Needs: Funds for expansion of projects.

Chile

Comite Nacional Pro Defensa de la Fauna y Flora, Casilla 3675, Santiago, Chile. Attn: Yerko Vilina. Contact organization: Smithsonian Migratory Bird Center.

Abstract: Comite Nacional Pro Defensa de la Fauna y Flora (CODEFF) promotes the conservation and wise use of Chile's natural resources through scientific study, environmental education, and activism. With regard to migratory birds, CODEFF has initiated conservation projects for the protection of migratory shorebirds and is currently seeking funding for the study of austral migrants in the temperate forests of southern and central Chile.

Needs: Funds for the continuation and expansion of its projects and for purchasing land for conservation; field equipment, including telescopes and binoculars.

Brazil

Funatura, SCLN 107, ED. Gemini Center II, Bloco "B", Salas 201/17, CEP 70743, Brasilia-DF. Attn: Maria Tereza Jorge Padua, Executive Superintendent. Contact organization: Smithsonian Migratory Bird Center.

Abstract: Funatura seeks to preserve Brazil's natural flora and fauna through the establishment of sanctuaries. To date, the organization has selected twenty-two sites for the creation of sanctuaries, eleven of which have been established.

Needs: Funds for the expansion and management of sanctuaries, travel and materials, and environmental education programs.

Fundacao Brasileira para a Conservacao da Natureza, Rue Miranda Valverde, 103 Botafogo, CEP 22281, Rio de Janeiro RJ, Brasil. Attn: Salvatore Siciliano. Contact organization: The Nature Conservancy.

Abstract: The Brazilian Foundation for Nature Conservation (FBCN) operates throughout Brazil to promote the preservation of biodiversity. The FBCN focuses its attention on scientific research applied to conservation, cultural patrimony, the management and conservation of natural areas and endangered species, and environmental education. It has assembled one of Brazil's most complete libraries on conservation issues. To realize and coordinate its projects, FBCN maintains exchanges with universities, nongovernmental organization, and public and private institutions.

Needs: Office equipment, video and photographic equipment; assistance in fund-raising.

Bolivia

Reserva de la Biosfera, Estación Biológica del Beni, La Paz, Av. 16 de Julio, No. 1732, P.O. Box 5828, La Paz, Bolivia. Attn: Carmen Miranda, Executive Director.

Abstract: The Beni Biological Station constitutes one of the most important efforts in the conservation and management of natural resources in Bolivia. The fundamental objective of the Beni Reserve is to promote the conservation of biotic resources while balancing the needs of the local human population. To achieve this goal, it develops programs in the areas of management and protection of the biota, basic and applied research, environmental education, and sustainable development. The reserve is characterized by a high diversity of bird fauna. Among the more than 470 species of birds found in the area are many of great importance for conservation.

Needs: Funds for research projects and laboratory equipment.

Centro de Datos Para la Conservación (CDC-Bolivia), Cota Cota, Calle 26 y Av. Munoz Reyes s/n, La Paz, Bolivia. Attn: Maria de Marconi, Executive Director. Contact organization: The Nature Conservancy.

Abstract: As part of the Nature Conservancy's network of databases in Latin America and the Caribbean, CDC-Bolivia maintains a computerized database on the natural resources of Bolivia, including the migratory and resident bird species. An important role of the CDC is to identify areas of critical conservation value.

Needs: Funds to create an illustrated guide to the migratory birds of Bolivia.

Making a Difference   Sam Droege, Russell Greenberg

The Neotropical migrant conservation program Partners in Flight was created in 1991 in response to reports of widespread declines in the populations of Neotropical migrants and troubling indications of extensive and continuing loss of their habitat on wintering and breeding grounds. The program's stated goals are to (1) determine the status and causes of population changes in migratory birds and (2) maintain stable populations and enhance and restore declining populations.

While these goals are admirable, they are also vague. With over two hundred species of birds under consideration in this conservation program and limited resources, the need for a focused set of achievable conservation priorities is clear. Up to now the highest priority has been given to inventories, establishment of monitoring programs, and research, rather than direct conservation action.

Although there is a need for solid information on the status and life history of Neotropical migrants, conservation action should not wait for the completion of many of these newly established long-term projects. We need to develop and start working toward active conservation goals now. Developing conservation priorities is straightforward. For most species, we have basic information about where they breed, where they winter, what habitats they use, their migratory paths, what they eat, where they forage, and, in most cases, what the trend in population numbers has been over the past twenty-five years. That collection of natural history information permits us to identify the species in greatest need of conservation in each region. In almost every case, the solution to the troubles facing these birds lies in restoring and reconditioning the habitat they have lost. Therefore, we already know that saving Neotropical migrants requires developing reasonable conservation goals for key habitats.

Neotropical migratory landbirds generally do not concentrate at specific sites at critical junctures in their migratory travels, as do shorebirds. Thus, there is seldom a discrete set of sites to focus on for conservation efforts. Preservation efforts must cover large geographic regions and be extensive in their approach.

The following are some ideas for regionally focused conservation efforts. Our suggestions are not based on rigorous analysis but on the following considerations: the habitat supports a high diversity of Neotropical migratory birds at some critical juncture in their life history; many of these species are found primarily in the particular bioregion; and the habitat is currently threatened by human-caused disturbance. In most cases, what we suggest is obvious and is already the focus of many regional efforts. What we are advocating is the formalization of a few key goals and the formation of a coalition of groups interested in these key regional issues.

The Arid West—riparian woodlands. In the arid portions of the western United States, the greatest diversity of Neotropical migrants is often found in the ribbons of vegetation along watercourses. The proportional loss of this habitat in the last two hundred years is perhaps the greatest of any in the region; it has suffered from flood control, grazing, agricultural clearing, and the introduction of exotic plants. Considerable research has been completed on the riparian avifauna. The remaining habitat is limited and often under governmental control. Conservation of riparian areas would concentrate on limiting grazing, restoring riparian woodlands in those areas where the potential still exists, and augmenting and connecting patches of existing riparian cover.

The Montane West. Montane meadow and thickets are very productive habitats. The large population of insects and the abundance of flowers and sap wells maintained by sapsuckers support the young of many species of birds as they prepare for migration. This includes species that breed in local upland habitats, as well as those that breed in the lowlands and move upmountain to take advantage of this productivity. Hummingbirds apparently time their migration to hit the peak of flowering in mountain meadows in the summer. These habitats are fragile and can be damaged by a number of human activities, including the grazing of livestock, off-road vehicle use, and even too much recreational hiking.

The Boreal North—flood plain habitats and mature spruce-fir woods. The boreal forest represents the greatest tract of temperate forest. Because of its size, it supports large numbers of Neotropical migrants. Many of the richest stands, particularly in the eastern lakes region, are already being exploited for timber, paper, and other resources. Improved management of these forests is critical for the high diversity of migrants, particularly warblers, that depend on them. The northern and western regions still contain large areas of old-growth forest. The forests of the floodplain support the highest diversity and density of migratory landbirds and waterbirds. Unfortunately, the most accessible tracts to logging often are found along the major rivers. In addition, these areas are vulnerable to hydroelectric development. The predictable annual flooding may be essential in replenishing nutrients in these otherwise unproductive regions.

Midwest—prairie grasslands. The midwestern prairies support a unique group of birds currently showing the greatest and most consistent declines of any group of Neotropical migrants. In addition to the obvious effects of turning most of the northern prairies into agricultural lands, many of the southern grasslands in the Chihuahua and Sonoran regions have been converted to thorn shrub associations, largely because of grazing. The Conservation Reserve Program, tall grass preserves, extensions and management of the National Grassland Systems, and incentives for change in hayfield and range management are just some of the many means of stabilizing and restoring native grasslands.

Northeast—large forest tracts. The forests of eastern North America support the highest numbers and diversity of tropical landbird migrants. Unlike the West, the vast majority of the forested land is under private ownership, held primarily in small lots. This makes the great eastern forests particularly susceptible to suburbanization and subdivision for second homes.

In many areas, forests are now growing on what was farmland thirty to fifty years ago; however, an increasing number of states are experiencing net forest loss due to development. While forest is still abundant in most states, it is rapidly degenerating in quality for many migratory species. Neotropical migratory bird conservation provides additional support for regional action on open-space policy and zoning issues.

Southeast—bottomland hardwoods. Agricultural conversion, flood control, and drainage continue to threaten the last remaining bottomland systems. With their hardwood forests and natural disturbance regimes, such as canebrake, these systems support such declining species as Swallow-tailed Kites and Cerulean and Swainson's warblers and supported the (probably) extinct Bachman's Warbler. Conservation activities such as legislative support for Swampbuster Initiatives, restoration of cleared agricultural fields, and initiation of progressive conservation zoning regulations will directly lead to increase in bottomland habitat.

Latin America. The conservation of migratory birds is facing an identity crisis. Do migrants from the temperate zone require different conservation strategies than those normally developed for overall biodiversity? We suggest that migratory birds can act as a flagship for managing agricultural lands in the tropics for biodiversity. Such management includes the promotion of small-scale forest conservation, use of shade crops such as coffee and cacao, and protection of riparian buffer zones.

Caribbean—mangrove swamps. Mangrove swamps support high densities of migratory birds as well as act as nurseries for island fisheries. Unfortunately, mangrove swamps are restricted in their distribution and highly threatened by coastal development and pollution.

We believe that the selection of a small set of specific conservation projects will catalyze future actions. Once discrete habitat conservation goals are defined, further actions can be focused on developing and implementing the political strategy for achieving them. Each participating organization can contribute to the effort to protect critical habitat according to its strengths. The concerned bird-watching public can become involved in the local and regional land-use decision-making process.

Successes and failures of the program can be easily judged in terms of the amount of land protected or placed under acceptable resource management regimes. Each participating organization and agency can be evaluated in terms of discrete and measurable criteria. Furthermore, the definition of discrete regional goals will lead to more focused research and monitoring programs.

Sam Droege is a biologist with the National Biological Service. Russell Greenberg is Director of the Smithsonian Migratory Bird Center.

Species Biographies

In this section we present brief biographies to acquaint you with 157 species of Neotropical migratory birds. Each biography includes a written species account and a map with breeding and wintering ranges. The species account briefly describes where and in what habitat each species breeds and spends the winter, along with an overview of diet and conservation status. Nonbreeding distributions are particularly difficult to define, since birds can be found in many areas outside their normal winter ranges during periods of migration. With this in mind, we have based winter ranges where birds are regularly present between December and March, based on our review of the regional literature. Finally, for many species we include fun facts that highlight some unusual or unique feature of their natural history.

The species recognized in the list are based on the Sixth Checklist of North American Birds of the American Ornithologists' Union and its supplements. The higher taxa are based on Sibley and Monroe (1990). Taxonomic classifications and sequence of families and species are according to Sibley and Monroe (1990) and the A.O.U. Checklist, 39th Supplement (1993). The exact composition of the list of Neotropical migrants depends upon the definition used, so we will provide ours here. We include birds that have populations that breed primarily north and winter primarily south of the Tropic of Cancer. By applying this definition we have excluded some species that might otherwise be considered Neotropical migrants (e.g., Kirtland's Warbler winters in the Bahamas, primarily north of the Tropic of Cancer). Thus, we hope to emphasize the truly tropical species.

The key at the top of each account explains the abbreviations used for the headings of the species accounts.

Biogeographic Regions

Our description of the distribution of Neotropical migratory species differs from other traditional treatments in the use of biogeographic regions instead of countries, states, and other politically defined areas; however, for strictly coastal species, we use political boundaries to describe ranges. We hope this provides a more biologically meaningful picture of the distribution of each species. The system we used is modified from Udvardy (1975). A biogeographic region is an area with shared history and climate; it is subjectively defined by biogeographers based on the distribution of numerous unrelated taxa. Since many of these regions will be unfamiliar to most readers, we provide a brief synopsis here.

Arctic Tundra. A fairly flat, treeless region with short summers and long winters. Nearly all the bird species are shorebirds and waterbirds that migrate to the south.

Taiga. A heavily forested region with conifers such as spruce, fir, and pine dominating the landscape. Bogs, marshes, and aspen and birch groves are scattered throughout. A few shorebirds nest in the wetlands. Many small forest birds are Neotropical migrants. Resident birds are the same as or closely related to Siberian and Scandinavian species.

Northeastern Forests. A transition from taiga to the more subtropical broadleaf forests in the southern United States. Conifers and northern hardwoods dominate. Many of the migratory, forest birds are also found in the southern taiga and follow their preferred northern, coniferous tree species south along the higher elevations of the Appalachian Mountains. This area has very warm summers and freezing winters. Deforestation through logging, agriculture, and suburban sprawl has greatly affected the migratory bird populations, although in some areas reforestation has increased available habitat from the previous century.

Southeastern Forests. A flat region with diverse mixed hardwood forests, extensive pinewoods, and cypress swamps and other wetlands. With hot, humid summers, the hardwood forests have a subtropical feel. Many migratory forest birds are primarily found in these forests, but some distributions extend slightly northward into the latter region. Much of the pine forests are in second growth following decades of logging, and in some areas hardwood forests are heavily fragmented because of deforestation for agriculture.

Great Plains. This flat, heavily cultivated region was once a continuous grassland. The western edge is (or was) a very arid shortgrass prairie, while the eastern portion is dotted with wetlands and is (or was) typically longgrass prairie. Winters are long and very cold, with summers hot and humid. The riparian areas are the most diverse in birds, but native grasslands are highly threatened and extremely important, as several grassland species are unique to the region.

Rocky Mountains. A region of high, conifer-clad mountains and sagebrush and grassland valleys. Winters are long and cold, with much snow, but summers are warm and bring daily rainstorms. Although many birds of the forests are resident, most are migratory along with birds of the wetlands and valleys. Many of the bird species are also found in bioregions to the north and west.

Great Basin. A cold desert, with scrubland and saline lakes in the valleys, pinyon-juniper in mid-elevations in the mountains, and pine and fir in the highest elevations. Aspen groves are found in wet areas in the mountains, and riparian forests are rare. Summers are hot and winters are cold, often with snow. Except for some of the montane species, most of the birds are migratory.

Pacific Northwestern Forests. This is a wet, cool, and mountainous region that has a relatively mild winter because of the maritime effect of the Pacific Ocean. It is dominated by coniferous forests. Coastal mountains have a tremendous amount of rainfall, which decreases toward the interior. Many of the forest birds are migratory, and are also found in nearby regions. The coastal wetlands are important feeding and staging areas for migrating shorebirds.

Sierra-Cascades. These tall mountain chains are dominated by coniferous forests. Winters are harsh and snow cover is usually high; summers are warm with regular rainfall. Many of the bird species found in these mountains are also found in nearby mountainous regions.

California. A mild climate throughout the year typifies this region. An area with a mosaic of oak savannas, chaparral (arid scrub), and deciduous and mixed coniferous and broadleaved forests, the region is mountainous, with broad valleys. Rain falls mostly in the cooler winter months, and the summers can be hot and dry. Many of the widespread western migratory birds breed in this region.

Baja California and Sonora. Primarily a hot, desert region with a few forest birds in the mountains, this area is important for some short-distance migratory birds, and is equally important as a breeding and wintering range for long-distance migrators.

West Mexican Lowlands. Much of the region consists of dry, deciduous forest important to many western migrants, but pockets of tropical, moist forest and coastal mangroves enrich the diversity by providing habitat for eastern migratory species. The coastal lagoons are also important as shorebird wintering areas.

Mexican Plateau and Cordillera. A complex region with arid, interior valleys and plateaus, and mountain ranges with forests that vary from dry, pine-oak woodland to lush, humid, cloud forests. In the north, winters are cool and summers hot. Many western migratory birds winter in this region.

Campechean Lowlands. A humid, warm, lowland region that has been greatly deforested. Much of the region has been converted for agriculture and cattle, although a few large patches of tropical rainforest remain. Savanna habitats are found locally. A number of eastern migratory birds winter in this region, although its current importance for these species is probably reduced by deforestation.

Mayan Highlands. A humid, mountainous region with broadleaved, evergreen cloud forests and pine-oak woodland in the drier areas. Numerous, distinct mountain ranges create a complex system of local weather patterns. Several arid valleys lie within the rain shadows of these mountains. An important area for migratory songbirds, these highlands harbor large populations for many western and eastern species.

Yucatan. A flat, low, limestone region with an annual average rainfall of from sixteen inches in the low, thorny, deciduous forests in the northwest to forty-two inches in the tall, moist, deciduous forests in the southeast. Rainfall occurs mostly between May and November. Much of the land had been cleared in the northern and western sections for cattle pastures or cornfields, and large areas of low, second-growth scrub have grown in abandoned fields. Lakes and rivers are almost nonexistent because of the porous nature of the limestone bedrock. Mangrove swamps and palmetto savannas are found along the coasts. This region is important for several migratory species.

Central American Caribbean Lowlands. A flat, humid region with an annual rainfall of up to two hundred inches, this area supports a luxuriant rainforest. The dry season, from December to April, is most pronounced in the West, where the forests are partly deciduous. Several eastern forest migrants are found primarily in this region.

Central American Pacific Lowlands. This region is the transitional zone from the dry, deciduous, thorn forest of western Mexican lowlands to the wet, evergreen, rainforest of the tropical Pacific lowlands. The dry season varies but at one site in Costa Rica it averages five months, from December to May, with an annual rainfall of seventy inches and a mean annual temperature of 82 degrees Fahrenheit. A number of eastern migratory birds are found in this region.

Chiriqui Highlands. A small, mountainous region dominated by a chain of large volcanoes that reach up to sixteen thousand feet in elevation. The climate varies drastically between sites because of the influences of the Caribbean weather system on the northern mountain chain and the Pacific weather system on the southern mountains. The vegetation is mostly humid, with cloud forests dominated by epiphyte-laden oaks and devoid of conifers. Alpine shrubland is found above tree line. Several western migrants reach their southern boundary here.

Caribbean Islands. An extremely complex system of islands and habitats. Rainfall patterns are complicated by the rainshadow effects of island topography, so that arid deserts and tropical rainforests can exist on the same island. The amount of deforestation varies among the islands, and severe hurricanes can

Regularly Wintering Migratory Bird Species			
Biogeographic Region	*Number of Migratory Landbirds*	*Number of Migratory Shorebirds*	*Number of Countries*
Baja California and Sonora	54	26	1
Mexican Plateau and Cordillera	73	0	1
West Mexican Lowlands	68	24	1
Campechean	61	17	3
Mayan Highlands	61	0	6
Yucatan	59	17	3
Central American Pacific Lowlands	28	21	6
Chiriqui Highlands	38	0	2
Caribbean Islands	36	15	
Tropical Pacific Rainforest	44	14	6
Pacific Coast Desert	5	19	3
Valdivian Rainforest	0	0	1
Caribbean Llanos and Dry Forest	14	6	2
Guianan Shield	2	4	4
Amazon Rainforest	19	5	9
Northern Andean Highlands	20	1	4
Altiplano and Puna Zones of High Andes	2	6	3
Southern Andean Highlands	5	0	3
Cerrado and Caatinga	11	11	3
Parana	0	7	3
Atlantic Rainforest	1	12	1
Chaco and Pampas	13	22	5
Patagonia	0	8	2

add greatly to the effects of logging. A number of migratory bird species are primarily found in this region.

Tropical Pacific Rainforests. With 118 to 524 inches of rain annually, this region boasts a luxuriant tropical forest. There is almost no seasonality, as rain falls nearly every afternoon (250–300 days per year). A few migratory bird species extend their ranges south to include this region.

Regularly Wintering Migratory Bird Species

Country	Number of Migratory Landbirds	Number of Migratory Shorebirds	Number of Migratory Raptors	Biogeographic Regions
Mexico	107	29	10	6
Guatemala	64	18	9	3
El Salvador	45	18	8	2
Belize	40	18	7	3
Honduras	57	17	8	3
Nicaragua	49	17	8	3
Costa Rica	46	23	8	3
Panama	40	18	7	2
Colombia	29	18	4	4
Ecuador	20	23	4	4
Peru	14	23	3	5
Chile	2	12	2	3
Venezuela	23	15	4	4
Guyana	6	21	2	2
Surinam	6	21	2	2
French Guiana	10	21	2	2
Brazil	16	22	4	7
Bolivia	10	18	4	5
Paraguay	9	17	4	3
Uruguay	3	21	4	1
Argentina	9	23	5	4

Pacific Coast Desert. One of the most arid regions in the world, this desert in places has not recorded rainfall in a century. The central area is the driest, and the vegetation grades from nonexistent to a dry, thorny, deciduous woodland in the north and a "Mediterranean" chaparral or shrubland in the south. There are very few landbirds, but several areas on the coast harbor large numbers of migratory shorebirds.

Valdivian Rainforest. One of very few temperate-zone rainforests in the world, this region receives up to 118 inches of rainfall annually. Evergreen, Southern Hemisphere conifers, and southern beech dominate the vegetation. In the rich, humid conditions, moss, lichen, and mistletoe cover the trees, and bamboo is mixed with extensive shrubs. None of the migratory land-bird species winter in this region.

Caribbean Llanos and Dry Forest. An extensive, flat, grassland-savanna that is usually flooded during the monsoon season, from May to November, the llanos contains a mosaic of vegetation types, from grassland to evergreen forests along rivers and streams. Annual rainfall averages from 63 inches near the coast to 118 inches at the base of the Andes. The dry forest is a small area of thorny, deciduous scrubland and cactus desert. This region's rainfall averages from 11.5 inches a year near the coast to 33.5 inches farther inland. The "wet" season is from mid-May to October. Temperatures average 83 to 87 degrees Fahrenheit, with little variation throughout the year. Some migratory species may use this region only temporarily before moving farther south. A number of others find this to be their southern boundary to their wintering range.

Amazon Rainforest. A large, complex region that is mostly broadleaved, evergreen forests, rivers, and oxbow lakes. Many of the forests are seasonally flooded. There are a few isolated savannas. There is little seasonal variation in the high temperatures, although rainfall patterns are highly seasonal but vary geographically. The western section, near the base of the Andes, has the highest biological diversity in the world. Most of the migratory birds that winter in this region have their highest densities along this western section.

Northern Andean Highlands. One of the most populated regions, this area has been heavily impacted by cattle pastures, coffee growing, and other agriculture. Deforestation in central valleys and some middle elevation zones has been rampant. In some areas large forested tracts persist as broadleaved evergreen cloud forests. Some inland valleys are arid, scrubby deserts, and at the upper elevations, above the tree line, grasslands and alpine scrublands predominate. Most migratory birds that winter in this region are found at lower to middle elevations.

Altiplano and Puna Zones of High Andes. A cold, arid region that is above the tree line. Grasslands, desert scrub, freshwater marshes and lakes, and large, saline lakes predominate. Migratory shorebirds are found in the wetland areas, especially during migration.

Southern Andean Highlands. A temperate region that has much less vegetation and animal diversity than its tropical counterpart, the Northern Andean Highlands. This region is much colder, with more pronounced seasons. Many of the resident birds that are found are unique to this region, and many migrate north during the southern winter. Migratory birds from the northern hemisphere are almost unknown here.

Cerrado. This is the savanna-forest transition from the Amazonian region to the Chaco and Pampas regions, and has intermediate characteristics. The

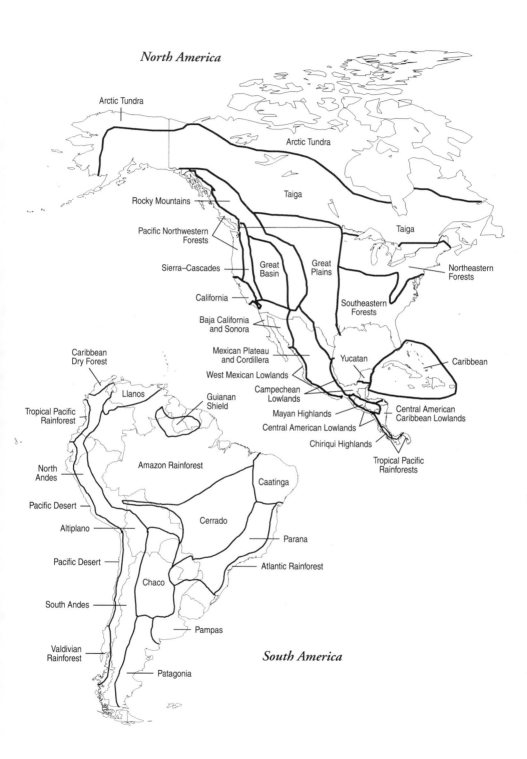

North America

Arctic Tundra

Arctic Tundra

Taiga

Rocky Mountains

Taiga

Pacific Northwestern
Forests

Sierra–Cascades

Great
Basin

Great
Plains

Northeastern
Forests

California

Southeastern
Forests

Baja California
and Sonora

Mexican Plateau
and Cordillera

Yucatan

Caribbean

West Mexican Lowlands

Campechean
Lowlands

Central American
Caribbean Lowlands

Caribbean
Dry Forest

Llanos

Guianan
Shield

Mayan Highlands

Central American Lowlands

Tropical Pacific
Rainforest

Chiriqui Highlands

Tropical Pacific
Rainforests

North
Andes

Amazon Rainforest

Pacific Desert

Caatinga

Altiplano

Cerrado

Pacific Desert

Parana

Chaco

Atlantic Rainforest

South Andes

Pampas

Valdivian
Rainforest

South America

Patagonia

fifty-six to seventy-six inches of annual rain falls mostly between October and April. The temperature extremes at one location in eastern Bolivia are from 41 to 95 degrees Fahrenheit, but the daily mean temperature varies only slightly throughout the year. The vegetation is a mosaic of grasslands, shrublands, and light woodlands. The trees are mostly deciduous except in the evergreen, river-edge forests. Some areas, such as the Pantanal, are seasonally flooded and attract many marsh-dwelling birds.

Caatinga. A region of dry, thorny scrubs, the Caatinga has a rainfall of only eight to thirty-eight inches a year. Much of the rain falls during a short wet season, during which the vegetation produces leaves and flowers. During the long dry season the vegetation loses its leaves and becomes dormant. This region harbors few if any migratory birds.

Parana. A transitional zone between the arid Cerrado and Caatinga and the humid Atlantic Rainforest. Some areas are dominated by *Auracaria* conifers. Very few migratory birds winter in this region.

Atlantic Rainforest. This heavily populated region was once heavily forested, but today only isolated pockets of rainforest survive. Only a few migratory landbirds winter in this region.

Chaco and Pampas. This is a low, flat, arid region that reaches an elevation of only thirteen hundred feet on its western boundary, at the foot of the Andes. Yearly mean temperatures range from 64 to 80 degrees Fahrenheit, with maximum temperatures up to 118 degrees. Rainfall varies from nineteen to thirty-eight inches a year, with the wettest area along the large Paraguay-Parana River—a major influence on the climate in the region. Up to 80 percent of this rainfall occurs from November to April, leaving a pronounced dry season for the remainder of the year. Because of this long, annual dry period, the region does not have major lakes or swamps, and waterbirds are confined to the few large rivers. The vegetation is mostly grassland on the Pampas (an important wintering area for several species of arctic-nesting shorebirds) and desert-scrub woodland with cacti in the Chaco. Many areas have been cultivated, and cattle farming is prevalent, especially in the Pampas. Most species of birds are characteristic of these desert and grassland conditions, but during the dry season many migrate north to the Amazonian region.

Patagonia. A cold, flat, windswept land of low shrubs and bunchgrass, this region has an annual rainfall of just eight inches. None of the migratory land birds and only a few of the shorebirds winter in this area.

BR BREEDING RANGE	WR WINTERING RANGE	D DIET	FF FUN FACTS
BH BREEDING HABITAT	WH WINTERING HABITAT	CS CONSERVATION STATUS	

ANATIDAE

Cinnamon Teal

Blue-winged Teal *(Anas discors)*

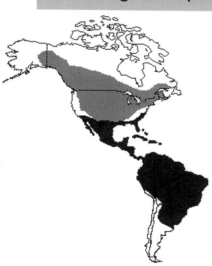

BR: Taiga, Northeastern Forests, Great Plains, northern Southeastern Forests, Rocky Mountains, Great Basin, northern Pacific

BH: marshes, ponds and lakes, prairies

WR: southern coastal, particularly southern Texas and peninsular Florida, throughout all bioregions in Caribbean and northern two thirds of South America, Central America, and the West Indies

WH: freshwater and brackish marsh

D: mainly stems, leaves, and seeds of aquatic plants; also aquatic insects, mollusks, crustaceans, marine worms

CS: common throughout range

FF: only duck species that migrates primarily to the tropics from the north

Cinnamon Teal *(Anas cyanoptera)*

PERMANENT
RANGE

PR: much of California, southwestern Arizona,
    southern New Mexico, southwestern Texas and
    most of central Mexico, northwestern and southern
    half of South America
BR: southern Rocky Mountains, Great Basin,
    Southern Pacific Northwestern Forests, California,
    northern Baja California, and Sonora
BH: marshes, ponds, and lakes
WR: California, Southern Great Basin, Southern
    Great Plains, south to tropical Pacific Lowlands
WH: freshwater and brackish wetlands
D: aquatic plants, insects, snails
CS: populations have declined because of human
    encroachment on nesting grounds, draining of wet-
    lands for cultivation, and water diversion for irriga-
    tion

PICIDAE

Yellow-bellied Sapsucker

Yellow-bellied Sapsucker *(Sphyrapicus varius)*

BR: Taiga, Northeastern Forests
BH: deciduous and mixed deciduous-coniferous
forest
WR: Southeastern Forests, southern West Mexican
Lowlands, Mexican Plateau and Cordillera,
Campechean Lowlands, Yucatan, Mayan High-
lands, Central American Pacific Lowlands,
Caribbean Islands
WH: montane, coniferous forest, clearings with
some large trees, light woodland, riparian
woodlands
D: insects, primarily adult and larval beetles and
ants, sap, some fruit and berries
CS: common
FF: bores horizontal rows of holes ("sapwells") into
trees for sap; sap attracts insect prey

CUCULIDAE

Black-billed cuckoo

Black-billed Cuckoo *(Coccyzus erythropthalmus)*

BR: Great Plains, Northeastern Forests, northern Southeastern Forests

BH: upland forest with substantial low, shrubby vegetation; also in overgrown pastures and orchards

WR: poorly known: records from Pacific Coast Rainforest, Amazon Rainforest, Cerrado

WH: prefers dense cover; occurs in second-growth woodland, scrubby areas, semi-open woodland, and forest edges

D: insects, especially caterpillars; in breeding range, feeds heavily on tent caterpillars and gypsy moth larvae, some fruit

CS: common

FF: often sings at night; both cuckoo species show tremendous year-to-year fluctuations in abundance

Yellow-billed Cuckoo *(Coccyzus americanus)*

BR: California, Sonora, Great Basin, Great Plains, Northeastern Forests, Southeastern Forests

BH: open woodlands, towns, riparian woodlands, overgrown pastures and orchards

WR: poorly known: records from Caribbean Dry Forest, central Tropical Pacific Rainforest, Cerrado, Amazon Rainforest, Atlantic Rainforest

WH: evergreen gallery forest, deciduous forest and scrub habitat

D: insects, especially caterpillars; feeds heavily on tent caterpillars and gypsy moth larvae on breeding grounds; also fruits and small frogs

CS: on endangered list in California (1990); candidate for U.S. federal listing (1991); nearly extinct in western riparian habitat of breeding range, also declining in the East because of habitat loss and pesticide contamination on breeding grounds, wintering grounds, and along migration routes

FF: in the western United States cuckoos are extremely late migrants and most arrive in June

APODIDAE

Chimney Swift

Black Swift *(Cypseloides niger)*

BR: Pacific Northwestern Forests, Sierra-Cascades, central Rocky Mountains, California, southern Mexican Plateau and Cordillera, Mayan Highlands, Chiriqui Highlands, Caribbean

BH: montane forests and seacoasts with rocky cliffs

WR: poorly known: records from Mayan Highlands, Chiriqui Highlands

WH: montane forests

D: flying insects

CS: rare or uncommon

FF: nests in colonies on cliffs, often near or beneath waterfalls

Chimney Swift *(Chaetura pelagica)*

BR: southern Taiga, Northeastern Forests, Southeastern Forests, Great Plains

BH: nests in chimneys, barns, and hollow trees; open country, woodlands, and towns

WR: poorly known: records from Tropical Pacific Lowlands, Pacific Coast Desert, western Amazon Rainforest, Cerrado

WH: deciduous, broadleaved evergreen, and gallery forest

D: flying insects

CS: common

FF: hundreds can be found roosting in a single chimney

Vaux's Swift *(Chaetura vauxi)*

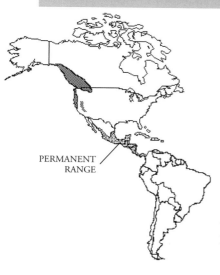

PERMANENT RANGE

PR: southern Mexico through Central America and Venezuela

BR: Pacific Northwestern Forests, Sierra-Cascades, northern Rocky Mountains

BH: coniferous forests, open country, and woodlands near lakes and rivers; nests in hollow trees, seldom in chimneys

WR: poorly known: confusion in field with resident races, West Mexican Lowlands, ?

WH: mixed, deciduous, and broadleaved evergreen forest, cities and open areas

D: flying insects

CS: uncommon

FF: migratory race in United States may be a species distinct from resident tropical races

TROCHILIDAE

Ruby-throated Hummingbird

Ruby-throated Hummingbird *(Archilochus colubris)*

BR: southern Taiga, Northeastern Forests, Southeastern Forests, Great Plains

BH: coniferous, deciduous, and mixed woodlands; yards, gardens, orchards

WR: West Mexican Lowlands, Campechean Lowlands, Yucatan, Mayan Highlands, Central American Caribbean Lowlands, Central American Pacific Lowlands

WH: prefers brushy second-growth and light deciduous forest, often along forest edges and in semi-open areas, in gallery forest and in shade trees on coffee plantations, flowering hedges

D: nectar from flowers (especially from red, orange, and pink flowers), also small insects, spiders, and tree sap from sapsucker wells

CS: widely reported to be declining

FF: only common hummingbird in eastern United States

Broad-tailed Hummingbird *(Selasphorus platycercus)*

BR: Great Basin, Rocky Mountains, Mexican Plateau and Cordillera

WR: Mexican Plateau and Cordillera

BH and WH: meadows and flowering patches in open coniferous forests, pinyon-juniper and pine-oak woodlands, gardens in towns and cities

D: flower nectar, also small insects

CS: common

FF: as in the following species, males make a loud trilling sound in flight from air passing through modified tail feathers

Rufous Hummingbird *(Selasphorus rufus)*

BR: Pacific Northwestern Forests, northern Rocky Mountains

WR: West Mexican Lowlands, Mexican Plateau and Cordillera

BH and WH: meadows, edges, and thickets of coniferous forests, chaparral, gardens in towns

D: flower nectar and insects

CS: common

FF: northernmost hummingbird

STRIGIDAE

Flammulated Owl

Flammulated Owl *(Otus flammeolus)*

BR: Pacific Northwestern Forests, California, Sierra-Cascades, Great Basin, southern Rocky Mountains, Mexican Plateau and Cordillera

WR: poorly known: few winter records, southern Mexican Plateau and Cordillera, Mayan Highlands

BH and WH: montane forest, oak and pine woodlands, especially ponderosa pine forests

D: primarily insects and other invertebrates, such as spiders, scorpions, and centipedes; will sometimes eat small mammals and birds

CS: rare to locally common

FF: one of few owls with dark eyes; difficult to see, as eyes do not reflect light (eyeshine) from a flashlight

Elf Owl *(Micrathene whitneyi)*

BR: Sonora, Mexican Plateau

WR: Baja California and Sonora, West Mexican Lowlands, Mexican Plateau and Cordillera

BH and WH: desert lowlands and wooded canyons, riparian woodlands, oak and sycamore woodlands, juniper and pinyon-pine (requires abandoned woodpecker holes for nesting)

D: mainly large insects, but also scorpions and sometimes lizards, snakes, and small birds

CS: common in some regions, declining in Texas and California; being reintroduced in California

FF: smallest owl in the world

CAPRIMULGIDAE

Whip-poor-will

Lesser Nighthawk *(Chordeiles acutipennis texensis)*

BR: (migratory race) California, Baja California and Sonora, Mexican Plateau, West Mexican Lowlands

BH: dry, open country, scrubland, and desert

WR: poorly known; (migratory race) central Mexico to western Colombia; difficult to distinguish from resident races in the field

WH: open areas with scattered woods or scrub, savanna, marsh, beaches, rivers, and rice paddies

D: feeds on insects in flight during the day and at night

CS: common

FF: because of its call, it was formerly named the Trilling Nighthawk

Common Nighthawk *(Chordeiles minor)*

BR: Taiga, Pacific Northwestern Forests, Sierra-Cascades, Great Basin, Rocky Mountains, Great Plains, Northeastern Forests, Southeastern Forests, northern Mexican Plateau and Cordillera

BH: open woodlands, grasslands, farmlands, towns

WR: western Amazon Rainforest, Cerrado

WH: grasslands and savanna, pastures, farmlands

D: flying insects

CS: declining in many parts of range primarily because of loss of breeding habitat and increased predation rates

FF: almost never seen in migration in nonbreeding areas in the western United States

Chuck-Will's Widow *(Caprimulgus carolinensis)*

PERMANENT RANGE

PR: southern Southeastern Forests and northeastern Caribbean

BR: southern Northeastern Forests, Southeastern Forests

BH: deciduous forests, prefers oak-pine woodlands

WR: Campechean Lowland, Yucatan, Central American Caribbean Lowland, Caribbean

WH: deciduous, broadleaved evergreen, and gallery forests

D: nocturnal low-flying insects; occasionally preys on small vertebrates

CS: locally common

Whip-poor-will *(Caprimulgus vociferus)*

PERMANENT
RANGE

PR: Mexican Plateau and Cordillera, Mayan
  Highlands
BR: Northeastern Forests, Southeastern Forests,
  Mexican Plateau and Cordillera, Mayan Highlands
BH: open coniferous and mixed woodlands in the
  East, wooded canyons in the West
WR: Campechean Lowland, Central American
  Caribbean Lowland
WH: coniferous, mixed coniferous-broadleaved,
  deciduous, and broadleaved evergreen forest
D: nocturnal flying insects
CS: declining throughout breeding range because of
  habitat fragmentation and loss
FF: Mexican and eastern United States races may be
  distinct species

SCOLOPACIDAE

Whimbrel

Hudsonian Godwit *(Limosa haemastica)*

BR: Tundra

BH: wet bogs and marshes, tidal mudflats, grassy tundra near water, flooded fields

WR: Pampas, Patagonia

WH: wet grasslands, brackish wetlands, lakes, ponds, and seashores, inlets and estuaries

D: marine worms, horseflies, other insects, mollusks and crustaceans

CS: locally common

FF: lost individuals in migration have shown up in New Zealand

Marbled Godwit *(Limosa fedoa)*

BR: Great Plains, Tundra

BH: marshes; flooded plains; usually near lakes, rivers, and streams; shortgrass prairies

WR: coastal areas from southern United States (coastal California, Gulf Coast, Atlantic Coast to North Carolina) to Chile and Venezuela

WH: tidal flats, wet grasslands, freshwater and brackish marshes, seashore

D: aquatic insects and mollusks, snails, small crustaceans, worms, leeches

CS: common, although range is contracting because of conversion of breeding habitat for agriculture

FF: most of West Coast population stages on Humboldt Bay during fall migration before turning inland

Eskimo Curlew *(Numenius borealis)*

BR: Tundra, historically in northwestern Mackenzie, possibly to western Alaska

BH: arctic tundra

WR: Pampas

WH: grasslands

D: mostly insects, also snails and berries

CS: Endangered on U.S. and Canadian federal lists, nearly extinct: last photograph 1962 in eastern Texas, last specimen 1963 from Barbados, 1976 sighting in west Hudson Bay; formerly abundant, decline due to intensive hunting in late 1800s and conversion of upland winter habitat

FF: very small population recently found nesting in arctic Canada

Whimbrel *(Numenius phaeopus)*

BR: Tundra

BH: open tundra

WR: Pacific Coast from northern California to southern Chile, Atlantic, Gulf, and Caribbean coasts
from Virginia to central Brazil

WH: mudflats, tidal creeks, sandy or rocky shores,
flooded fields near coast, mangroves

D: crustaceans, mollusks, marine worms, insects,
berries (breeding)

CS: locally common along coast; rare inland

FF: the very distinctive Asian and European races are
occasionally found in North America; the long,
curved bill is the same shape as the burrows of the
ghost crabs on which whimbrels commonly feed

Upland Sandpiper *(Bartramia longicauda)*

BR: Taiga, Great Plains, northern Great Basin,
Northeastern Forests

BH: grassy open areas, pastures, fields, shortgrass
prairies

WR: southern Cerrado, Pampas

WH: pastures, airstrips, shortgrass savannas

D: mostly insects, especially grasshoppers and
crickets; weevils, ants, berries, seeds, and grains

CS: once abundant, but on demise of passenger
pigeon in 1880s became focus of intensive hunting,
which resulted in drastic declines. Afforded protection by Migratory Bird Treaty Act in 1918. Populations recovered somewhat, but continued habitat
loss in both breeding and wintering ranges means
species is still in peril. In eastern part of breeding
range, much of decline is due to development and
to succession of old fields to woodland. In the West,
overgrazing has deteriorated habitat, and on wintering grounds, habitat is lost as converted to agriculture and grazing lands.

FF: old name was Upland Plover for its ploverlike
qualities

Lesser Yellowlegs *(Tringa flavipes)*

BR: Taiga, Tundra

BH: tundra, grassy meadows, bogs, and clearings in coniferous forest zone

WR: coastal southern United States to southern South America including the Caribbean, Altiplano and Puna Zones of High Andes

WH: mudflats, marshes, estuaries, shores of ponds and lakes

D: adult insects and larvae, small fish, crustaceans, worms

CS: common

Greater Yellowlegs *(Tringa melanoleuca)*

BR: Taiga

BH: tundra, swampy muskegs, bogs, clearings in boreal region

WR: coastal Oregon and California, southern Nevada to southern Texas, Gulf Coast and Atlantic Coast to Massachusetts, south in many lowland areas to Tierra del Fuego, also Altiplano and Puna Zones of High Andes

WH: mudflats, marshes, shores of ponds, lakes, rivers

D: tadpoles, worms, mollusks, snails, crabs, insects

CS: common

Solitary Sandpiper *(Tringa solitaria)*

BR: Taiga

BH: taiga, muskeg with scattered trees, near freshwater lakes and ponds in boreal and subarctic coniferous forest zone

WR: along coasts from southeastern Georgia, Florida, and the Gulf Coast to Argentina, Pacific Coast of west Mexico to Peru, Amazon Rainforest, Cerrado, Pampas

WH: freshwater ponds, marshes, flooded pastures

D: aquatic insects, spiders, small crustaceans, and frogs

CS: common

FF: uses old nests of songbirds in trees

Spotted Sandpiper *(Tringa macularia)*

BR: Taiga, Sierra-Cascades, Pacific Northwestern Forests, Rocky Mountains, northern Great Plains, Northeastern Forests

BH: rivers, lakes

WR: bioregions throughout southern United States to Amazon Rainforest, Pampas, Altiplano and Puna Zones of High Andes

WH: rivers, ponds, lakes, seacoasts

D: invertebrates

CS: common

FF: female is dominant during courtship display and mates with more than one male

Wandering Tattler *(Heteroscelus incanus)*

BR: Taiga

BH: scrubby vegetation along stream banks, damp meadows, forest clearings, lakes

WR: Pacific Coast from southern California to Peru, southern and central Pacific islands

WH: rocky seacoasts, islets, sandy beaches

D: small crustaceans, mollusks, insects

CS: common

FF: main wintering range is in eastern Polynesian islands

Ruddy Turnstone *(Arenaria interpres)*

BR: Tundra

BH: coastal tundra

WR: Pacific, Atlantic and Gulf Coastal United States south along coasts to Tierra del Fuego, Pacific islands

WH: rocky or sandy shores, mudflats, tidal creeks, river mouths

D: mollusks, crustaceans, adult and larval insects (particularly in summer), eggs of gulls and terns

CS: common

FF: commonly hunts by turning over rocks and flotsam

Short-billed Dowitcher *(Limnodromus griseus)*

BR: Tundra
BH: swampy coastal tundra, muskeg, boreal-forest
  bogs
WR: Pacific Coast from northern California to cen-
  tral Peru, Atlantic, Gulf, and Caribbean coasts from
  Virginia to central Brazil
WH: tidal mudflats, usually saltwater habitat
D: insects, marine worms, snails, crustaceans, seeds
CS: common (formerly a popular game bird, num-
  bers have been drastically reduced)
FF: detects prey tactilely by probing rapidly in a
  sewing-machine motion

Surfbird *(Aphriza virgata)*

BR: Tundra
BH: mountain tundra, open, rocky ground above
  tree line
WR: southeastern Alaska, Pacific Coast from south-
  eastern Alaska to Tierra del Fuego
WH: rocky seacoasts
D: small mollusks and crustaceans, insects in summer
CS: common
FF: nests and eggs unknown until 1926

Red Knot *(Calidris canutus)*

BR: Tundra

BH: barren or stony tundra

WR: very locally along Pacific, Atlantic, and Caribbean coasts from southern California and New York to Tierra del Fuego

WH: sandy and pebbly beaches, especially at coastal river mouths, mudflats

D: insects, mollusks, crustaceans, crab eggs, some seeds, plant buds and shoots

CS: locally common; once most abundant shorebird in North America, numbers were reduced by hunting in late nineteenth century

FF: congregates in Delaware Bay to eat horseshoe crab eggs in May

Sanderling *(Calidris alba)*

BR: Tundra

BH: high arctic tundra

WR: Pacific Coast from southern Alaska to Chile, Atlantic, Gulf, Caribbean coasts from Nova Scotia to Argentina

WH: sandy beaches, mudflats

D: insects in summer, small crustaceans in winter

CS: common, although has shown a drop in numbers of as much as 80 percent along eastern coast of United States in recent years

FF: defends small territories within flocks on beaches; locks hind toe as an adaptation for running on beaches

Semipalmated Sandpiper *(Calidris pusilla)*

BR: Tundra

BH: subarctic and arctic tundra

WR: southeastern Mexico along coast through the West Indies to northern Chile and Argentina

WH: flat, muddy, sandy, or gravelly shore

D: insects in summer, small mollusks, marine worms, small crustaceans

CS: abundant

FF: one of the few monogamous sandpipers

Western Sandpiper *(Calidris mauri)*

BR: Tundra

BH: marshes, coastal sedge tundra, wetlands of sub-arctic boreal forests

WR: Pacific and Atlantic-Caribbean coasts from California and North Carolina to northern Peru and Surinam, West Indies

WH: flat, sandy, muddy, or gravelly shore

D: insects in summer, marine worms, snails, small crustaceans

CS: common

FF: most of the world population gathers at Copper River Delta, Alaska, in early May

Least Sandpiper *(Calidris minutilla)*

BR: Tundra, Taiga
BH: wetlands of subarctic boreal forests and tundra
WR: coastal California, across southern United States to southern Peru and eastern Brazil
WH: muddy borders of fresh or saltwater ponds, mudflats
D: insects in summer, small crustaceans, mollusks and worms
CS: very common
FF: males do most parental care

White-rumped Sandpiper *(Calidris fusciollis)*

BR: Tundra
BH: mossy and grassy tundra near water
WR: Patagonia, Pampas
WH: freshwater and saltwater marsh
D: insects in summer, tiny mollusks, marine worms, small crustaceans
CS: uncommon
FF: has longest migration for shorebirds

Baird's Sandpiper *(Calidris bairdii)*

BR: Tundra
BH: barren tundra
WR: Altiplano and Puna Zones of High Andes, Cerrado, Pampas, Patagonia, Pacific Coast Desert
WH: coastal flats
D: insects in summer, small crustaceans, insects
CS: uncommon
FF: only "peep" to migrate primarily through interior United States

Pectoral Sandpiper *(Calidris melanotos)*

BR: Tundra
BH: arctic tundra
WR: Altiplano and Puna Zones of High Andes, Cerrado, Pampas, Patagonia, coastal Peru
WH: grassy freshwater wetlands, seashore
D: insects, especially adult and larval flies in summer; also beetles, crickets, grasshoppers, small crustaceans, algae, seeds
CS: uncommon in West and East, but common in central United States in migration
FF: polygynous (female will have several males as mates)

Stilt Sandpiper *(Calidris himantopus)*

BR: Tundra

BH: arctic sedge tundra usually near wooded border of taiga

WR: Cerrado, Pampas, locally northward along both coasts to extreme southern United States

WH: shallow salt or freshwater marshes, pond margins

D: adult and larval beetles and other insects, small snails

CS: uncommon

FF: commonly found in dowitcher flocks feeding in a similar sewing-machine fashion

Buff-breasted Sandpiper *(Tryngites subruficollis)*

BR: Tundra

BH: dry, grassy tundra

WR: southern Cerrado, Pampas

WH: freshwater wetlands, grasslands

D: adult and larval insects, especially beetles and flies; spiders; seeds

CS: once abundant, but numbers were severely reduced by hunting pressures in late 1800s, now suffers from habitat loss due to agricultural conversion of upland winter habitat

FF: males form leks and attract females by flashing white underwings

Wilson's Phalarope *(Steganopus tricolor)*

BR: Taiga, Great Basin, northern Rocky Mountains, northern Great Plains, Great Lakes region

BH: marshes and wet meadows, taiga

WR: Altiplano and Puna Zones of High Andes, Cerrado, Pampas, Patagonia, coastal Peru

WH: inland wetlands, coastal lagoons, freshwater ponds, marshes and tidal mudflats, saline and alkaline lakes

D: adult and larval insects, small crustaceans, aquatic plant seeds, plankton

CS: uncommon, threatened by wetland habitat loss in breeding range and along migration routes

FF: sometimes polyandrous; females more brightly colored than males, have several males as mates, and leave males, which then incubate eggs and feed young

CHARADRIIDAE

American Golden-Plover

American Oystercatcher *(Haematopus palliatus)*

BR: Atlantic and Caribbean coasts from Massachusetts to southern Mexico and from Venezuela to
  Argentina; Pacific Coast from northwestern Mexico
  to central Chile; West Indies

BH: rocky and sandy seacoasts

WR: northern populations winter from coasts of
  southeastern United States, Mexico, and West
  Indies to southern South America

WH: brackish wetlands and seacoasts

D: mollusks, crustaceans, worms, and insects

CS: displaced from much of former breeding habitat
  by development

FF: feeds on mollusks by stabbing contents of or
  hammering shell

Black-necked Stilt *(Himantopus mexicanus)*

BR: California, Great Basin, Great Plains, Atlantic
   Coast from Virginia south along Gulf Coast,
   Mexico, throughout bioregions to southern South
   America
BH: shallow freshwater and brackish ponds and
   marshes, alkaline lakes, flooded fields and pastures
WR: northern populations winter from bioregions in
   southern United States to southern South America
WH: freshwater and brackish wetlands, seacoasts
D: adult and larval insects, small crustaceans, snails,
   small fish, and seeds of aquatic plants
CS: common

American Golden-Plover *(Pluvialis dominica)*

BR: Tundra
BH: arctic and subarctic tundra above tree line
WR: Cerrado, Pampas, Patagonia
WH: grassland and savanna, freshwater wetlands,
   seacoast
D: insects, crustaceans, mollusks, small fish, berries
CS: common; once abundant, but numbers declined
   because of hunting at end of nineteenth century;
   recovering
FF: breeding display consists of slow, languid flap-
   ping—perhaps to enhance appearance of large size

Pacific Golden-Plover *(Pluvialis fulva)*

BR: western Tundra

BH: arctic and subarctic tundra above tree line

WR: California, Pacific Islands

WH: grassland, agricultural fields, beaches, rocky
seacoast

D: insects, crustaceans, mollusks, small fish

CS: common; a few winter in North American
continent

FF: until recently, regarded as race of Lesser (American) Golden-Plover

Semipalmated Plover *(Charadrius semipalmatus)*

BR: Tundra

BH: dry, arctic tundra, sandy areas

WR: coasts from central California and Virginia
south to central Chile and northern Argentina

WH: mudflats; mangroves; sandy and rocky shores,
especially at river mouths

D: insects (particularly in breeding season), small
mollusks, crustaceans, marine worms, insects

CS: declined drastically in 1890s because of hunting,
now recovered

Wilson's Plover *(Charadrius wilsonia)*

BR: Atlantic, Gulf, and Caribbean coasts from New
Jersey to Belize and West Indies, and from coastal
Colombia to eastern Brazil; Pacific Coast from Baja
California to northwestern Peru

BH: sandy beaches and mudflats

WR: coasts from breeding grounds to northern Peru
and central Brazil

WH: beaches, coastal mudflats, estuaries, muddy
banks of rivers near coast

D: small crustaceans and other invertebrates

CS: fairly common but declining

FF: unlike many shorebirds, plovers are strictly visual
foragers

LARIDAE

Franklin's Gull

Black Skimmer *(Rynchops niger)*

BR: locally in southwestern United States and north-western Mexico, along Atlantic and Gulf coasts from Massachusetts to southeastern Mexico, and along coasts and rivers of much of South America

BH: sandy beaches, coastal islands, tropical rivers

WR: northern birds winter from southern United States throughout lowland bioregions to Argentina and Chile; southern birds winter north in small numbers to Costa Rica

WH: along calm waters of rivers, estuaries, lakes, tidewaters, coastal lagoons

D: fish, crustaceans, aquatic insects

CS: locally common; sensitive to human disturbance at or near nesting colonies

FF: scoops up prey by skimming surface of water with elongated, lower mandible

Franklin's Gull *(Larus pipixcan)*

BR: Great Plains, northern Great Basin

BH: shallow freshwater marsh

WR: Tropical Pacific Rainforest, Pacific Coast Desert, few in Central American Pacific Lowlands

WH: river mouths, harbors, mudflats, salt ponds, flooded fields, and marshes

D: insects, amphibians, seeds and grains, some small mammals; in winter, fish and crustaceans

CS: common, but showing sharp declines

FF: nearly entire population migrates to and from Peru by crossing Isthmus of Tehuantepec in southern Mexico

Sandwich Tern *(Sterna sandvicensis)*

BR: along coasts from Virginia through the West Indies

BH: sandy seacoasts

WR: southeastern United States along coasts to Uruguay, Pacific Coast from southern Mexico to Peru

WH: river mouths, estuaries, harbors, lagoons, seacoasts

D: fish, shrimp, squid

CS: common

Common Tern *(Sterna hirundo)*

BR: Tundra, Taiga

BH: areas near water with little or no vegetation, sandy seacoasts, small islands in salt marshes, rocky islands in lakes and rivers

WR: along Pacific Coast from Mexico to central Peru, and Atlantic-Gulf Coast from North Carolina to northern Argentina, Caribbean Islands

WH: harbors, estuaries, salt ponds, less often on sandy or rocky shores

D: mostly fish, also shrimp and other crustaceans, worms, insects

CS: in early twentieth century, millinery trade devastated population; still declining on East Coast because of beach erosion and development, Great Lakes populations declining because of rising water levels (interfere with nesting) and expanding Ring-billed Gull populations (compete for nest sites)

Least Tern *(Sterna antillarum)*

BR: Pacific Coast from central California to Honduras; Atlantic, Gulf, and Caribbean coasts from Maine to Honduras; West Indies and islands off Venezuela; central United States along Colorado, Red, Missouri, and Mississippi River systems

BH: river sandbars, broad areas of sand or gravel beaches, salt plains

WR: coastal Baja California along Pacific Coast to southern Mexico, probably northwestern South America, coastal Colombia to eastern Brazil

WH: inshore coastal waters such as bays, estuaries, salt ponds and lagoons

D: mostly fish, sand eels, and crustaceans

CS: added to U.S. federal endangered species list in 1985; almost exterminated by plume hunters near turn of century, inland nesting habitat now being destroyed by channelization and damming of rivers (eliminates sandbars and beaches), coastal colonies often deserted because of disturbance created by humans and human-associated predators

FF: will sometimes spear fish with closed bill

Black Tern *(Chlidonias niger)*

BR: Great Basin, Great Plains, Northeastern Forests, Taiga

BH: freshwater marshes, taiga, plains, prairies, wet meadows, ponds, lakes, river oxbows and impoundments

WR: along both coasts from Panama to Peru and Surinam

WH: seacoasts, bays, estuaries, lagoons, lakes, rivers

D: aquatic and land insects, worms, small mollusks, crustaceans, plankton, and fish

CS: overall population decreasing (5.6 percent a year) because of contaminants and loss and disturbance of wetland nesting areas, especially in upper Midwest

FF: only tern in Western Hemisphere to drastically change plumage color from black breeding plumage to light winter plumage

ACCIPITRIDAE

American Swallow-tailed Kite

American Swallow-tailed Kite *(Elanoides forficatus)*

PERMANENT RANGE

PR: throughout bioregions in Mexico, Central America, and South America to northern Argentina

BR: Southeastern Forests

BH: open woodlands, bottomlands, wetlands

WR: poorly known: confusion with resident races

WH: broadleaved evergreen and gallery forests

D: primarily insects, but also small snakes, lizards, frogs, nestling birds, and fruit

CS: candidate for U.S. federal endangered species listing; locally common, although marsh drainage, deforestation, and hunting have reduced population and range

FF: known to pluck fruit from tropical forest canopy in flight

Mississippi Kite *(Ictina mississippiensis)*

BR: Southeastern Forests, southern Great Plains
BH: Riverine forest, open woodland, prairies
WR: poorly known: records from Cerrado, Chaco
WH: broadleaved deciduous and gallery forest, savanna
D: insects, mice, lizards, and frogs
CS: common in southern Great Plains, uncommon in southeast; increasing since 1950s, breeding range expanding west, possibly because of tree planting for erosion control
FF: catches and eats dragonflies in midair

Broad-winged Hawk *(Buteo platypterus)*

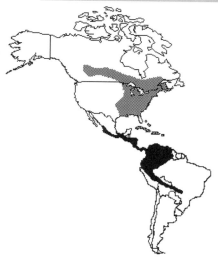

BR: Taiga, Northeastern Forests, Southeastern Forests
BH: deciduous and mixed forest and open woodland
WR: West Mexican Lowlands, Campechean Lowlands, Central American Caribbean Lowlands, Central American Pacific Lowlands, Tropical Pacific Rainforest, Northern Andean Highlands, Amazon Rainforest
WH: deciduous broadleaved, broadleaved evergreen, and gallery forest; prefers open areas, forest edge, broken forest, semi-open woodlands
D: small mammals; also frogs, snakes, lizards, and insects; occasionally small fish and birds
CS: common throughout range
FF: may not eat during fall migration between United States and South America

Swainson's Hawk (Buteo swainsoni)

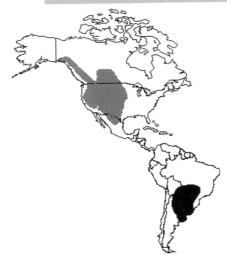

BR: interior Pacific Northwestern Forests, Great Basin, Great Plains

BH: prairies, open pine-oak woodland, farmlands, grasslands, desert

WR: Cerrado, Chaco, Pampas

WH: grassland, savanna, scrub

D: mainly small mammals, lizards, and birds

CS: candidate for U.S. federal endangered species listing; decline due to loss of habitat, human disturbance, hunting; will readily abandon nest if disturbed

FF: sometimes seen hunting in large flocks in migration

Osprey (Pandion haliaetus)

PERMANENT RANGE

PR: southern California, Baja California, western Mexico, Gulf Coast, and Florida

BR: Taiga, Pacific Northwestern Forests, Rocky Mountains, Great Basin, Northeastern Forests, Atlantic Coast in southern United States, Caribbean Islands

WR: throughout bioregions from Mexico to Pampas, northern Chile

BH and WH: occurs in variety of habitat types associated with fresh or salt water along rivers, lakes, and seacoasts

D: feeds almost exclusively on live-caught fish, will also eat small mammals, reptiles, amphibians, and birds

CS: conservation programs and reduction of DDT have halted more rapid decline of species; although locally common and cosmopolitan, is declining in areas because of habitat destruction, reduction in food resources, and pesticide use; (population crashed especially in 1950s–1970s from DDT contamination, hunting, and encroachment)

FF: found throughout world

CICONIIDAE

Turkey Vulture

Turkey Vulture *(Cathartes aura)*

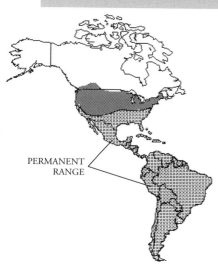

PERMANENT RANGE

PR: southern half of United States throughout Central and South America

BR: southern British Columbia, Alberta and Saskatchewan, throughout bioregions from continental United States to Tierra del Fuego

WR: poorly known for migrant populations: confusion with resident individuals

BH and WH: open habitats in lowlands and mountains, grasslands, deserts

D: carrion

CS: reportedly decreasing in southern Great Plains and parts of South; thinning of eggshells because of pesticide contamination is still a problem

FF: has one of keenest senses of smells of any bird; will vomit on attackers as defense

TYRANNIDAE

Great-crested Flycatcher

Olive-sided Flycatcher *(Contopus borealis)*

BR: Taiga, Pacific Northwestern Forests, Sierra-Cascades, Rocky Mountains, Northeastern Forests

BH: semi-open coniferous forest with tall snags; in mixed woodlands near edges and clearings

WR: Chiriqui Highlands, Northern Andean Highlands, rare and local Mayan Highlands, Amazon Rainforests

WH: around edges, clearings, and gaps of highland forest; occurs in deciduous, evergreen, and gallery forests

D: hawks insects from high, exposed tree limbs

CS: declining across entire North American range because of removal of standing dead trees (snags) and fire suppression combined with suburban sprawl (particularly in the Northeast)

FF: known for its "quick three beers" song

Western Wood-Pewee *(Contopus sordidulus)*

BR: Pacific Northwestern Forests, California, Sierra-Cascades, Great Basin, Rocky Mountains, western Great Plains, Mexican Plateau and Cordillera, West Mexican Lowlands

BH: open woodlands, primarily conifer-dominated forests, also floodplain and riparian forest and wooded canyons

WR: Northern Andean Highlands

WH: evergreen, broadleaved forest, clearings, and forest edges

D: flying insects, spiders, and some berries

CS: common; rare cowbird host

FF: one of the few western migrants to winter in South America

Eastern Wood-Pewee *(Contopus virens)*

BR: Northeastern Forests, Southeastern Forests, eastern Great Plains

BH: primarily deciduous forests (especially oak-dominated forest); also mixed forests, woodlots, orchards, and towns

WR: Tropical Pacific Rainforests, Amazon Rainforests

WH: clearings and edges of second-growth forest, river edges; found in variety of forest types

D: flying insects

CS: common

FF: defends territories in migration

Yellow-bellied Flycatcher *(Empidonax flaviventris)*

BR: Taiga, Northeastern Forests

BH: moist coniferous forest, bogs, swamps

WR: Campechean Lowlands, Yucatan, Central American Caribbean Lowlands

WH: deciduous, evergreen, or gallery forest, shaded clearings, and coffee plantations

D: foliage and flying insects, occasionally small fruit

CS: common; rare cowbird host

FF: in winter defends territory in mature rainforest

Acadian Flycatcher *(Empidonax virescens)*

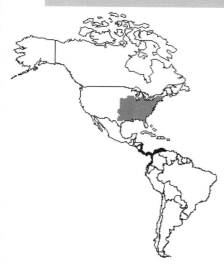

BR: Southeastern Forests, southern Northeastern Forests

BH: lower canopy and understory of humid, shady forest (bottomlands and swamps), riparian thickets; prefers beech forests in northeast

WR: Central American Caribbean Lowlands, Tropical Pacific Rainforests, Northern Andean Highlands

WH: thickets and gaps in humid forests, and shady second-growth woodland

D: mostly foliage and flying insects, occasionally small fruits

CS: common; common cowbird host

Alder Flycatcher *(Empidonax alnorum)*

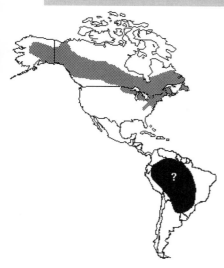

BR: Taiga, Northeastern Forests

BH: moist thickets, bogs, swamps, sides of streams and ponds

WR: Amazon Rainforests

WH: open shrubby areas and woodland borders, river edges

D: foliage and flying insects, especially beetles; some fruit

CS: common; occasional cowbird host

FF: silent individuals nearly impossible to distinguish in field from the Willow Flycatcher

Willow Flycatcher *(Empidonax traillii)*

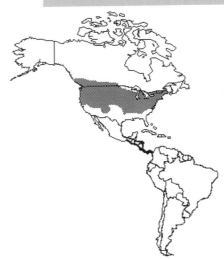

BR: Pacific Northwestern Forests, Sierra-Cascades, Great Basin, Rocky Mountains, Great Plains, Northeastern Forests

BH: mountain meadows, brushy fields; prefers woodland edges and borders of riparian forests

WR: Central American Pacific Lowlands, Central American Caribbean Lowlands

WH: brushy edges and second-growth woodlands

D: foliage and flying insects

CS: candidate for U.S. federal endangered listing (as of 1991); West Coast populations especially declining because of habitat destruction and degradation and cowbird parasitism

Least Flycatcher *(Empidonax minimus)*

BR: Taiga, northern Rocky Mountains, northern Great Plains, Northeastern Forests

BH: open deciduous forest; prefers forest edges and clearings

WR: West Mexican Lowlands, Campechean Lowlands, Yucatan, Central American Caribbean Lowlands, Central American Pacific Lowlands

WH: brushy clearings and borders of second-growth deciduous and gallery forest

D: foliage and flying insects and occasionally fruit

CS: declining

FF: breeds in woodlands but winters in scrublands

Hammond's Flycatcher *(Empidonax hammondii)*

BR: Pacific Northwestern Forests, Sierra-Cascades,
   Rocky Mountains
BH: mostly montane, coniferous forest
WR: Mexican Plateau and Cordillera, Mayan
   Highlands
WH: mostly pine-oak woodland, also edge of decidu-
   ous, evergreen, mixed, or gallery forest
D: foliage and flying insects
CS: common
FF: President Theodore Roosevelt once asked John
   Muir how to distinguish from the Dusky Flycatcher

Dusky Flycatcher *(Empidonax oberholseri)*

BR: Pacific Northwestern Forests, Sierra-Cascades,
   Rocky Mountains, Great Basin
BH: prefers open coniferous and mixed forests with
   shrubby understory, aspen groves, montane
   chaparral
WR: Mexican Plateau and Cordillera
WH: scrub and gallery forest, pine-oak woodland
D: foliage and flying insects
CS: common
FF: defends interspecific territories against the Gray
   Flycatcher

Gray Flycatcher *(Empidonax wrightii)*

BR: Great Basin, southern Rocky Mountains

BH: arid woodlands, especially areas of yellow pine and pinyon-juniper mixed with sagebrush

WR: Baja California and Sonora, West Mexican Lowlands, Mexican Plateau and Cordillera

WH: arid scrub, savanna, and gallery forest

D: insects

CS: fairly common

FF: differs from other *Empidonax* by flicking tail downward instead of upward

Pacific-slope Flycatcher *(Empidonax difficilis)*

BR: Pacific Northwestern Forests, Californian, Sierra-Cascades

BH: coniferous and mixed forest, oak woodlands, usually near streams

WR: West Mexican Lowlands

WH: forest

D: foliage and flying insects

CS: common

FF: can raise up to three broods of young in one nesting season

Cordilleran Flycatcher *(Empidonax occidentalis)*

BR: Great Basin, Rocky Mountains, Mexican Plateau and Cordillera

BH: coniferous forest, riparian woodland

WR: West Mexican Lowlands?

WH: forest

D: foliage and flying insects

CS: common

FF: until recently, this and the Pacific Coast Flycatcher were thought to be the same species

Buff-breasted Flycatcher *(Empidonax fulvifrons)*

PERMANENT RANGE

PR: Mayan Highlands, southern Mexican Plateau and Cordillera

BR: Mexican Plateau and Cordillera

BH: open pine and pine-oak woodland

WR: Mexican Plateau and Cordillera, Mayan Highlands

WH: canyon groves, oak-pine forest, brush

D: foliage and flying insects

CS: rare and local in United States (Arizona), numbers have declined and range decreased markedly since 1920

Ash-throated Flycatcher *(Myiarchus cinerascens)*

BR: California, Baja California and Sonora, Great Basin, southern Great Plains, Sierra-Cascades, southern Rocky Mountains, Mexican Plateau and Cordillera, West Mexican Lowlands, northern Campechean Lowlands

BH: desert scrub, pinyon-juniper and oak woodland, chaparral, riparian woodland

WR: Baja California and Sonora, West Mexican Lowlands, Mexican Plateau and Cordillera, Mayan Highlands

WH: tropical dry forest, savanna and dry scrub

D: foliage and flying insects, some fruit

CS: common

FF: one of the few Neotropical migrants to nest in tree cavities

Great-crested Flycatcher *(Myiarchus crinitus)*

BR: Northeastern Forests, Southeastern Forests, southern Taiga, Great Plains

BH: prefers mature hardwood forests; also in wooded suburbs, orchards, and woodlots

WR: Campechean Lowlands, Central American Caribbean Lowlands, Central American Pacific Lowlands, Caribbean Dry Forest, northern Tropical Pacific Rainforest, Amazon Rainforests (rare?), Cuba

WH: semi-open woodlands, evergreen broadleaved forests

D: insects, small fruit (has also been observed eating hummingbirds)

CS: fairly common

FF: uses snakeskins in its nests

Cassin's Kingbird *(Tyrannus vociferans)*

BR: California, Baja California and Sonora, Mexican Plateau and Cordillera, Rocky Mountains

WR: southern Baja California and Sonora, West Mexican Lowlands, Mayan Highlands, northern Central American Pacific Lowlands

BH and WH: semi-open areas in scrub, pinyon-juniper, pinyon-yucca, pine-oak woodlands, and semi-open plains

D: flying insects, some fruit

CS: fairly common

Western Kingbird *(Tyrannus verticales)*

BR: southern Pacific Northwestern Forests, California, Great Basin, Rocky Mountains, Great Plains, Sonora, northern Mexican Plateau and Cordillera

BH: open country with scattered trees, especially in agricultural areas, woodland edges

WR: West Mexican Lowlands, Central American Pacific Lowlands, Campechean Lowlands

WH: open country with scattered trees, farms, roadsides

D: flying insects and some fruit

CS: common, range expanding since 1900 with spread of agriculture

Eastern Kingbird *(Tyrannus tyrannus)*

BR: Taiga, northern Great Basin, Rocky Mountains, Great Plains, Northeastern Forests, Southeastern Forests

WR: Amazon Rainforests, Cerrado

BH and WH: open areas with scattered trees, river edge, forest edge, farmlands, towns

D: flying insects, mostly fruit in winter

CS: common

FF: migrate and winter in large flocks that overwhelm the aggressive, territorial defenses of larger, tropical flycatchers, which defend fruiting trees

Scissor-tailed Flycatcher *(Tyrannus forficatus)*

BR: southern Great Plains

WR: Campechean Lowlands, Central American Pacific Lowlands

BH and WH: open country with scattered trees, around pastures, clearings, and farms (savanna, plains, prairies, fields)

D: flying insects, some fruit

CS: common

FF: often roosts in large flocks on antennas in cities on their wintering grounds

VIREONIDAE

Yellow-throated Vireo

Black-capped Vireo *(Vireo atricapillus)*

BR: locally from central Oklahoma through Edward's
  Plateau to Big Bend area of Texas and Mexico.
BH: oak scrub
WR: West Mexican Lowlands
WH: thickets
D: foliage insects, fruit
CS: U.S. endangered species; threatened by habitat
  loss and cowbird parasitism
FF: one of few songbirds with red eyes

Bell's Vireo (*Vireo bellii*)

BR: Great Plains, Baja California and Sonora, northern Mexican Plateau and Cordillera

BH: mesquite thickets, riparian thickets, scrub oak

WR: West Mexican Lowlands, Central American Pacific Lowlands

WH: scrub and riparian woodland

D: foliage insects, some fruit

CS: rare to absent from some former ranges in California, declining in Kansas, Oklahoma, and Texas; decline is caused by cowbird parasitism and elimination of riparian habitat

White-eyed Vireo (*Vireo griseus*)

BR: Southeastern Forests, southern Northeastern Forests, southeastern Great Plains

BH: thickets, undergrowth, scrubby forest edge, brushy woodland

WR: southern Southeastern Forests, southern Great Plains, Campechean Lowlands, Yucatan, Caribbean Islands

WH: dense, shrubby forest

D: foliage insects, some fruit, especially in fall and winter (20–30 percent); defends fruiting gumbo-limbo trees all winter

CS: common; common cowbird host

FF: one of few species whose mouth lining is black

Solitary Vireo *(Vireo solitarius)*

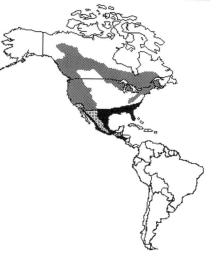

BR: Pacific Northwestern Forests, Taiga, Californian, Sierra-Cascades, Great Basin, Rocky Mountains, Northeastern Forests, Mexican Plateau and Cordillera, Mayan Highlands

BH: open coniferous or coniferous-deciduous forest

WR: West Mexican Lowlands, Campechean Lowland, Mayan Highlands, Central American Caribbean Lowlands, Central American Pacific Lowlands

WH: forest edge and semi-open woodland, pine-oak woodland

D: foliage insects and some fruit

CS: common; common cowbird host

FF: several distinct races that may prove to be different species—differ in plumage and song

Yellow-throated Vireo *(Vireo flavifrons)*

BR: Southeastern Forests, Northeastern Forests, eastern Great Plains

BH: mature, moist deciduous forest, less frequently in wooded residential areas

WR: Campechean Lowlands, Yucatan, Central American Caribbean Lowlands, Caribbean Islands, northern Tropical Pacific Rainforest, Caribbean Dry Forest

WH: tall, second-growth forest, forest edge, shaded gardens, coffee plantations

D: foliage insects, some fruit

CS: rather uncommon to common; common cowbird host; pesticide use has reduced numbers in suburban areas, especially in New England

Philadelphia Vireo *(Vireo philadelphicus)*

BR: Taiga, northern Northeastern Forests

BH: open deciduous, coniferous, or mixed forests, woodland edges, streamside thickets, aspen groves

WR: Campechean Lowlands, Central American Caribbean Lowlands

WH: light woodland, forest edge, coffee plantations, gardens

D: foliage insects, some fruit

CS: uncommon to rare

FF: defends territories against following vireo species in taiga birch forests; commonly found in pairs in winter

Red-eyed Vireo *(Vireo olivaceus olivaceus)*

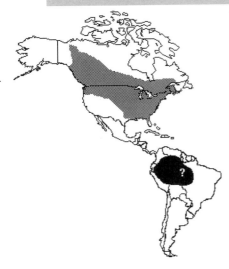

BR: Taiga, northern Cascades, northern Rocky Mountains, Great Plains, Northeastern Forests, Southeastern Forests

BH: deciduous or mixed forest with dense understory, clearings, and edges; wooded suburban areas

WR: probable confusion with resident race *V. o. chivi* in South America; Amazon Rainforests

WH: evergreen broadleaved forest

D: foliage insects, some fruit in winter

CS: abundant; one of most common cowbird hosts, once considered one of three most common species in eastern deciduous forests, now declining

FF: found in flocks at fruiting trees in tropics

Warbling Vireo *(Vireo gilvus)*

BR: Pacific Northwestern Forests, Taiga, California, Sierra-Cascades, Great Basin, Rocky Mountains, Great Plains, Northeastern Forests, Southeastern Forests, Mexican Plateau and Cordillera

BH: open deciduous and mixed forest, riparian woodlands, thickets, towns

WR: West Mexican Lowlands, Mexican Plateau and Cordillera, Central American Pacific Lowlands

WH: light woodlands, savanna groves, dry deciduous forest, coffee plantations

D: foliage insects, some fruit

CS: common and widespread; common cowbird host, has declined in urban areas because of pesticide contamination

FF: males and females forage together

MUSCICAPIDAE

Wood Thrush

Veery *(Catharus fuscescens)*

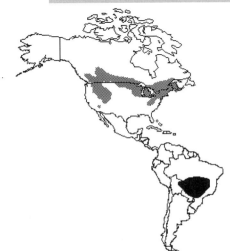

BR: Taiga, Northeastern Forests, northern Great Basin, northern Rocky Mountains

BH: open, moist deciduous woods with dense understory of trees, shrubs, and ferns; bottomland and riparian forests

WR: poorly known: Cerrado

D: evenly divided between insects and fruit (forages primarily on forest floor)

CS: common; common cowbird host

Gray-cheeked Thrush *(Catharus minimus)*

BR: Taiga
BH: coniferous forest and taiga
WR: poorly known: a few records from Amazon
  Rainforest
WH: streamside thickets, old cacao plantations, open
  woodland
D: leaf litter insects, earthworms, and some fruit
CS: common in portions of its range

Bicknell's Thrush *(Catharus bicknelli)*

BR: eastern Northeastern Forests
BH: montane coniferous forest, montane scrub
WR: Caribbean Islands (island of Hispaniola), west-
  ern and southern Venezuela?
WH: forest, thickets
D: foliage and ground insects, earthworms, fruit
CS: has small range and found only in highest eleva-
  tions on breeding grounds
FF: until recently, regarded as race of Gray-cheeked
  Thrush

Swainson's Thrush *(Catharus ustulatus)*

BR: Taiga, Pacific Northwestern Forests, California, Sierra-Cascades, Great Basin, Rocky Mountains, Northeastern Forests

BH: dense coniferous forest, riparian thickets, alder groves, mixed forests

WR: Mayan Highlands, Chiriqui Highlands, Northern Andean Highlands, Tropical Pacific Rainforests, Amazon Rainforests

WH: humid forests and thickets, old second-growth forests

D: ground and foliage insects, much fruit, particularly on wintering grounds

CS: declining, especially in West

FF: known to roost at night in flocks on wintering grounds

Wood Thrush *(Catharus mustelinus)*

BR: Northeastern Forests, Southeastern Forests, eastern Great Plains

BH: moist deciduous and mixed forest, swamps, gardens and urban parks in the Northeast

WR: Campechean Lowlands, Yucatan, Central American Caribbean Lowlands, northern Tropical Pacific Lowlands

WH: moist thickets and forests, cacao plantations, second-growth forest

D: insects, earthworms, some small fruit

CS: declining in some parts of range; frequent cowbird host

FF: migrant that is most dependent on rainforest on wintering grounds

STURNIDAE

Gray Catbird

Gray Catbird *(Dumetella carolinensis)*

BR: Taiga, Northeastern Forests, Southeastern Forests, northern Great Basin, Rocky Mountains, Great Plains

BH: dense thickets in deciduous woodlands and residential areas, riparian thickets, shrubby edge habitat, marsh edges, overgrown fields

WR: Campechean Lowlands, Yucatan, Mayan Highlands, Central American Caribbean Lowlands, Caribbean Islands

WH: forest edge, dense second-growth woodlands, scrub and shrub, hedgerows

D: insects, small fruit and seeds; fruit and seeds constitute larger proportion of diet in fall and winter

CS: common

FF: named after its catlike "mew" call

CERTHIIDAE

Blue-gray Gnatcatcher

Blue-gray Gnatcatcher *(Polioptila caerulea)*

BR: California, Great Basin, southern Rocky Mountains, southern Great Plains, Northeastern Forests, Southeastern Forests, Baja California, Mexican Plateau and Cordillera

BH: bottomlands, oak-pine forest, scrub and open woodland, pinyon-juniper and chaparral, evergreen broadleaved forest

WR: Baja California and Sonora, West Mexican Lowlands, Campechean Lowlands, Mexican Plateau and Cordillera, Mayan Highlands, Central American Pacific Lowlands, Caribbean Islands, (resident race on Yucatan)

WH: scrub woodland, evergreen, and deciduous tropical forest; oak woodland; riparian forest

D: foliage and bark insects

CS: common in parts of range; common cowbird host

FF: lichen-covered nest mimics exterior of tree forks

HIRUNDINIDAE

Purple Martin

Tree Swallow *(Tachycineta bicolor)*

BR: Taiga, Sierra-Cascades, Great Basin, Rocky Mountain, Northeastern Forests

BH: open woodland near water such as ponds, marshes, river bottoms, swamps, especially in areas with snags in or near water (nests in tree cavities)

WR: Southern California, southern Southeastern Forests, south through bioregions to Costa Rica and Caribbean

WH: pastures or savannas near water (ponds, marshes, etc.)

D: flying insects, berries

CS: common

FF: up to a million roost annually in a single farm field in Chiapas, Mexico, from December through March

Violet-green Swallow *(Tachycineta thalassina)*

BR: Pacific Northwestern Forests, California, Sierra-Cascades, Great Basin, Rocky Mountains, West Mexican Lowlands, Mexican Plateau and Cordillera

BH: open woodlands, suburbs, edges of dense forests (coniferous, deciduous, or mixed), woodland clearings, especially near water

WR: West Mexican Lowlands, Mexican Plateau and Cordillera, Mayan Highlands

WH: montane forests, open areas in lowlands, especially near water

D: flying insects

CS: common

Purple Martin *(Progne subis)*

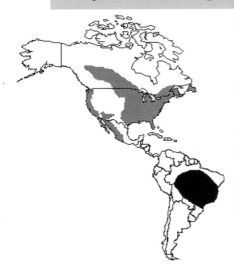

BR: Taiga, southern Pacific Northeastern Forests, California, Sierra-Cascades, Great Plains, Sonora, West Mexican Lowlands, Northeastern Forests, Southeastern Forests

BH: coniferous and mixed forests with large snags, open woodlands near water, suburban areas, *saguaro* deserts

WR: southern Amazon Rainforests, Cerrado

WH: open areas around towns (and oilfields), savanna, scrubland

D: flying insects

CS: locally common, western population decreasing because of starling competition, combined with elimination of nest sites (removal of snags); readily accepts colonial nest boxes in the East; current focus of effort to locate and monitor all active breeding colonies

FF: commonly nests in artificial houses set up in suburban and rural areas in eastern United States, but does not use these houses in western United States; gathers in large premigratory communal roosts of up to one hundred thousand birds at end of summer

Northern Rough-winged Swallow
(Stelgidopteryx serripennis)

BR: Pacific Northwestern Forests, California, Sierra-Cascades, Great Basin, Rocky Mountains, Great Plains, Northeastern Forests, Southeastern Forests, throughout Mexico

WR: southern Florida, Louisiana, and Texas, Campechean Lowlands, West Mexican Lowlands, southern Mexican Plateau and Cordillera, Mayan Highlands

BH and WH: open areas especially near streams, river valleys, and gorges; areas with embankments

D: flying insects

CS: fairly common

FF: recently split from Southern Rough-winged Swallow from Central America; as with following swallow species, nests in burrows in riverbanks and cliffs

Bank Swallow (Riparia riparia)
also known as Sand Martin

BR: Taiga, Great Basin, California, Great Plains, Northeastern Forests

WR: Amazon Rainforests, Cerrado?

BH and WH: open areas usually near water, grasslands, agricultural fields, nests in burrows in riverbanks and cliffs

D: flying insects

CS: locally common, declining over parts of range

FF: gathers in huge premigratory communal roosts, found throughout Europe, Africa, and Asia

Barn Swallow *(Hirundo rustica)*

BR: Taiga, Pacific Northwestern Forests, Sierra-Cascades, California, Great Basin, Rocky Mountains, Great Plains, Northeastern Forests, Southeastern Forests, Mexican Plateau and Cordillera, West Mexican Lowlands

BH: open forest, rural and suburban areas, agricultural lands

WR: bioregions from Costa Rica south throughout South America, Puerto Rico, Lesser Antilles

WH: open areas such as pastures, marshes, rice fields

D: flying insects, especially flies

CS: common

FF: also found in Europe, Africa, and Asia

Cliff Swallow *(Hirundo pyrrhonta)*

BR: Taiga, Pacific Northwestern Forests, California, Sierra-Cascades, Great Basin, Rocky Mountains, Great Plains, Northeastern Forests, northern Southeastern Forests, Sonora, West Mexican Lowlands, Mexican Plateau and Cordillera

WR: Cerrado, Parana, Pampas, Chaco, Atlantic Rainforest

BH and WH: open country near freshwater; near dams, bridges, agricultural fields, towns, and cliffs

D: flying insects

CS: common in western United States, locally common in the East, overall populations stable or increasing, except in some northeastern states where it is declining; house sparrows will take over nests belonging to cliff swallows

FF: females are known to lay eggs in conspecific nests

FRINGILLIDAE

Magnolia Warbler

Lincoln's Sparrow *(Melospiza lincolnii)*

BR: Taiga, Pacific Northwestern Forests, Sierra-Cascades, Rocky Mountains

BH: prefers bogs, wet meadows, riparian thickets; also occurs along forest edges, clearings

WR: southern Pacific Northwestern Forests, California, Baja California and Sonora, West Mexican Lowlands, Mexican Plateau and Cordillera, Campechean Lowlands, Mayan Highlands

WH: brushy fields

D: insects (particularly in summer) and seeds

CS: common

FF: only true Neotropical, migratory sparrow

Bachman's Warbler *(Vermivora bachmanii)*

BR: formerly ranged throughout southeastern United States, may still breed in South Carolina

BH: low, moist, deciduous forest, swamps, canebrakes (bamboo thickets), bottomlands

WR: Cuba and Isle of Pines

WH: bamboo?

D: insects, probably nectar in winter

CS: on U.S. federal list of endangered species; rarest songbird in North America, on verge of extinction (if not already extinct), last confirmed sighting in Cuba in mid-1980s; removal of canebrakes in southeastern United States for agriculture and flood and fire control, loss of wintering habitat likely causes for decline; apparently always rare

FF: painting of this species by J. S. Audubon in 1800s shows the birds on a plant that is now extinct in the wild

Blue-winged Warbler *(Vermivora pinus)*

BR: Northeastern Forests, northern Southeastern Forests

BH: second-growth woods, overgrown fields and pastures, woodland edges, especially brushy borders of swamps and streams

WR: Campechean Lowlands, Yucatan, Mayan Highlands, Central American Caribbean Lowlands, Central American Pacific Lowlands, Chiriqui Highlands (few)

WH: second-growth and semi-open woodlands, especially near gaps and at edges

D: foliage insects

CS: uncommon; frequent cowbird host

FF: commonly breeds with next warbler species to form hybrids that are named Lawrence's and Brewster's warblers

Golden-winged Warbler *(Vermivora chrysoptera)*

BR: Northeastern Forests

BH: edges of deciduous forest, overgrown pastures, thickets; prefers early-successional, old fields

WR: Campechean Lowlands, Mayan Highlands, Central American Caribbean Lowlands, Chiriqui Highlands, northern Tropical Pacific Rainforest, northern Northern Andean Highlands

WH: along edges and gaps of wooded areas, second-growth forest

D: foliage insects

CS: locally common but seriously declining in some regions, especially in southern part of breeding range; decrease in recently abandoned farmland, competition with Blue-winged Warbler (with which it hybridizes), deforestation in wintering range, and parasitism by Brown-headed Cowbirds have contributed to decline

FF: commonly probes dead leaves in hunting for hidden insect prey

Tennessee Warbler *(Vermivora peregrina)*

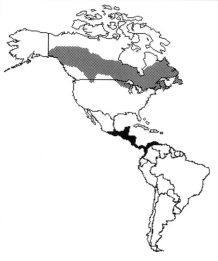

BR: Taiga, northern Northeastern Forests

BH: openings in coniferous and deciduous woodlands with dense ground layer

WR: Campechean Lowlands, Yucatan, Central American Caribbean Lowlands, Central American Pacific Lowlands, Chiriqui Highlands, Tropical Pacific Rainforest, northern Northern Andean Highlands

WH: second-growth forest, particularly in flowering trees (including introduced eucalyptus), coffee plantations, gardens

D: foliage insects; in winter feeds commonly on nectar and berries

CS: common

FF: known to defend tiny territories within flocks at flowering trees in tropics

Orange-crowned Warbler *(Vermivora celata)*

BR: Taiga, Pacific Northwestern Forests, California, Sierra-Cascades, Great Basin, Rocky Mountains

BH: edges of second-growth forest, brushy openings, riparian thickets, chaparral, oak and oak-coniferous woodlands

WR: California, Baja California and Sonora, West Mexican Lowlands, Mexican Plateau and Cordillera, southern Southeastern Forests, Texas to northern Campechean Lowlands

WH: oak woodlands, gardens, riparian woodlands, brushy fields

D: foliage insects; fruit, and nectar in winter

CS: common in western United States, rare in the East

FF: four distinct races; all four may be found in winter at same location in southern California

Nashville Warbler *(Vermivora ruficapilla)*

BR: Taiga, Northeastern Forests, Pacific Northwestern Forests, Sierra-Cascades

BH: coniferous and mixed forests, open second-growth woodlands, bogs, overgrown pastures and fields, woodland edges, brushy, mixed forests,

WR: West Mexican Lowlands, Campechean Lowlands, Mayan Highlands

WH: evergreen broadleaved forests, deciduous forests, coffee plantations

D: insects; more berries and nectar in winter

CS: common

FF: occurs in large single-species flocks in the winter

Virginia's Warbler *(Vermivora virginiae)*

BR: Great Basin, southern Rocky Mountains
WR: southern West Mexican Lowlands, southern
    Mexican Plateau and Cordillera
BH and WH: pinyon-juniper woods, chaparral,
    scrubby montane woodlands, riparian thickets,
    pine-oak woodland
D: foliage insects
CS: common
FF: differs from Nashville Warbler primarily in lower
    concentration of yellow pigment in feathers—a
    common feature in arid-land species

Colima Warbler *(Vermivora crissalis)*

BR: Chisos Mountains of extreme western Texas,
    northern Mexican Plateau and Cordillera
WR: southern Mexican Plateau and Cordillera
BH and WH: montane thickets, forested canyons,
    scrubby woodland
D: foliage insects
CS: candidate for U.S. federal endangered species list-
    ing; rare and local
FF: natural history not well known; very few studies
    of this warbler

Lucy's Warbler *(Vermivora luciae)*

BR: Sonora

WR: southern West Mexican Lowlands

BH and WH: deserts, mesquite and cottonwoods
along watercourses

D: foliage insects

CS: common

FF: the only true desert warbler; one of only two
cavity-nesting warblers

Northern Parula *(Parula americana)*

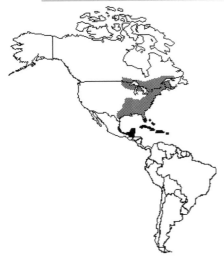

BR: Northeastern Forests, Southeastern Forests

BH: swampy forest, bogs, coniferous and deciduous
woodlands, particularly with abundance of Spanish
moss and lichens

WR: Caribbean Islands, Campechean Lowlands,
Yucatan

WH: semi-open, tall, second-growth woodland and
edges

D: foliage insects; some nectar in winter

CS: common

FF: have nested in several locations in California

Yellow Warbler *(Dendroica petechia aestiva)*

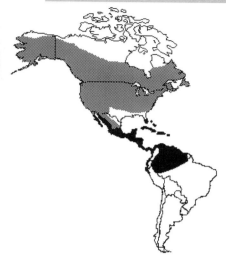

BR: Pacific Northwestern Forests, Taiga, California, Sierra-Cascades, Great Basin, Baja California and Sonora, Rocky Mountain, Great Plains, Northeastern Forests, northern Southeastern Forests, Mexican Plateau and Cordillera

BH: edges of streams, ponds, swamps and marshes, hedgerows, roadside thickets, orchards, gardens, agricultural lands, mangroves in southern Florida, riparian woodland in the West, brush fields

WR: Baja California and Sonoran, West Mexican Lowlands, Campechean Lowlands, Yucatan, Central American Caribbean Lowlands, Central American Pacific Lowlands, Tropical Pacific Rainforests, Amazon Rainforests, Caribbean Islands

WH: second-growth woodland, particularly along streams, brushy pastures and hedgerows, agricultural lands, gardens, mangroves

D: foliage insects; some small fruit and nectar in winter

CS: declines in many areas across range, especially in Idaho, Dakotas, California, and Arizona, due to loss of habitat and heavy cowbird parasitism; populations in the West increasing again wherever reduction of grazing has allowed regrowth of riparian vegetation; one of the three most common cowbird hosts

FF: in winter, aggressively defends territories against other species

Chestnut-sided Warbler *(Dendroica pensylvanica)*

BR: Northeastern Forests, eastern Taiga

BH: brushy second-growth forest, abandoned fields and pastures, woodland edges, roadside thickets

WR: southern West Mexican Lowlands, Campechean Lowlands, Mayan Highlands, Central American Caribbean Lowlands, northern Tropical Pacific Rainforest, Chiriqui Highlands

WH: second-growth, a variety of woodlands, shady gardens

D: foliage insects; small fruit in winter

CS: common; frequent cowbird host

FF: much more common today than in early nineteenth century

Magnolia Warbler *(Dendroica magnolia)*

BR: Taiga, Northeastern Forests

BH: open coniferous and mixed coniferous-deciduous woodlands, bogs, second-growth woodland, woodland edges, coniferous Alder thickets

WR: Campechean Lowlands, Yucatan, Mayan Highlands, Central American Caribbean Lowlands, Central American Pacific Lowlands

WH: a variety of woodlands, open groves, thickets, deciduous forest

D: foliage insects

CS: common

FF: extremely vocal on breeding and wintering grounds, but silent during fall migration

Cape May Warbler *(Dendroica tigrina)*

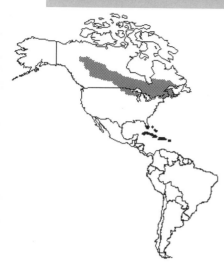

BR: Taiga, northern Northeastern Forests

BH: open boreal coniferous forest, coniferous edges and woodland

WR: Caribbean Islands

WH: evergreen and deciduous forests, gardens, mangroves, thickets

D: foliage insects; more fruit and nectar in winter

CS: uncommon

FF: populations closely tied to irruptions of spruce budworm populations; often extremely aggressive, defending trees from a number of species

Black-throated Blue Warbler *(Dendroica caerulescens)*

BR: southern Taiga, Northeastern Forests

BH: northern hardwood forests, mature coniferous-deciduous forests with brushy undergrowth, mountain laurel thickets in Appalachians

WR: Caribbean Islands

WH: forest canopy, edges, semi-open in hilly country

D: foliage insects, some berries

CS: common

FF: males tend to occur in forests and females in shrubby habitat, in winter

Black-throated Gray Warbler *(Dendroica nigrescens)*

BR: southern Pacific Northwestern Forests, California, Sierra-Cascades, Great Basin, southern Rocky Mountains, Baja California and Sonora

WR: Baja California and Sonora, West Mexican Lowlands, Mexican Plateau and Cordillera

BH and WH: open oak-coniferous forests, oak woodlands, pinyon-juniper and oak scrub

D: mostly foliage insects, some fruit, nectar

CS: common

FF: songs similar to Hermit Warbler's songs, species may mimic each other if nesting in close proximity

Townsend's Warbler *(Dendroica townsendi)*

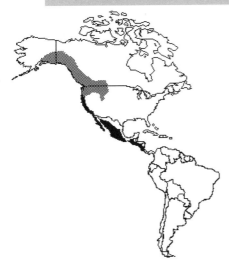

BR: Pacific Northwestern Forests, northern Sierra-Cascades, northern Rocky Mountains

BH: montane coniferous forests and mixed coniferous-deciduous forests

WR: southern Pacific Northwestern Forests, California, Mexican Plateau and Cordillera, West Mexican Lowlands, Mayan Highlands, Chiriqui Highlands

WH: humid forests, pine-oak woodlands, forest edges, second-growth woodland, and clearings

D: foliage insects; some fruit in winter

CS: common in coniferous forests of Pacific Northwest

FF: population that winters in California is from the Queen Charlotte Islands

Hermit Warbler *(Dendroica occidentalis)*

BR: southern Pacific Northwestern Forests, southern Sierra-Cascades

BH: coniferous forest

WR: Mexican Plateau and Cordillera, Mayan Highlands, Chiriqui Highlands

WH: coniferous forest, pine-oak woodland, particularly pines

D: foliage insects

CS: common

FF: will sometimes breed with Townsend's Warblers to form hybrid offspring

Black-throated Green Warbler *(Dendroica virens)*

BR: Taiga, Northeastern Forests

BH: open mixed woodlands, northern coniferous forests; less often inhabits second-growth hardwoods

WR: Campechean Lowlands, West Mexican Lowlands, Mexican Plateau and Cordillera, Mayan Highlands, Yucatan, Central American Caribbean Lowlands, Chiriqui Highlands, Central American Pacific Lowlands, Caribbean Islands

WH: evergreen and deciduous forests, second-growth woodlands, pine-oak woodland

D: foliage insects, some fruit

CS: common

FF: while wintering in lowlands, primarily found in acacia-type trees with thin, needlelike leaves; in highlands, favors oaks and conifers

Golden-cheeked Warbler *(Dendroica chrysoparia)*

BR: locally on Edward's Plateau of central Texas

BH: requires mature stands of Ashe juniper (builds nest using bark strips from only these trees)

WR: Mayan Highlands

WH: pine-oak forests and thickets

D: foliage insects

CS: on Federal Endangered Species List; uncommon and very local—an extreme habitat specialist; populations have been decimated by removal and conversion of "cedar brakes" (Ashe juniper stands); mature cedar brakes ranging from several hundred to a thousand or more acres are necessary to ensure adequate habitat; heavily parasitized by cowbirds

FF: on wintering grounds, found alone or one or two in mixed-species flocks with Townsend's, Hermit, and Black-throated Green warblers

Blackburnian Warbler *(Dendroica fusca)*

BR: eastern Taiga, Northeastern Forests

BH: mature coniferous forests, oak-hickory forests of the Appalachians

WR: Chiriqui Highlands, Northern Andean Highlands

WH: evergreen, broadleaved forest and edge, second-growth woodland

D: foliage insects

CS: common

FF: squeaky notes of song are among the highest-frequency bird vocalizations

Yellow-throated Warbler *(Dendroica dominica)*

PERMANENT
RANGE

PR: central and northern Florida and southern
   Georgia
BR: Southeastern Forests
BH: riparian woodland, swamps, oak-pine forests
WR: Campechean Lowlands, Yucatan, Central
   American Caribbean Lowlands, southern West
   Mexican Lowlands, Central American Pacific Low-
   lands, Caribbean Islands
WH: palms in lowland savanna and towns, pine
   forests
D: bark and foliage insects
CS: common in southeastern United States
FF: commonly found in gardens in town plazas in
   Mexico

Prairie Warbler *(Dendroica discolor)*

BR: Northeastern Forests, Southeastern Forests
BH: brushy pine-oak woodlands, mangroves, brushy
   second-growth woodlands, and farmlands
WR: Caribbean Islands, Yucatan
WH: lowland pine savanna, associated with palm
   trees in Florida and Caribbean
D: foliage insects
CS: common; frequent cowbird host; listed as vul-
   nerable in Canada
FF: not found on prairies

Palm Warbler *(Dendroica palmarum)*

BR: Taiga

BH: bogs, open coniferous forest

WR: southern Atlantic and Gulf coasts of United States, Caribbean Islands, Campechean Lowlands, Yucatan, Central American Caribbean Lowlands, coastal California (uncommon)

WH: second-growth woodland, edges, open groves, coastal scrub

D: foliage insects, berries, also nectar

CS: fairly common

FF: wags tail frequently and feeds on ground like the pipit

Bay-breasted Warbler *(Dendroica castanea)*

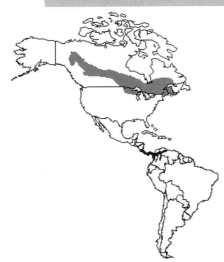

BR: Taiga, northern Northeastern Forests

BH: open coniferous forest, mixed woodland borders of streams, highways, and lakes

WR: Central American Caribbean Lowlands, Tropical Pacific Rainforest, northern Northern Andean Highlands (low elevations)

WH: evergreen broadleaved forests and edges, dry deciduous woodland

D: mostly foliage insects; fruit in winter

CS: fairly common

FF: breeding populations closely tied to irruptions of spruce budworm populations, but eats much fruit in winter

Blackpoll Warbler *(Dendroica striata)*

BR: Taiga, eastern Northeastern Forests
BH: boreal coniferous forest
WR: Amazon Rainforest, Caribbean Llanos
WH: evergreen broadleaved forests, second-growth
   woodland, thickets, and gardens
D: foliage insects; small fruit in fall and winter
CS: common
FF: makes round-trip migration at least twenty-five
   hundred miles, overwater flight from eastern United
   States to northern South America

Cerulean Warbler *(Dendroica cerulea)*

BR: Northeastern Forests, northern Southeastern
   Forests
BH: mature deciduous forest
WR: Northern Andean Highlands
WH: evergreen broadleaved forests and edges
D: foliage insects; some small fruit in winter
CS: locally common; sensitive to fragmentation of
   breeding habitat; population size has declined across
   range in eastern United States despite range expan-
   sion to east and north; listed as vulnerable in
   Canada
FF: found in mixed-species flocks in Andes, but only
   one or two individuals per flock; often found in
   male-female pairs

Black-and-white Warbler *(Mniotilta varia)*

BR: Taiga, Northeastern Forests, Southeastern Forests, Great Plains

BH: mature or second-growth deciduous or mixed forest

WR: Gulf Coast of United States, southern West Mexican Lowlands, southern Mexican Plateau and Cordillera, Campechean Lowlands, Yucatan, Mayan Highlands, Central American Caribbean Lowlands, Central American Pacific Lowlands, Chiriqui Highlands, Tropical Pacific Rainforest, northern Northern Andean Highlands

WH: pine-oak woodland, deciduous and evergreen broadleaved forests, old second-growth forest, and gardens

D: bark insects

CS: common; frequent cowbird host, very sensitive to fragmentation of breeding habitat

FF: found in mixed-species flocks on wintering grounds—only one per flock and will aggressively chase others that try to join flock; one of earliest warblers to arrive on breeding grounds; forages on bark and so not dependent on leaves being out

American Redstart *(Setophaga ruticilla)*

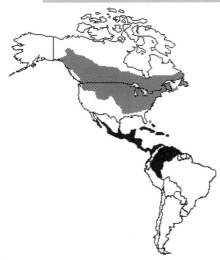

BR: northern Cascades, northern Rocky Mountains, northern Great Plains, Taiga, Northeastern Forests, Southeastern Forests

BH: open deciduous woodlands, also mixed forest

WR: West Mexican Lowlands, Campechean Lowlands, Yucatan, Mayan Highlands, Central American Caribbean Lowlands, Central American Pacific Lowlands, Chiriqui Highlands, Tropical Pacific Rainforest, Northern Andean Highlands, Caribbean Llanos, eastern Amazon Rainforest

WH: light woods, second-growth woodland, gaps and edges

D: foliage and flying insects

CS: abundant; frequent cowbird host

FF: feeds mostly on small leafhoppers, which it flushes by flashing wings and tail

Prothonotary Warbler *(Protonotaria citrea)*

BR: western Northeastern Forests, Southeastern Forests

BH: swamps, wet lowland forest

WR: Campechean Lowlands, Central American Caribbean Lowlands, Central American Pacific Lowlands, Tropical Pacific Rainforest, Caribbean Llanos, Caribbean Islands

WH: prefers streamside thickets, rivers and ponds, mangroves

D: insects, occasionally fruit and nectar

CS: uncommon; frequent cowbird host, may be declining because of habitat loss; listed as vulnerable in Canada

FF: may occur in male-female pairs in winter, also in single-species flocks; hole-nesting species, will accept nest boxes; roosts communally

Worm-eating Warbler *(Helmitheros vermivorus)*

BR: northern Southeastern Forests, southern Northeastern Forests

BH: deciduous forest undergrowth, along wooded slopes, ravines, and streamsides

WR: Campechean Lowlands, Yucatan, Central American Caribbean Lowlands, West Mexican Lowlands, Central American Pacific Lowlands, Caribbean Islands

WH: undergrowth in evergreen, broadleaved forests

D: mostly insects

CS: uncommon; sensitive to forest fragmentation on breeding grounds; rarely cowbird host

FF: foraging specialist on wintering grounds, feeds by probing into dead, curled leaves on trees and vines

Swainson's Warbler *(Limnothlypis swainsonii)*

BR: Southeastern Forests

BH: moist forest with dense undergrowth, cane-brakes, swamps

WR: southern Campechean Lowlands, Yucatan, Caribbean Islands

WH: evergreen, broadleaved, and riparian forests

D: insects on ground and in low brush

CS: uncommon; has experienced sharp declines, is threatened by loss of canebrake habitat and cowbird parasitism

FF: only warbler besides Bachman's that lays white eggs; both species thought to depend on canebrakes and use bamboo in nest

Ovenbird *(Seiurus aurocapillis)*

BR: Taiga, Northeastern Forests, Southeastern Forests, northern Great Plains

BH: mature, deciduous forest; occasionally inhabits moist or swampy forest

WR: Campechean Lowlands, West Mexican Lowlands, southern Mexican Plateau and Cordillera, Mayan Highlands, Yucatan, Central American Caribbean Lowlands, Chiriqui Highlands, Central American Pacific Lowlands, Caribbean Islands

WH: tall scrub, well-shaded understory of broadleaved and riparian forest

D: gleans insects, earthworms, other invertebrates, seeds, and other vegetation from forest floor

CS: common; frequent cowbird host, very sensitive to fragmentation of breeding habitat

FF: builds domed-shaped nests that look similar to old-style ovens

Northern Waterthrush *(Seiurus noveboracensis)*

BR: Taiga, Northeastern Forests, northern Rocky Mountains

BH: thickets along edges of swamps, ponds, and streams

WR: southern Baja California, West Mexican Lowlands, Campechean Lowlands, southern Mexican Plateau and Cordillera, Yucatan, Central American Caribbean Lowlands, Central American Pacific Lowlands, Tropical Pacific Rainforest, Caribbean Llanos, Caribbean Islands, northern Amazon Rainforest

WH: well-shaded woodland along streams, rivers, ponds, swamps, and mangroves

D: aquatic and terrestrial insects, small crustaceans, mollusks, and some minnows and worms

CS: common

FF: in wintering grounds, defends territory from Louisiana Waterthrush

Louisiana Waterthrush *(Seiurus motacilla)*

BR: Northeastern Forests, northern Southeastern Forests

BH: prefers bottomland forest along swiftly moving streams; also in swampland

WR: West Mexican Lowlands, Mexican Plateau and Cordillera, Campechean Lowlands, Mayan Highlands, Central American Caribbean Lowlands, Chiriqui Highlands, Central American Pacific Lowlands, Caribbean Islands

WH: wooded areas along clear, swiftly moving streams

D: terrestrial and aquatic insects, spiders, small mollusks, and fish

CS: uncommon; common cowbird host; listed as vulnerable in Canada

FF: scientific name translates to "wagtail wagtail" in Greek and Latin

Kentucky Warbler *(Oporornis formosus)*

BR: southern Northeastern Forests, northern Southeastern Forests

BH: humid deciduous forest

WR: West Mexican Lowlands, Campechean Lowlands, Yucatan, Central American Caribbean Lowlands, Mayan Highlands, Chiriqui Highlands,
Tropical Pacific Rainforest, northern Northern
Andean Highlands

WH: wet forest with shady understory; thickets along
forest edge or gaps

D: gleans insects from ground litter and low
groundcover

CS: common; frequent cowbird host, very sensitive to
fragmentation of breeding habitat

FF: one of most forest-dependent migrants on breeding and wintering grounds

Connecticut Warbler *(Oporornis agilis)*

BR: Taiga

BH: spruce and tamarack bogs, poplar woodland

WR: poorly known: few winter records, Cerrado?

WH: riparian forest? thickets? almost unknown in
winter

D: insects gleaned from ground or low branches

CS: uncommon and local

FF: one of few warblers that doesn't hop, but walks;
rare in Connecticut

Mourning Warbler *(Oporornis philadelphia)*

BR: Northeastern Forests, Taiga

BH: deciduous woodlands with dense undergrowth, shrubby second-growth woodlands, bogs, swamp and marsh edges

WR: Central American Caribbean Lowlands, Chiriqui Highlands, Central American Pacific Lowlands, Tropical Pacific Rainforest

WH: thickets, overgrown pastures, often near brackish or freshwater wetlands

D: insects from ground and low shrubs

CS: locally common to uncommon

FF: so named because of dark hood and black "crepe" on throat

MacGillivray's Warbler *(Oporornis tolmiei)*

BR: Pacific Northwestern Forests, Sierra-Cascades, northern Great Basin, Rocky Mountains,

BH: young second-growth, shrubby areas, riparian thickets

WR: southern Baja California and Sonora, West Mexican Lowlands, Campechean Lowlands, Mexican Plateau and Cordillera, Mayan Highlands, Central American Caribbean Lowlands, Central American Pacific Lowlands, Chiriqui Highlands

WH: second-growth woodland, scrubby fields, thickets

D: insects from ground and low shrubs

CS: common to uncommon

FF: known to interbreed with Mourning Warbler

Common Yellowthroat *(Geothlypis trichas)*

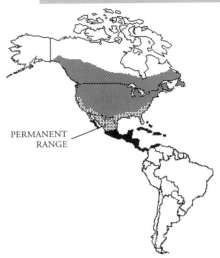

PERMANENT
RANGE

PR: Southern California, northern Baja California and Sonora, Southern Great Plains, Southeastern Forests

BR: Pacific Northwestern Forests, California, Great Basin, Great Plains, Northeastern Forests, Southeastern Forests

BH: marshes, thickets near water, brushy pastures, old fields

WR: southern United States, Baja California and Sonora, West Mexican Lowlands, Mexican Plateau and Cordillera, Campechean Lowlands, Yucatan, Central American Caribbean Lowlands, Central American Pacific Lowlands, Caribbean Islands

WH: reedy marshes and dense, scrubby wetlands; pastures and fields

D: gleans insects from low vegetation

CS: common to abundant

FF: only warbler that is true wetland species, particularly in western North America, but can winter in dry cattle pasture

Hooded Warbler *(Wilsonia citrina)*

BR: southern Northeastern Forests, Southeastern Forests

BH: moist hardwood forest with dense undergrowth, cypress-gum swampland

WR: central West Mexican Lowlands, southern Campechean Lowlands, Yucatan, Mayan Highlands, Central American Caribbean Lowlands, Central American Pacific Lowlands, Chiriqui Highlands

WH: moist thickets, forest edge, second-growth woods

D: foliage and ground insects

CS: common; frequent cowbird host

FF: in winter, males occur in forests more so than females

Wilson's Warbler *(Wilsonia pusilla)*

BR: Pacific Northwestern Forests, Sierra-Cascades, Rocky Mountains, Taiga

BH: bogs, thickets, moist brushy areas

WR: southern Baja California and Sonora, West Mexican Lowlands, Mexican Plateau and Cordillera, Campechean Lowlands, Mayan Highlands, Central American Caribbean Lowlands, Central American Pacific Lowlands, Chiriqui Highlands

WH: broadleaved evergreen and deciduous forests, montane scrub, second-growth woodland, coffee plantations

D: foliage insects

CS: common

FF: polygynous (males in some areas will have more than one mate)

Canada Warbler *(Wilsonia canadensis)*

BR: Northeastern Forests, Taiga

BH: cool, moist woodlands with shrubby undergrowth, streamside thickets, bogs

WR: Northern Andean Highlands

WH: evergreen, broadleaved forests

D: foliage insects

CS: locally common; common cowbird host

FF: thought to migrate in pairs

Yellow-breasted Chat *(Icteria virens)*

BR: southern Pacific Northwestern Forests, California, Great Basin, Rocky Mountains, Great Plains, Northeastern Forests, Southeastern Forests, Baja California and Sonora, Mexican Plateau and Cordillera, northern West Mexican Lowlands

BH: second-growth forest, scrub, streamside thickets, forest edge, overgrown pastures

WR: West Mexican Lowlands, Campechean Lowlands, Yucatan, Mayan Highlands, Central American Caribbean Lowlands, Central American Pacific Lowlands, Chiriqui Highlands

WH: second-growth forest, forest edge, brushy fields

D: insects; mostly fruit in winter

CS: common; frequent cowbird host

FF: complex song, with ventriloquial qualities; mimics other species

Summer Tanager *(Piranga rubra)*

BR: Southeastern Forests, southern Great Plains, Baja California and Sonora, northern Mexican Plateau and Cordillera

BH: open mixed and deciduous woodlands, bottomland forest, riparian woodland

WR: Baja California and Sonora, West Mexican Lowlands, Campechean Lowlands, Mexican Plateau and Cordillera, Mayan Highlands, Yucatan, Central American Caribbean Lowlands, Central American Pacific Lowlands, Chiriqui Highlands, Tropical Pacific Rainforest, Northern Andean Highlands, western Amazon Rainforest

WH: evergreen and deciduous forest, riparian woodland, shady gardens, clearings and pastures with scattered trees

D: tears open nests of wasps and bees to extract larvae and pupae; also eats adult wasps and bees, fruit

CS: common; range reportedly contracting in eastern United States

FF: males take two years to acquire full red plumage

Scarlet Tanager *(Piranga olivacea)*

BR: Northeastern Forests, southern Taiga, eastern Great Plains

BH: mature deciduous and mixed deciduous-coniferous woodlands, wooded parks and suburban areas

WR: Tropical Pacific Rainforest, Northern Andean Highlands, western Amazon Rainforest (near base of Andes)

WH: evergreen broadleaved forests, river edge

D: foliage and flying insects, fruit (especially on wintering grounds)

CS: common; common cowbird host

FF: the only tanagers in which males molt into dull plumage in winter

Western Tanager *(Piranga ludovicianus)*

BR: Pacific Northwestern Forests, California, Sierra-Cascades, Great Basin, Rocky Mountains, northern Baja California

BH: open, mature coniferous forest, less often in mixed and deciduous forests

WR: southern Baja California and Sonora, West Mexican Lowlands, Mexican Plateau and Cordillera, Campechean Lowlands, Mayan Highlands, Central American Pacific Lowlands

WH: pine-oak woodland, evergreen broadleaved and deciduous forests, second-growth forest

D: foliage and flying insects; also fruit, especially on wintering grounds

CS: common

FF: found in male-female pairs in winter

Dickcissel *(Spiza americana)*

BR: Great Plains, western Northeastern Forests,
    northern Southeastern Forests
BH: tall grasslands, cultivated and abandoned fields
WR: West Mexican Lowlands, Central American
    Pacific Lowlands, Caribbean Llanos and Dry Forest
WH: grasslands, rice fields
D: insects in summer; seeds and grains in winter
CS: common in Plains, rare and local in the East;
    overall population appears to be declining; frequent
    cowbird host, active nests in fields often destroyed
    by farming machines
FF: named after its song

Rose-breasted Grosbeak *(Pheucticus ludovicianus)*

BR: Northeastern Forests, Great Plains, Taiga
BH: second-growth deciduous or mixed woods, edges
    of forests, swamps, streams and pastures, wooded
    parks and suburbs
WR: West Mexican Lowlands, Campechean Low-
    lands, southern Mexican Plateau and Cordillera,
    Mayan Highlands, Yucatan, Central American
    Caribbean Lowlands, Central American Pacific
    Lowlands, Chiriqui Highlands, Tropical Pacific
    Rainforest, Northern Andean Highlands
WH: open woods, forest edge, scattered trees in plan-
    tations, gardens and clearings
D: insectivorous in summer; seeds, fruit, buds, some
    insects and nectar in winter
CS: common; common cowbird host, showing large
    declines
FF: known to interbreed with next species where
    breeding ranges overlap

Rose-breasted Grosbeak

Black-headed Grosbeak *(Pheucticus melanocephalus)*

BR: Pacific Northwestern Forests, California, Sierra-Cascades, Great Basin, Rocky Mountains, Great Plains, West Mexican Lowlands, Mexican Plateau and Cordillera

BH: open deciduous forest, chaparral, woodland edges, riparian thickets, wooded parks and suburbs

WR: West Mexican Lowlands, Mexican Plateau and Cordillera, Mayan Highlands, northern Campechean Lowlands, southern Baja California

WH: pine-oak forest, broadleaved evergreen and deciduous forest, riparian woodland, second-growth woodland

D: mostly insects, also fruit and seeds

CS: common

FF: will sometimes mimic other birds in its songs

Blue Grosbeak *(Guiraca caerulea)*

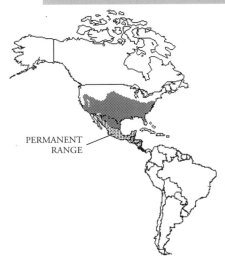

PERMANENT RANGE

PR: throughout bioregions from central Mexico to Costa Rica

BR: California, Great Basin, Baja California and Sonora, southern Rocky Mountains, Great Plains, Southeastern Forests

BH: weedy pastures, old fields, forest edges, stream-side thickets, hedgerows, mesquite woods

WR: West Mexican Lowlands, Mexican Plateau and Cordillera, Campechean Lowlands, Mayan Highlands, Yucatan, Central American Caribbean Lowlands, Central American Pacific Lowlands, Chiriqui Highlands

WH: agricultural areas with scattered trees and hedgerows, second-growth woodland, edges of deciduous forest, dry scrub

D: insects, seeds, and fruit

CS: fairly common, but rare and local in northeastern part of breeding range; frequent cowbird host

FF: one of few birds found in cornfields in wintering grounds

Lazuli Bunting *(Passerina amoena)*

BR: California, Sierra-Cascades, Great Basin, Rocky Mountains, Great Plains, northern Baja California

BH: arid brush, chaparral, riparian thickets, aspen groves, open woodlands

WR: southern Baja California and Sonora, West Mexican Lowlands, western Mexican Plateau and Cordillera

WH: weedy fields, grassland edges, croplands, second-growth woodland

D: mostly insects; seeds in winter

CS: common to uncommon; disappearing in some parts of range because of human encroachment, increasing in other parts because of increases in appropriate habitat due to logging and irrigation projects (more early successional habitat and riparian thickets)

FF: young males learn how to refine singing by listening to older male "tutors"

Indigo Bunting *(Passerina cyanea)*

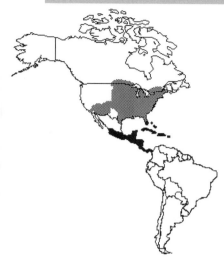

BR: Northeastern Forests, Southeastern Forests, Great Plains, southern Rocky Mountains, Sonora

BH: woodland edges, brushy fields and ravines, roadside and streamside thickets

WR: southern West Mexican Lowlands, southern Mexican Plateau and Cordillera, Campechean Lowlands, Yucatan, Mayan Highlands, Central American Caribbean Lowlands, Central American Pacific Lowlands, Chiriqui Highlands, Caribbean Islands

WH: weedy fields, grassland edges, croplands, second-growth woodland

D: insects, seeds, small fruit

CS: common in eastern breeding range; frequent cowbird host

FF: in winter male looks all brown, but reveals brilliant blue in spring when brown edges of feathers wear off

Painted Bunting *(Passerina ciris)*

BR: eastern Southeastern Forests, southern Great Plains, Sonora, northern Mexican Plateau and Cordillera

BH: brushy fields and woodlands, hedgerows, streamside and roadside edges

WR: West Mexican Lowlands, Campechean Lowlands, Yucatan, Central American Caribbean Lowlands, Central American Pacific Lowlands, Cuba and Bahamas, southern Florida

WH: overgrown pastures and brushy, second-growth woodland

D: mostly insects on breeding grounds; mostly seeds, fruit, some insects in winter

CS: locally common; frequent cowbird host

FF: common cagebird in Mexico

Northern Oriole *(Icterus galbula)*

BR: Northeastern Forests, northern Southeastern Forests, Great Plains, Rocky Mountains, Great Basin, Sierra-Cascades, California, Pacific Northwestern Forests, northern Baja California and Sonora, northern Mexican Plateau and Cordillera

BH: orchards, deciduous forest edge, wooded suburbs and parks, mesquite groves, prairies, riparian woodland

WR: West Mexican Lowlands, Campechean Lowlands, Mexican Plateau and Cordillera, Mayan Highlands, Central American Caribbean Lowlands, Central American Pacific Lowlands, Tropical Pacific Rainforest, Caribbean Dry Forest, Caribbean Islands

WH: pine-oak forest, broadleaved evergreen and deciduous forests, cacao and coffee plantations, semi-open woodland, savanna groves

D: insects, spiders; much fruit and nectar in winter

CS: common; eastern populations declining

FF: probably two species—the Bullock's and Baltimore orioles; Baltimore Orioles winter primarily in shade coffee and cacao plantations

Orchard Oriole *(Icterus spurius)*

BR: Northeastern Forests, Southeastern Forests, Great Plains, northern Mexican Plateau and Cordillera

BH: orchards; open areas with scattered trees, including farmlands and suburban areas; scrub; mesquite

WR: southern West Mexican Lowlands, Campechean Lowlands, Yucatan, Central American Caribbean Lowlands, Central American Pacific Lowlands, Tropical Pacific Rainforest, Caribbean Dry Forest

WH: scrubby, second-growth woodland, savanna, hedgerows, gardens

D: mostly insects; more fruit and nectar on wintering grounds

CS: locally common, populations decreasing in many parts of range, mostly because of cowbird parasitism and loss of tropical forest habitat

FF: possibly migrates north from wintering range by following the flowering of trees such as *Inga*

Bobolink *(Dolichonyx oryzivorus)*

BR: Northeastern Forests, northern Great Plains, northern Great Basin

BH: grass fields, meadows

WR: Cerrado, Chaco, northern Pampas

WH: grassy clearings, fields, scrub, rice fields

D: forages in cultivated grain fields for seeds, grains, and insects

CS: locally common, numbers decreasing in northeastern United States because of decline in agriculture and in the Southeast because of hunting for food and rice crop protection, range extending in the West because of irrigation

FF: landbird with one of longest migration routes; known as "rice bird" for its common association with that crop

Selected Reference List

CHAPTER 1
General
Diamond, Anthony W., et al. *Save the Birds*. Boston: Houghton Mifflin Company, 1989.
Ehrlich, P. S., D. S. Dobkin, and D. Wheye. *The Birder's Handbook*. New York: Simon and Schuster, Inc., 1988.
————. *Birds in Jeopardy*. Stanford: Stanford University Press, 1992.
Finch, D. M., and P. W. Stangel, eds. *Status and Management of Neotropical Migratory Birds*. USDA Forest Service Technical Report RM-229. Ft. Collins, Col.: Rocky Mountain Experimental Station, 1993.
Gollop, J. B., T. W. Barry, and E. H. Iverson. *Eskimo Curlew: A Vanishing Species?* Regina: Saskatchewan Natural History Society, 1986.
Gorup, P. D. *Ecology and Conservation of Grassland Birds*. ICBP Technical Publ. no. 7, 1988.
Greenberg, R. *El Sur de Mexico: Cruces de los Caminos para Pajaros Migratorios*. (Southern Mexico: Crossroads for Migratory Birds.) Washington, D.C.: Smithsonian Migratory Bird Center, 1991.
————. *Uniendo las Americas: Aves Migratorias en Costa Rica y Panama*. (Bridging the Americas: Migratory Birds in Costa Rica and Panama.) Washington, D.C.: Smithsonian Migratory Bird Center, 1994.
Greenberg, R., and S. Lumpkin. *Birds Over Troubled Forests*. Washington, D.C.: Smithsonian Migratory Bird Center, 1990.
Griscom, L., and A. Sprunt. *The Warblers of North America*. New York: Devin-Adair. Reprinted by Doubleday, 1957.
Hagan, J. M., and D. Johnston, eds. *Ecology and Conservation of Neotropical Migrant Landbirds*. Washington, D.C.: Smithsonian Institution Press, 1992.
Hamel, P. *The Bachman's Warbler: A Species in Peril*. Washington, D.C.: Smithsonian Institution Press, 1986.
Helmers, D. L. *Shorebird Management Manual*. Manomet, Mass.: Wetlands for the Americas, 1992.
Johnsgard, P. A. *The Hummingbirds of North America*. Washington, D.C.: Smithsonian Institution Press, 1983.
Keast, A., and E. S. Morton. *Migrant Birds in the Neotropics: Ecology, Behavior, Distribution, and Conservation*. Washington, D.C.: Smithsonian Institution Press, 1980.

Matthiassen, P. *The Wind Birds.* New York: The Viking Press, 1973,

McCabe, R. A. *The Little Green Bird: Ecology of the Willow Flycatcher.* Madison, Wis.: Rusty Rock Press, 1992.

Morse, D. H. *American Warblers.* Cambridge: Harvard University Press, 1989.

Nolan, V., Jr. *The Ecology and Behavior of the Prairie Warbler.* Ornithological Monograph No. 26, 1978.

Rappole, J. H., E. S. Morton, T. E. Lovejoy, and J. L. Ruos. *Nearctic Migrants in the Neotropics.* Washington, D.C.: U.S. Fish and Wildlife Service, 1983.

———. *Aves Migratorias Nearcticas en los Neotropicos.* Front Royal, Va.: Conservation Research Center, National Zoological Park, 1983.

Terborgh, J. *Where Have All the Birds Gone?* Princeton: Princeton University Press, 1989.

Walkinshaw, L. H. *The Kirtland's Warbler.* Bloomfield, Mich.: Cranbrook Institute of Science, 1983.

Environmental Issues
General
State of the World. World Watch Institute. New York: Norton Press (annual).

World Resources. World Resources Institute, IIED, UNEP. New York: Oxford University Press (annual).

The Conservation of Biological Diversity
Ehrlich, P. R., and A. Ehrlich. *Extinctions.* New York: Random House, 1981.

Ehrlich, P. R. *Machinery of Nature.* New York: Simon and Schuster, 1986.

McKibben, B. *The End of Nature.* New York: Random House, 1989.

Soule, M., ed. *The Science of Scarcity and Diversity.* Sunderland, Mass.: Sinauer Associates, 1986.

Wilson, E. O., ed. *Biodiversity.* Washington, D.C.: National Academy Press, 1988.

Wilson, E. O. *The Diversity of Life.* Cambridge: Harvard University Press, 1992.

Population
Ehrlich, P. R., and A. H. Ehrlich. *The Population Explosion.* New York: Simon and Schuster, 1989.

Lappe, F. M., and R. Schurman. *Taking Population Seriously.* San Francisco: Institute for Food Policy Studies, 1988.

Economics of Consumption
Daly, H. E., and J. B. Cobb. *For the Common Good: Redirecting the Economy Towards Community, the Environment, and a Sustainable Future.* New York: Beacon Press, 1989.

Daly, H. E., and K. E. Townsend. *Valuing the Earth: Economics, Ecology, and Ethics.* Cambridge: MIT Press, 1993.

Repetto, R. C. *World Enough and Time: Successful Strategies for Resource Management.* New Haven: Yale University Press, 1986.

Pesticides and Toxin Contamination
Carson, R. *Silent Spring.* Boston: Houghton-Mifflin, 1962.

National Toxics Campaign. *Citizen's Toxic Protection Manual.* Boston: 1988.

Natural Resource Defense Council. *Harvest of Hope: Alternative Agriculture's Potential to Reduce Pesticide Use.* New York: NRDC, 1991.

Weir, D., and M. Schapiro. *Circle of Poisons: Pesticides and People in a Hungry World*. San Francisco: Institute for Food and Development Policy, 1981.

Global Change

Frior, J. *The Changing Atmosphere: A Global Challenge*. New Haven: Yale University Press, 1990.

Schneider, S. H. *Global Warming*. Vintage Books, 1989.

North American Habitat Conservation

Cox, T. R., et al. *This Well-wooded Land: Americans and Their Forests from Colonial Times to the Present*. Lincoln: University of Nebraska Press, 1985.

Drushka, K. *STUMPED: The Forest Industry in Transition*. Toronto: Douglas and Macintyre, 1985.

Ferguson, D., and N. Ferguson. *Sacred Cows at the Public Trough*. Bend, Ore: Maverick Press, 1983.

Harris, L. D. *The Fragmented Forest: Island Biogeography Theory and the Preservation of Biotic Diversity*. Chicago: University of Chicago Press, 1984.

Hunter, M. L., Jr. *Wildlife, Forests, and Forestry: Principles of Managing Forests for Biological Diversity*. Englewood Cliffs, N.J.: Regents/Prentice Hall, 1990.

Ireland, L. C. *The Study of New England's Forests*. University Press of New England, 1982.

Kusler, J., and M. E. Kentula, eds. *Wetland Creation and Restoration: The Status of the Science*. Washington, D.C.: Island Press, 1990.

Matthiessen, P. *Wildlife in America*. New York: Viking Press, 1959.

National Research Council. *Alternative Agriculture*. Washington, D.C.: National Academy Press, 1989.

Norse, E. A. *Ancient Forests of the Pacific Northwest*. Washington, D.C.: Island Press, 1990.

O'Conner, R., and M. Shrubb. *Farming and Birds*. Cambridge, England: Cambridge University Press, 1986.

Perlin, J. *A Forest Journey: The Role of Wood in the Development of Civilization*. New York: W. W. Norton & Co., 1989.

Richards, J. F., and R. P. Tucker, eds. *World Deforestation in the Twentieth Century*. Durham, N.C.: Duke University Press, 1988.

Robinson, G. *The Forest and the Trees: A Guide to Excellent Forestry*. Washington, D.C.: Island Press, 1988.

Verner, J., M. L. Morrison, and C. J. Ralph, eds. *Wildlife 2000: Modeling Habitat Relationships of Terrestrial Vertebrates*. Madison: University of Wisconsin Press, 1986.

Werner, R. E., and Kim Hendrix. *California Riparian Systems: Ecology, Conservation and Productive Management*. Berkeley: University of California Press, 1984.

Williams, M. *Americans and Their Forests*. Cambridge, England: Cambridge University Press, 1989.

Tropical Habitat Conservation

Caufield, C. *In the Rainforest*. New York: Knopf, Inc., 1985.

Collins, M., ed. *The Last Rainforests: A World Conservation Atlas*. New York: Oxford University Press, 1990.

Forsyth, A., and K. Miyata. *Tropical Nature: Life and Death of the Rainforest of Central and South America*. New York: Charles Scribner's Sons, 1984.

Gentry, A. H., ed. *Four Neotropical Rainforests*. New Haven: Yale University Press, 1990.

Goodland, R. *Race to Save the Tropics: Ecology and Economics for a Sustainable Future.* Washington, D.C.: Island Press, 1990.

Gradwohl, J., and R. Greenberg. *Saving Tropical Rainforests.* Washington, D.C.: Island Press, 1988.

Head, S., and R. Heinyman. *Lessons of the Rainforest.* San Francisco: Sierra Club Books, 1990.

Hecht, S., and A. Cockburn. *The Fate of the Forest.* New York: Harper Perennial, 1990.

Janzen, D. *Costa Rican Natural History.* Chicago: University of Chicago Press, 1984.

Kricher, J. C. *A Neotropical Companion.* Princeton: Princeton University Press, 1990.

Leonard, H. J. *Natural Resources and Economic Development in Central America.* New Brunswick, N.J.: Transaction Books, 1987.

McNeely, J. *Economics and Biological Diversity: Developing and Using Economic Incentives to Conserve Biological Resources.* Gland, Switzerland: International Union for the Conservation of Nature and Natural Resources, 1988.

Myers, N. *The Primary Source: Tropical Forests and Our Future.* New York: W. W. Norton and Co., 1984.

National Academy of Sciences. *Conservation of Tropical Moist Forests.* Washington, D.C.: National Academy Press, 1980.

National Research Council. *Sustainable Agriculture and the Environment.* Washington, D.C.: National Academy Press, 1993.

Nations, J. *Tropical Rainforests: Endangered Environments.* New York: Franklin Watts, 1993.

CHAPTER 2

American Birding Association. *Directory of Volunteer Opportunities for Birders.* P.O. Box 6599, Colorado Springs, CO 80934.

American Ornithologists' Union. *Biographies of North American Birds.* Continuing series of fascicles, Philadelphia, Pa.

Bent, A. C. *Life Histories of North American Birds.* (Nineteen different volumes). New York: Dover Press, 1961–1989.

Bonney, R. E., Jr. "Counting in the Cold." *Living Bird Quarterly.* Autumn 1991:8–9.

———. "Good Hawking." *Living Bird Quarterly.* Summer 1991:36–37.

———. "You Can Make a Difference." *Birder's World.* 4 (1990):35–39.

DeSante, D. F. "Monitoring Avian Productivity and Survivorship (MAPS) program: A Sharp, Rather Than Blunt, Tool for Monitoring and Assessing Landbird Populations." *Wildlife 2001: Populations,* edited by D.C. Mccullough and R. H. Barrett. London: Elsevier Applied Science, 1992, pp. 511–521.

Ehrlich, P. S., D. S. Dobkin, and D. Wheye. *The Birder's Handbook.* New York: Simon and Schuster, Inc., 1988.

Gemmill, D. "Directory of Volunteer Opportunities for Birders." *Winging It.* 4 (1992):1–48.

Greenberg, R. *A Primer for Studying Avian Foraging Behavior.* 25 pp. ms. available upon request from the Smithsonian Migratory Bird Center, 1992.

Grubb, T. C. *Beyond Birding: Field Projects for Inquisitive Birders.* Pacific Grove, Calif.: The Boxwood Press, 1986.

Hanley, W. *Natural History in America.* Massachusetts Audubon Society, 1977, pp. 3–15.

Heinrich, B. *Ravens in Winter.* New York: Summit Books, 1989.

Howell, T. R. "Eugene Eisenmann and the Study of Neotropical Birds." *Ornithological Monographs* 36 (1985):1–4.

Hvenegaard G. T., et al. "Economic Values of Bird Watching at Point Pelee National Park, Canada." *Wildlife Society Bulletin* 17 (1989):526–531.

Isler, M. L., and P. R. Isler. *The Tanagers: Natural History, Distribution, and Identification.* Washington, D.C.: Smithsonian Institution Press, 1987.

Morse, D. H. *American Warblers.* Cambridge: Harvard University Press, 1989.

Nice, M. M. *Research Is a Passion with Me.* Toronto: Consolidated Amethyst Communications, Inc., 1976.

Page, G. W., et al. "Shorebird Numbers in Wetlands of the Pacific Flyway: A Summary of Counts from April 1988 to January 1992." *Point Reyes Bird Observatory Newsletter,* 1992.

Ralph, C. J., G. R. Geupel, P. Pyle, T. E. Martin, and D. F. DeSante. *Field Methods for Monitoring Landbirds.* Arcata, Calif.: USDA Forest Service, 1993.

Ralph, C. J. and Scott, J. M. "Estimating Numbers of Terrestrial Birds." *Studies in Avian Biology.* 6: 34–41.

Remsen, J. V. Jr. "On Taking Field Notes." *American Birds.* 31 (1977):946–953.

Root, T. *Atlas of Wintering North American Birds.* Chicago: University of Chicago Press, 1988.

Skutch, A. F. *Life of the Tanager.* Ithaca: Cornell University Press, 1989.

Smith, C. R., ed. *Handbook for Atlasing American Breeding Birds.* The North American Ornithological Atlas Committee, 1990.

Temple, S. A., and J. R. Cary. "Description of the Wisconsin Checklist Program." *Biol. Report.* 1 (1990):14–17.

————. *Wisconsin Birds: A Seasonal and Geographical Guide.* Madison: University of Wisconsin Press, 1987.

Tinbergen, N. *Curious Naturalists.* New York: Anchor Books, 1958.

Wauer, R. H. "The Average Birder Is Not a Little Old Lady in Tennis Shoes." *Birding.* 12 (1980):138–145.

Wiedner, D., and P. Kerlinger. "Economics of Birding: A National Survey of Active Birders." *American Birds.* 44 (1990).

Bird Field Guides

A Field Guide to the Songs of Eastern and Central America. Ithaca, N.Y.: Cornell Laboratory of Ornithology, 1990. Recording.

A Field Guide to the Western Bird Songs. Ithaca, N.Y.: Cornell Laboratory of Ornithology, 1992. Recording.

National Geographic Society. *Field Guide to the Birds of North America.* Washington, D.C.: National Geographic Society, 1987.

National Geographic Society's Guide to Bird Sounds. Washington, D.C.: National Geographic Society, 1985. Recording.

Peterson, Roger Tory. *A Field Guide to the Birds East of the Rockies.* Boston: Houghton Mifflin Company, 1980.

————. *A Field Guide to the Western Birds.* Boston: Houghton Mifflin Company, 1961.

Robbins, C., Bruun, Zim, and A. Singer. *A Field Guide to the Birds of North America.* New York: Golden Press, 1983.

Warblers of North America, Ithaca, N.Y.: Cornell Laboratory of Ornithology, 1985. Recording.

CHAPTER 3

Bissell, S. J., K. Demarest, and D. L. Schrupp. "The Use of Zoning Ordinances in the Protection and Development of Wildlife Habitat." *Integrating Man and Nature in the Metropolitan Environment.* 37–42. Washington, D.C.: National Institute for Urban Wildlife, 1986.

Bobo, K., J. Kendall, and S. Max. *Organizing for Social Change: A Manual for Activists in the 1990s.* Midwest Academy, 1991.

Brenneman, R. L., and S. M. Bates, eds., *Land-Saving Action*. Washington, D.C.: Island Press, 1984.

Cox, J. *Landscaping with Nature*. Emmaus, Pa.: Rodale Press, 1991.

DeGraff, R., and G. Wit. *Trees, Shrubs, and Vines for Attracting Birds*. Amherst: University of Massachusetts Press, 1979.

Dennis, J. V. *The Wildlife Gardener*. New York: Alfred A. Knopf, 1985.

Diekelmann, J., and C. Diekelmann. *Natural Landscaping*. New York: McGraw Hill, 1982.

Fremont-Smith, M. R., and R. E. Koontz, "Becoming and Remaining a Tax-Exempt Organization." *Land Saving Action*. Washington, D.C.: Island Press, 1984.

Harrison, G. H. "Is There a Killer in Your House?" *National Wildlife*. Oct./Nov. 1992:10–13.

Henderson, C. L. *Landscaping for Wildlife*. St. Paul: Minnesota Department of Natural Resources, 1987.

Hoose, P. M. *Building an Ark: Tools for the Preservation of Natural Diversity through Land Protection*. San Francisco: Island Press, 1981.

Horwich, R. H. "How to Develop a Community Sanctuary: An Experimental Approach to the Conservation of Private Lands." *Oryx*, 24 (1990):95–102.

Klem, D., Jr. "Bird Injuries, Cause of Death, and Recuperation from Collisions with Windows." *J. Field Ornithology*, 61 (1990):115–119.

———. "Collisions between Birds and Windows: Mortality and Prevention." *J. Field Ornithology*, 61 (1990):120–128.

Kress, S. W. *The Audubon Society Guide to Attracting Birds*. New York: Charles Scribner's Sons, 1985.

Lipkis, A., K. Lipkis, and M. Pick. *How to Save Your Neighborhood, City, or Town*. San Francisco: Sierra Club, 1993.

———. *The Simple Act of Planting a Tree: Tree People*. Jeremy P. Tarcher, Inc., 1990.

Mantell, M. A., S. F. Harper, and L. Propst. *Creating Successful Communities*. Washington, D.C.: Island Press, 1990.

Marinelli, J. "Going Native." *The Amicus Journal*. Fall 1992:28–29.

Martin, A. C., H. S. Zim, and A. L. Nelson. *American Wildlife and Plants: A Guide to Wildlife Food Habits*. New York: Dover, 1961.

Mitchell, J. C. "Exotic Delights—Pleasures or Plagues?" *Virginia Wildlife*, June 1992:4–8.

Mitchell, J. C., and R. A. Beck. "Free-Ranging Domestic Cat Predation on Native Vertebrates in Rural and Urban Virginia." *Virginia Journal of Science*. Vol 43 No. 1B (1992).

Otis, D. R. "Landscaping for Birds." *The Living Bird Quarterly*. Winter 1991.

Patterson, R., and M. Patterson, "The Joys of Natural Landscaping." *American Forests*, March/April 1992:32–35.

Smyser, C. A. *Nature's Design*. Emmaus, Pa.: Rodale Press, 1982.

Stallcup, R. "A Reversible Catastrophe." *Point Reyes Bird Observatory Newsletter*, Spring/Summer 1991:8–9.

Stinson, E. R., and P. T. Bromley. *Pesticides and Wildlife: A Guide to Reducing Impacts on Animals and Their Habitat*. Richmond: Virginia Department of Game and Inland Fisheries, 1991.

Stokes, D. W. *The Natural History of Wild Shrubs and Vines*. Chester, Conn.: The Globe Pequot Press, 1989.

Tekulsky, M. *The Hummingbird Garden*. New York: Crown Publishers, Inc., 1990.

Terres, J. K. *Songbirds in Your Garden*. New York: Harper and Row, 1987.

Tufts, C. *The Backyard Naturalist*. Washington, D.C.: National Wildlife Federation, 1988.

———. "The National Wildlife Federation's Urban Wildlife Programs . . . Working for the Nature of Tomorrow." *Integrating Man and Nature in the Metropolitan Environment*, edited by L. W. Adams, and D. L. Leedy, 241–242. Washington, D.C.: National Institute for Urban Wildlife, 1987.

Wilcove, D. S. "Nest Predation in Forest Tracts and the Decline of Migratory Songbirds." *Ecology* 66:(1985):1211–1214.

Wilkins, S. C., and R. E. Koontz. "How to Form a Land Trust." *Land Saving Action.* Washington, D.C.: Island Press, 1984.

Wolfe, J. *Making Things Happen: How to Be an Effective Volunteer.* Washington, D.C.: Island Press, 1991.

CHAPTER 4

Audubon Wildlife Reports. National Audubon Society 1985–1989.

Bean, M. J. *The Evolution of National Wildlife Law.* New York: Praeger, 1983.

Boardman, R., ed. *Canadian Environmental Policy: Ecosystem, Politics, and Process.* New York: Oxford University Press, 1992.

Ferguson, D. and N. Ferguson. *Sacred Cows at the Public Trough.* Bend, Ore.: Maverick Publications, 1983.

Gradwohl, J., and R. S. Greenberg. "Conserving Nongame Migratory Birds." *Audubon Wildlife Report 89/90.* New York: Academic Press.

Howe, M. A. "Conservation of U.S. Nongame Birds" *Conserving Migratory Birds.* ICBP Technical Publication No. 12, pp. 225–257. Cambridge, UK: ICBP, 1991.

Hummel, M. *Endangered Spaces.* Canada: World Wildlife Fund, 1989.

Hunt, C. E., and National Wildlife Federation. *Down by the River: The Impact of Federal Water Projects and Policies on Biological Diversity.* Washington, D.C.: Island Press, 1986.

Ledec, G., and R. Goodland. *Wildlands: Their Protection and Management in Economic Development.* Washington, D.C.: The World Bank, 1988.

MacKintosh, G. *Preserving Communities and Corridors.* Washington, D.C.: Defenders of Wildlife, 1989.

Murray, S. *Aid Agencies and the Environment in Central America: A Directory.* Washington, D.C.: National Audubon Society, 1994.

Rich, B. *Mortgaging the Earth: The World Bank, Environmental Impoverishment, and the Crisis of Development.* New York: Beacon Press, 1993.

Stein, E. C. *The Environmental Sourcebook.* New York: Lyons and Burford, 1992.

U.S. Fish and Wildlife Service. Endangered and Threatened Wildlife and Plants: Animals Candidate Review for Listing as Endangered or Threatened Species, Proposed Rule. Federal Register. Part VIII. Washington, D.C., 1991.

Wald, J., K. Raitt, R. Strickland, and J. Feller. *How Not to Be Cowed.* Salt Lake City: Southern Utah Wilderness Alliance and the Natural Resources Defense Council, 1991.

World Wildlife Fund. *Endangered Spaces Progress Report.* Canada, 1992.

CHAPTER 5

Cornell Laboratory of Ornithology. *Organizer's Kit for International Migratory Bird Day* (in English; appropriate for U.S. and Canadian groups).

Equal Exchange. *Making Coffee Strong.* Stoughton, Mass., 1994.

Gordon R., ed. *Conservation Directory.* Washington, D.C.: National Wildlife Federation, 1994.

Lanier-Graham, S. D. *The Nature Directory.* New York: Walker and Company, 1991.

National Audubon Society. *Birds in the Balance: Action Packet.* Washington, D.C., 1993.

Pick, M. *How to Save Your Neighborhood, City, or Town.* San Francisco: Sierra Club Books, 1993.

Plotkin, M., and L. Famolare. *Sustainable Harvest and Marketing Rain Forest Products.* Washington, D.C.: Island Press, 1992.

Stein, E. C. *The Environmental Sourcebook.* New York: Lyon and Burford Publishers, 1992.

Uhl, C., and G. Parker. "Is a One-Quarter Pound Hamburger Worth a Half-Ton of Rain Forest?" *Interciencia.* Vol 11 (1986):213.

CHAPTER 7

American Ornithologists' Union. *The A.O.U. Checklist of North American Birds, Sixth Edition.* Lawrence: American Ornithologists' Union, 1983.

Bond, J. *Birds of the West Indies; Fifth Edition.* Boston: Houghton Mifflin Co., 1985.

Davis, S. E. "Seasonal Status, Relative Abundance, and Behavior of the Birds of Concepcion, Departmento Santa Cruz, Bolivia.," *Fieldiana New Series* 71 (1993):1–33.

Ehrlich, P. H., D. Dobkin, and P. Wheye. *The Birder's Handbook.* New York: Simon and Schuster, Inc., 1988.

————. *Birds in Jeopardy.* Stanford: Stanford University Press, 1992.

Finch, D. "Population Ecology, Habitat Requirements and Conservation of Neotropical Migratory Birds." USDA Forest Service General Technical Report RM-205, 1991.

Fjeldsa, J., and N. Krabbe. *Birds of the High Andes.* Svendborg, Denmark: Apollo Books, 1990.

Godfrey, W. E. *The Birds of Canada.* Ottawa: National Museum of Canada, 1986.

Haverschmidt, F. *Birds of Surinbam.* London and Edinburgh, Great Britain: Oliver & Boyd, 1968.

Hayes, F., et al. "North American Bird Migrants in Paraguay." *Condor* (1990) 92:947–960.

Hilty, S. *The Birds of Columbia.* Princeton: Princeton University Press, 1985.

Johnson, A. W., *The Birds of Chile* (two volumes). Buenos Aires: Platt Establecimientos Graficos SA, 1965, 1967.

Koepke, M. *The Birds of the Department of Lima, Peru.* Newton Square, Pa.: Harrowood Books, 1970.

Monroe, B. L., Jr. *A Distributional Survey of the Birds of Honduras.* Lawrence: American Ornithologists' Union: Ornithological Monogr. No. 7, 1968.

Narosky, T., and D. Yzurieta. *Guia para la Identificacion de las Aves de Argentian y Uruguay.* Buenos Aires: Asociacion Ornitologica del Plata, 1987.

National Geographic Society. *Field Guide to the Birds of North America.* Washington, D.C.: The National Geographic Society, 1987.

Ortiz, F., P. Greenfield, and J. C. Matheus. *Aves del Ecuador.* Quito, Ecuador: FEPROTUR, 1990.

Parker, T. A. III, S. A. Parker, and M. A. Plenge. *An Annotated Checklist of Peruvian Birds.* Vermillion, S.D.: Buteo Books, 1982.

Peterson, R. T,. and E. L. Chalif. *A Field Guide to Mexican Birds.* Boston: Houghton Mifflin Co., 1973.

Rand, A. L., and M. A. Traylor. *Manual de las Aves de El Salvador.* San Salvador: Universidad de El Salvador, 1954.

Rappole, J. H., E. S. Morton, T. E. Lovejoy, III, and J. L. Ruos. *Nearctic Avian Migrants in the Neotropics.* Washington, D.C.: U.S. Fish and Wildlife Service, 1984.

Remsen, J. V., Jr. and M. A. Traylor, Jr. *An Annotated List of the Birds of Bolivia.* Vermillion, S.D.: Buteo Books, 1989.

Ridgely, R. S. *The Birds of South America; vol. 1.* Austin: University of Texas Press, 1989.

Ridgely, R. S., and J. A. Gwynne. *A Guide to the Birds of Panama, Second Edition.* Princeton: Princeton University Press, 1989.

Root, T. *Atlas of North American Birds: An Analysis of Christmas Bird Count Data*. Chicago: The University of Chicago Press, 1988.

Russell, S. *A Distributional Study of the Birds of British Honduras*. Lawrence: American Ornithologists' Union: Ornithological Monogr. No. 1, 1964.

de Schauensee, R. M., and W. H. Phelps, Jr. *A Guide to the Birds of Venezuela*. Princeton: Princeton University Press, 1978.

Schneider, K. J., and D. M. Pence, eds. *Migratory Nongame Birds of Management Concern in the Northeast*. Newton Corner, Mass.: U.S. Fish and Wildlife Service, 1992.

Sibley, C., and B. L. Monroe, Jr. *Distribution and Taxonomy of the Birds of the World*. New Haven: Yale University Press, 1990.

Sick, H. *Birds in Brazil*. Princeton: Princeton University Press, 1993.

Stiles, F. G., and A. F. Skutch. *A Guide to the Birds of Costa Rica*. Ithaca, N.Y.: Cornell University Press, 1989.

Stotz, D., et al. "The Status of North American Migrants in Central Amazonian Brazil." *Condor* 94 (1992):608–621.

USDA Forest Service. *Forest and Rangeland Birds of the United States*. Agricultural Handbook 688, 1983.

Wilbur, S. *Birds of Baja California*. Berkeley: University of California Press, 1987.

ADDITIONAL RESOURCES
Children's Books and Materials for Teachers

Birds, Birds, Birds!: Ranger Rick's NatureScope Series, #75004, and *Rainforests: Tropical Treasures: Ranger Rick's NatureScope Series, #75044*. Contact the National Wildlife Federation, 1400 16th Street, NW, Washington, DC 20026-2266.

Birds of Two Worlds (poster). Contact the Missouri Department of Conservation, P.O. Box 180, Jefferson City, MO 65201.

Bird Wise. Reading, Mass.: Addison Wesley Publishing Co., Inc., 1989.

Disappearing Habitat, Disappearing Birds (teacher's packet and poster). Contact the National Audubon Society, Education Division, 700 Broadway, New York, NY 10003.

Migration Mysteries: Disappearing Neotropicals and *Animal Superheroes* (four-page newsletters for children). Contact the Minnesota Valley National Wildlife Refuge, 3815 E. 80th Street, Bloomington, MN 55425.

One Bird—Two Habitats (a middle school environmental education curriculum on migratory birds). Write to Susan Gilchrist, Wisconsin Department of Natural Resources, Residents Circle, 1350 Femrite Drive, Manona, WI 53716.

Audio-Visual Materials
Film

For the Birds. A film series on migratory birds and habitat protection narrated by Peter Gzowski and available from Missing Links Production, 455 12th Street, NW, Calgary, Alberta, Canada T2N 1Y9 (FAX: 403-283-6214). The series includes: *Singing in the Rainforest,* featuring wood warblers filmed in Costa Rica and Northern Alberta; *For the Birds,* featuring the comeback of Peregrine Falcons into Edmonton, Alberta; and *Birders of a Feather,* focusing on birds and birders moving from Canada to Costa Rica.

On a Wing and a Song. One-hour video from "The Nature of Things with David Suzuki." Transcript is available from: Transcripts—The Nature of Things, Canadian Broadcasting Company, P.O. Box 500, Station "A" Toronto, Ontario M5W 1E6, Canada. Video cassette is available from CBC-Educational Sales (same address).

Spring and Summer Songbirds of the Backyard. George Harrison. Ithaca, N.Y.: Cornell Laboratory of Ornithology.

What Good Is a Warbler? 12.5 minute, 16mm color, narrated, award-winning film that examines the life of the endangered Golden-cheeked Warbler. Appropriate for all grade levels, but particularly fourth through seventh. Subject area covers science, social studies, and language arts. Comes with follow-up discussion and activity ideas. Available from Adams & Adams Films, 706 Wayside Drive, Austin, TX 78703 (512) 477-8846.

Slide Shows

Migrants: A Troubled Future? (Partners in Flight Slide Show). Available from Cornell Laboratory of Ornithology, 159 Sapsucker Woods Road, Ithaca, NY 14850.

Individual slides can be purchased from *Vireo,* Philadelphia Academy of Natural Science, and the Cornell Laboratory of Ornithology (address above).

Migratory Bird Games

Shorebird Migration Game (ages 9–12). Write to Manomet Observatory, Box 1770, Manomet, MA 02345.

Index

Page numbers in *italics* indicate illustrations.